DON'T GET ME STARTED

Jewish Journal Books

Don't Get Me Started
A Collection of Columns on Life, Israel and the Jewish World

Published by Jewish Journal Books, an imprint of The Jewish Journal of Greater Los Angeles.

Copyright © 2011 by David Suissa.

ISBN: 9780983814504

First Printing September 2011.

Printed in the United States of America.

10 9 8 7 6 5 4 3 2 1

Dedicated to my beloved mother and father
and to the fruits of my labor:

Tova

Shanni

Mia

Noah

and

Eva

Contents

FOREWORD

Although Jewish unity has always been a chimera – Jews have always disagreed, sometimes very vigorously – there is a clear sense that in the modern age there is a loosening of the bonds. Communities don't speak to one another. Some Rabbis will not recognize others; some Jews disparage the movement, ideology, commitment or courage of other Jews.

In the twenty-eighth chapter of Genesis we read that Jacob put stones under his head. Yet after his dream when he arose they became one stone. The Midrash teaches that originally the stones quarreled about who would get to be the lucky stone resting under Jacob's head. But his dream and his mission forged unity among the stones. Similarly, when all Israel looks in the same direction, is animated by the same purpose, there is a unity that eludes us at other times. Everyone can pull together, if only briefly, when a tone of urgency and authenticity strikes.

So we believe in oneness, not only the Oneness of God but the ideal oneness of God's people in this world. Yet for all the lip service we pay to Jewish unity there are very few figures in the Jewish world who can move easily among Jews of all descriptions. Most stay in their segregated world. Among those who can traverse boundaries are people who, as they stand for nothing, can fit in with everything. Others simply pay no attention to boundaries because their vision overrides division.

David Suissa stands powerfully for certain ideals. Every reader of these essays will see clear, clever, forceful advocacy. Yet David Suissa also exudes something else, something different: a loving passion.

Suissa's embrace is wide; he is at home with ultra-orthodox Rabbis and adamant secularists; young and old, learned and unlearned; the grand and important as well as the unassuming and unknown. Suissa's background in advertising taught him a great truth: that ideas are always more powerful when wrapped up in a person. He exemplifies ahavat Yisrael – love of the land and people of Israel. It is not an exclusionary or mean love – though he can be tart and witty. It is a love that elevates and inspires.

You will find in these pages an impatience with those who hold Israel to unreasonable standards. You will find a willingness to listen to words of Torah whatever the source, so long as it is insightful and heartfelt. And you will hear the genuine voice of Torah, which speaks wisdom. In other words, in these essays, alternately personal, ideological, quotable and downright funny, you get Suissa.

Lucky reader.

David Wolpe

Senior Rabbi,

Sinai Temple, Los Angeles

INTRODUCTION

I've always loved the short essay form. If the essay is well crafted, I get a fresh, concise take on a subject of my choice—and I still have the whole night ahead of me. Not that I don't admire thick books of non-fiction, but often, when I dive into one, I find myself asking: I wonder how the writer would summarize these 400 pages into a short and powerful essay? What is the main idea of the book?

What is the essence?

"Don't Get Me Started" is a book of essence. In every column, whether writing about the Middle East or the meaning of death, I try to offer something fresh that will light a spark.

These columns were originally published in the Jewish Journal of Greater Los Angeles, and, over the years, many of them have been picked up in publications and Web sites around the country, most notably The Huffington Post.

The column began in August 2006, when my friend Rob Eshman, editor-in-chief of the Jewish Journal, made me an offer I couldn't refuse: "Why don't you write about whatever you feel passionately about that week?" So I did, under the moniker "Live in the Hood," and I have filed every week since – whether I found myself in a refugee camp in Ramallah,

Cottage cheese woke the people up.
The people were broke, and breaking.

Can't afford my landlord.
Can't look at my overdraft.
Can't afford to drive my car
Or put the kids in day care.

My vote's been stolen
By the fake heroes in Volvos.
Who can remember where we left our future?
Still no peace — only a miracle in pieces.

Crazy gaps everywhere.
Workers subsidizing schnorrers.
Those in green defending; those in black learning.
Hoarding in the Towers; sweating in the streets.
The elite can build while the poor can leave.

Jews can't dream any better than this?

Off to Rothschild they trekked
Half a million strangers reintroducing themselves.
Sushi eaters, chakchouka eaters
Mothers, strollers, comedians, professors
Settlers, anarchists, laborers, Saturday nighters
Pitching their tents in a shouk of causes
Marching, sleeping, singing, arguing
Reclaiming the miracle
Leading a nation back to renewal.

The innocents have returned
And the cynics are stuck in reverse.
In the outdoor salons of the shouk of causes
It is the merchants of meaning who rule.

Look at the fear peddlers now
Running for cover — scrambling behind their blue ribbons.
Reform or not, it is already the morning after.

The people are back in the desert
And they won't settle for fool's gold.

The Israelites are in tents — and Israel is coming home.

THE COLUMNS

"That feminine energy, which honors the holy act of receiving, helps us better connect with God and with each other. It's a spiritual energy that doesn't belong exclusively to women, and can be creatively embraced within halachah."

A WOMAN'S EDGE

August 10, 2011

It's not politically correct to talk about differences between men and women. In a society that values equality, this is understandable. As my friend Rabbi Yosef Kanefsky wrote this week on the Morethodoxy blog, "I believe fervently that Orthodoxy has yet to grapple fully or satisfactorily with the dignity of womankind."

The rabbi was especially disturbed by the prayer that blesses God every morning for "not having made me a woman," which he said "has the effect today of justifying our lack of progress."

Kanefsky's focus was on inequality. Women in Orthodoxy have fewer rights than men in several areas, including divorce, the prayer space and the rabbinate, and he lamented that while progress has been made, the community still "falls short of this goal in many ways."

These sentiments speak to a modern sensibility against discrimination of any kind, whether based on race, religion, gender, lifestyle, disability or age.

But while Kanefsky's sentiments were justifiably focused on a man's halachic "edge" over women, it seems to me that an important idea got lost.

That idea is a woman's spiritual edge over man.

I got a taste of that edge last Friday night at Temple Beth Am, where a packed house welcomed their new cantor, Magda Fishman, a soulful trumpet player who sings Shlomo Carlebach melodies like Billie Holliday sings the blues.

This was not my natural habitat. I pray in Orthodox shuls, so I'm clearly biased toward male cantors. Give me a Sephardic baritone with Ladino melodies and I'm in davening heaven. For me, the depth of a powerful male voice is like a surge of adrenaline. It charges me up. And it's what I'm used to.

So, how do I explain that I was so moved on Friday night by a female cantor leading services on the rooftop of a Conservative synagogue?

I think it started with the amazing rooftop setting, which was like being immersed in a mikveh of Godly air. Instead of being distracted by memorial plaques or stained-glass artwork, I was distracted only by an endless sky and a whispering breeze.

Into this open-air setting landed Magda Fishman. With the Los Angeles sunset framing her angelic face, Fishman picked up her trumpet and played a slow and moving solo that opened the evening. Then we all sang "Shalom Aleichem."

I confess — I felt a frisson of spirituality. I know "spirituality" is a nebulous term, so I'll say it more clearly: I lost myself. I stopped thinking and started feeling. It helped that every time I looked up at Fishman, she also looked lost. Lost in her prayers, her melodies and the moment.

She was receiving from God as much as she was giving to us.

She read the opening words of the "Hashkiveinu" prayer — "Help us lie down, O Lord our God, in peace, and rise up, O our King, to life" — and spoke, in her subtle Israeli accent, about the simple gratitude we owe God for waking up each morning. She then sang part of the prayer in English, and it sounded as if she was in a blues club singing her own lyrics.

Our mystics teach us that the Shekhina represents the feminine attribute of God. As meditation teacher Rabbi Yoel Glick writes: "The Shekhina is the essential creative force in the universe. It is also the creative power of the woman that forms new life in her womb. The introduction of more spiritual creativity into the prayer service is the introduction of the energy and power of the Shekhina."

On this night, Magda Fishman was the "Shabbat bride" who brought down a Shekhina strong enough to make me forget my bias for male cantors. In harmony with Rabbi Adam Kligfeld's Torah insights, as well as his own singing and that of Rabbi Susan Leider, I could feel a spiritual energy throughout the congregation that transcended the very idea of gender.

Later, it struck me that the Orthodox davening that I'm so used to, while often passionate and powerful, has a certain macho and business-like quality that can use a little softening up — a little feminine energy, if you will. It's the kind of energy that puts more emphasis on opening up our vessels to receive God's blessings than it does on the satisfaction of "a job well done."

That feminine energy, which honors the holy act of receiving, helps us better connect with God and with each other. It's a spiritual energy that doesn't belong exclusively to women, and can be creatively embraced within halachah.

"The Lurianic tradition emphasizes that it is the original separation of the Shekhina from the masculine that is the source of much suffering in the world, that the rebalancing is crucial for the Messianic era, " said Rabbi Mel Gottlieb, head of the Academy for Jewish Religion, California.

In other words, we men have a lot of rebalancing to do. Not just in recognizing the rights and dignity of women, as Rabbi Kanefsky pointedly reminded us, but also in learning how to receive the spiritual Shekhina from women.

I can say with all political incorrectness that, in my experience, women have an innate spiritual edge over men.

It almost makes me want to complain to God.

"So, here's my question. You're a progressive supporter of Israel and you see the government doing things that really upset you. What do you look at — the government's mistakes or the 'corrective mechanism' that's working on the ground to correct these mistakes?"

FAIR-WEATHER ZIONISTS

August 2, 2011

What do you do if an annoying and exasperating friend gets in trouble and really needs your help? And what do you do if that friend is also a blood relative, like Israel? I often ask myself that question about progressive, pro-Israel Jews who are furious at the direction in which their beloved Israel is going.

Is there a point when they will just decide to "dump" Israel?

I got a sobering answer last week when I read in Haaretz about a Jew whose "resume reads like a love poem to the world of Jewish activism." According to the article by Adam Chandler, this Jew has been "an extremely visible advocate for progressive Israeli and Jewish causes as well as an outspoken watchdog against anti-Semitism."

It turns out that a few weeks ago, this progressive, pro-Israel Jewish activist, Daniel Sieradski, announced to his 2,400 followers on Twitter that he had had enough.

"I've decided that after 10 years of fighting for a progressive Israeli course correction, that our efforts are futile," he wrote in June. "I officially give up. As the Jewish nation proceeds to march off a cliff, I will now go back to caring about everything else I cared about before Israel."

Sayonara, Israel. I'm done with you, and I will make sure all my followers know that I'm done with you.

As Chandler warns us: "Considering Sieradski's large following and his pioneer status, one might expect his declaration to precipitate a similar wave of emotional and ideological disengagement from Israel by other young, like-minded American Jews."

But in Chandler's view, Israel had it coming: "It's no surprise that progressives are disillusioned. The continuing expansion of settlements and the Boycott Law are manifestations of trends in Israel that make it increasingly difficult for many of us to speak in its favor in public forums abroad, on college campuses, even at kitchen tables."

Well, what do you readers think? Does Israel really have it coming? Has it screwed up so badly that it deserves to be "dumped" by disappointed Jewish progressives?

I took that question to my friend Gerald Bubis' house last week, where he was hosting a salon in honor of Daniel Sokatch, CEO of the New Israel Fund.

After hearing Sokatch rattle off a long list of progressive projects that his organization supports in Israel — programs dealing with civil and human rights, social and economic justice, religious pluralism and tolerance, Israeli Arabs and Bedouin citizens, the environment and women's rights — the only question on my mind was: Is Sieradski out of his mind? Has he not seen the progressive activity happening all over Israel?

Sokatch didn't try to hide his dismay with some recent decisions by the Israeli government. But the extraordinary effect of his presentation was this: Government policy notwithstanding, there's a whole lot of democratic action going on in Israel.

In fact, I think a great PR idea to engage young liberal Jews would be to have Sokatch go on college campuses and talk about how his group is helping advance progressive efforts in Israel: helping disadvantaged children of immigrants integrate into Israeli society; promoting empowerment activities for women and youth in Arab villages; providing legal help to establish and protect civil and human rights throughout the country; advancing the status of Jewish women whose rights have been violated by religious laws; helping protect the environment in the Galilee; and so on.

Sure, critics on the right have accused the New Israel Fund of supporting groups with anti-Israel views — but that kind of extreme liberalism is even more of a reason for progressives like Sieradski not to jump the Zionist ship.

Even a paper like the Los Angeles Times, while reporting on the Boycott Law, tried to keep things in perspective: "Examples of free speech in Israel are easy to find. Arab-Israeli lawmakers frequently attack the government as 'racist' on the Knesset floor ... newspaper pundits don't hesitate to launch character attacks against the prime minister."

So, here's my question. You're a progressive supporter of Israel and you see the government doing things that really upset you. What do you look at — the government's mistakes or the "corrective mechanism" that's working on the ground to correct these mistakes? Do you get demoralized by the faults or rejuvenated by the freedom to fight these faults?

When you look at the thousands of people protesting right now throughout Israel, many of them sleeping in tents, do you think only of criticizing the government or do you also think of helping the protesters?

Someone like Sokatch looks at Israel's faults and says, "What can I do to help?" Someone like Sieradski, after years of helping, now looks at Israel's faults and says, "What can I do but bail?"

The truth is, Israel is a mess in progress. It is a country surrounded by enemies that has nevertheless created a civil society like no other in the Middle East. For all its many faults, there is a restless energy to make things better — what Sokatch calls "democracy in action."

Progressive Zionists who don't appreciate this duality, and who end up bailing on Israel, are like friends who only love you when you're not around.

"Personally, I'm torn between two lovers. I have a deep sense of Judaism as a way of life and as a source of meaning and mission, but I also have a deep sense of Judaism as belonging to a miraculous people."

PEOPLEHOOD IS HISTORY

July 19, 2011

The latest buzzword in the Jewish world is "peoplehood." In a recent article in The Jewish Daily Forward titled "Funding Peoplehood," Misha Galperin, a top official with the Jewish Agency, writes that for the past few years "the organized Jewish community worldwide has recognized that the next major task facing us is strengthening Jewish identity, which we've come to call 'the price of peoplehood.'"

As he writes: "Prominent Jewish sociologists have identified the declining bonds of peoplehood as one of the most significant challenges posed by modernity and by a culture of universalism. Having been raised in a world of pluralism and tolerance, Jews younger than 45 do not necessarily privilege their Jewish brothers and sisters above others when it comes to friendship, marriage, volunteerism and charitable giving."

This new "peoplehood" buzzword is just the latest iteration of a broader issue that's been around for decades, using terms like "Jewish continuity," "assimilation," "intermarriage," and so on. "Peoplehood" is the latest reminder of a familiar problem for the organized Jewish community: American Jews in general don't feel compelled to connect to their Jewish tradition.

What I find fascinating about this latest emphasis on "peoplehood," however, is its tribal connotation. It's like an admission of failure. We couldn't get you to connect to Judaism so let's try something more primal: Connect to your tribe! To your people! It's the outreach of last resort.

No wonder Galperin's piece got some heated responses. Ruth Messinger, president of the American Jewish World Services, which focuses on Jews helping the world (and not just other Jews), wrote: "What's missing from this piece is a more expansive, values-based understanding of how Jewish peoplehood is expressed."

Another critique came from Daniel Septimus, of myjewishlearning. com, who wrote: "What is the content of Galperin's 'bond of peoplehood'? What is this bonded people supposed to do? What values do they cherish and share? What mission do they work to achieve? The Jewish community's inability to articulate answers to these questions, while at the same time fetishizing 'peoplehood' to the brink of idolatry, is exactly the reason the younger generation has drifted away."

Personally, I'm torn between two lovers. I have a deep sense of Judaism as a way of life and as a source of meaning and mission, but I also have a deep sense of Judaism as belonging to a miraculous people. If I moved to the desert and did absolutely nothing Jewish for three years, I would still feel nourished by my Jewish identity. The mere fact of "belonging" to my people is enough. It is the very transcendent nature of this feeling that moves me.

In the same way that faith and belief in God transcend reason, my connection to the Jewish people does the same. If I had to constantly justify this connection through reason — if I made it conditional on common actions or values — it wouldn't have the same power or emotion.

In fact, it's a mistake to assume that a deeper connection to Judaism and Jewish values will naturally lead to a deeper connection between Jews. Not necessarily. If I see "Jewish values," for example, as being synonymous with humanistic values like compassion, social justice and freedom, how does that connect me with Jews in yeshivas? Similarly, if I pray and learn Talmud all day, how does that connect me with Jews who express their Judaism by helping Muslims in Darfur?

Given all that, how might we promote a sense of peoplehood with Jews who feel no special or transcendent connection with their Jewish brethren?

If you ask me, the most natural way to promote Jewish peoplehood is to teach the extraordinary history of the Jewish people.

And I don't just mean biblical stories with all their grand moral lessons. I mean history, pure and simple. I mean the history of the migration of Sephardi Jews throughout the centuries; the history of the Jews of Europe and the Jews of Persia; the beginning of the Chasidic movement; the golden age of the medieval philosophers; the Jewish contributions to humanity; the beginning of the Zionist movement, and so on.

I mean teaching Jews (yes, even in day schools and yeshivas) not just our master story, but also our cultural and ancestral stories — warts and all — and how those myriad journeys have improbably converged in our generation.

Our sense of solidarity can only be enhanced by a greater familiarity with our incredible journey.

Unfortunately, history is the ugly stepchild of Jewish outreach. It doesn't have the romance of spirituality, the imperative of Torah study, the headiness of repairing the world or the practical relevance of daily rituals. What it does have, however, is narrative. Hundreds and thousands of narratives that have the power to bond us with the collective Jewish experience.

A few weeks ago, I reconnected with my cousin Sydney Suissa, who I grew up with in Casablanca and Montreal. Sydney was always a history buff. He ran programming at the History Channel and is now doing the same thing at National Geographic. My cousin is not Torah observant, but he has a deep connection to his people.

Why? Because he's been learning Jewish history for most of his life. His connection to his people didn't come from studying Torah, or from doing tikkun olam, which are important acts in their own right. It came because he embraced a remarkable story and heritage he feels he belongs to and would like to continue.

Galperin and the Jewish Agency are onto something. But maybe Galperin's next piece should be titled "Finding Peoplehood." He should invite and help Jews everywhere to discover the amazing story — and stories — of their people.

Values, rituals and study are important, but to build real human connections, you also need great stories.

Just ask any Jewish screenwriter.

"Our souls live on in everything we have done in this life, in every person we have touched, every word we have shared, every song we have sung."

THE MEANING OF DEATH (AND LIFE)

July 5, 2011

I hope you die and never come back!" the woman screamed at her husband as he left for work. Although the couple loved each other, it didn't stop them from having the occasional quarrel. That morning's quarrel, however, was worse than usual.

As fate would have it, the man never made it to work. He died of a heart attack shortly after leaving the house. We'll never know if the argument contributed to his death, but it doesn't matter. The woman, widowed now for 10 years, lives with the regret that she and her husband gave such ridiculous importance to their disagreements.

She now knows, all too well, that the nastiest disagreement is utterly insignificant when compared with the awesome finality of death.

I came across this story in a manuscript for a new book written by my friend Rabbi Benjamin Blech, with the working title "Why We Shouldn't Fear Death." The book is full of these little stories and anecdotes, mixed in with the spiritual musings of one of the leading lights of Modern Orthodoxy.

Blech himself spent many months fearing death after a routine doctor visit in February 2010. "There is no known cure," his doctor told him, after announcing he had a rare fatal disease called cardiac amyloidosis. Amyloids are proteins that can attack different parts of the body. If they invade the brain, the result is Alzheimer's. Blech's problem is in his heart. The amyloids are hardening the heart muscle, making it more difficult for the blood to be pumped to the rest of the body.

For nearly four decades, as a community rabbi, Blech would counsel and comfort congregants as they approached death. Now he had to do it for himself. He wasn't sure how. He found something on Google that suggested he had six months to live. He went to two specialists who were more careful with their prognosis: Intensive research is being done on the disease, they told him, but no one can predict what the lifespan will be.

So Blech is banking on meds, prayers and attitude.

It's the attitude part that's been the biggest challenge. After many months of "just being scared," he decided to start writing again. Only this time, instead of working on a book (he has published 12 books on various Jewish themes), he wrote short columns for Aish.com. The reason was simple: if he doesn't know how long he has to live, better not start a book he can't finish.

Then, four months ago, Passover came.

"It was like a fire came over me," he told me last week at a café in the neighborhood where he lives with his wife on the Upper West Side. Blech might be 77, but he has the face of a bright-eyed child who sees his first rainbow. He seems to always be amazed.

"I got this incredible urge to write a book about death," he said. "To dive into it and see what would happen."

Right after Passover, still unsure of how much longer he had to live, he sat down to write. The words just poured out. He finished the book in two months.

The result is an intelligent and soulful exploration of the unknowable. Blech doesn't try to conquer death or "spin" it or sugarcoat it. He's amazed by death, but not fazed by it. He looks it squarely in the eye, turns it around, peels back the layers, and, ultimately, infuses it with meaning.

Blech finds meaning in death by discerning divine meaning in life. If God is eternal, and we are created in God's image, then we share in that eternity. Our physical bodies might die, but our little piece of God—our individual souls—never die.

Our souls live on in everything we have done in this life, in every person we have touched, every word we have shared, every song we have sung. Living with that awareness is what creates a meaningful life.

Rabbi Blech says he doesn't fear death, and I believe him. Many years ago, my rabbi, Manis Friedman, asked me if I knew what people feared most. I mentioned the obvious: Loss of health? Loss of livelihood? Death?

"No," he said. "The biggest fear people have is that their life has no meaning."

On that basis, I can see how Rabbi Blech has lost his fear of death. His diagnosis, he says, was "God's way of telling me to write this book, to complete my mission. I would never have written a book about death otherwise."

He's right. Blech is too sweet and optimistic a man to think of writing a book about death. Ironically, it was the hardening of a muscle in his heart that led him eventually to take a hard and honest look at this most difficult of subjects.

By transforming a fatal diagnosis into a moment of purpose, Rabbi Blech has re-energized his life. Now, because his condition has "not worsened," he's wondering if there is still more he can do to fulfill his mission on earth. He's looking for another sign from God.

In the meantime, one thing you can bet he won't do is argue with his wife.

"Our community's problems are already pretty intimidating. As I see it, intimidating lingo just adds needless weight and complexity to those problems."

PEOPLE OF THE JARGON

June 15, 2011

For those of you who live in the real world and not in professional Jewish circles, consider yourselves blessed that you don't have to attend one of those all-day conferences on "The Future of Judaism." I've attended my fair share, and what I remember most is constantly being on the hunt for another cup of coffee. It's not that I don't love the mission of these gatherings; it's just that professional lingo has a way of putting me to sleep.

I was reminded of this weakness when I came across a report on a conference titled "Judaism 2030: A Working Conference for a Vibrant Jewish Future and the Steps Necessary to Get Us There" in ZEEK magazine. As soon as I read the term "New Jewish Culture activist," I felt that familiar onset of drowsiness.

What on earth is a New Jewish Culture activist?

Apparently, it's someone who likes to "talk with participants from a variety of institutional backgrounds about their visions of a 'vibrant Jewish future.'" Sounds wonderful, I thought. So why does it put me to sleep? Consider this perfectly reasonable paragraph:

"We also wanted to ask the questions in order to bring the visions that are presented into reality. How do we first identify the needs of individuals, communities, organizations, etc.? How do we really step back and look at what we're doing now and what we'll be doing in the future to meet both the present needs and to be ready to meet future needs? What kinds of policy changes do we have to make, what kinds of cultural changes must we make in order, for example, to embrace the increasingly fluid nature of identity in the future? What kinds of programmatic shifts must we make, and how do our institutional agendas need to change? Our goal is really to bring people from all of these different kinds of institutions to have this conversation about the future. Because it's really not taking place in this kind of context, and we want to really outline some of those steps so we can work to make these ideas and these visions — the viable ones — into reality."

ZZZZZZ.

I think my problem may actually be deeper than mere boredom. Professional language can also be intimidating, as in: "What kinds of cultural changes must we make in order to embrace the increasingly fluid nature of identity in the future?" That's scary stuff.

Sometimes, the lingo is just too hip: "Judaism can be employed as a tool in the world's toolbox of wisdom traditions." Other times, it just seems like you've heard it a million times, especially any sentence with the word "relevant" in it: "I think the vision for Judaism 2030 is: How do we, as synagogues and small communities around the country, manage to remain relevant to the lives of our constituents while they live in a global world?"

The Olympic champion of sleep-inducing jargon must be the word "paradigm." It didn't take long for the dreaded P word to make its appearance in the Judaism 2030 report: "My present concern is that Jewish community — and certainly Jewish education — has been in a totally isolationist paradigm for a long time."

There's nothing inherently wrong with jargon. For one thing, it makes the speaker feel important. Saying "paradigm" sounds a lot more sophisticated than saying "mode" or "position." Also, there's something comforting about having an inside lingo — it helps you bond with your fellow professionals.

The problem, of course, is that it doesn't help you bond with the community you're serving.

Our community's problems are already pretty intimidating. As I see it, intimidating lingo just adds needless weight and complexity to those problems, and creates needless distance between the professionals and the people.

Think of the most successful Jewish organization in the world today — the group that arguably has done more for Jewish continuity than any other. You know, those devoted "culture activists" who serve Jews around the globe? That's right, Chabad.

As I waded through the sophisticated verbiage in the Judaism 2030 report, it dawned on me that the beauty of the Chabad approach is in its intimacy — and simplicity.

In my view, Chabad's approach boils down to three words: Create. Invite. Serve. Whether in Uzbekistan or in Bakersfield, that's what Chabadniks do all day long. They create Jewish activities, they invite Jews to participate, and they serve them with love. Organizations like Chabad don't need fancy surveys to tell them that Jews need more Judaism; they're too busy planning Shabbat dinners, Chanukah parties and study programs to worry about five-year plans.

They understand that ideas are worth more than paradigms, action speaks louder than surveys, and love conquers all.

Not every Jewish organization is the same, but whether you're promoting spirituality, tikkun olam, Torah study, Jewish culture, Israel or Jewish ethics, you could do worse than throw away your strategic plans and follow this simple model: Create an idea or an event that fits what you do, invite the people you want, and serve them with love. Keep coming up with new ideas, and repeat until the Messiah comes.

And if it makes you feel better, you can call it The CIS Paradigm for a More Vibrant Jewish Future.

Coffee, anyone?

"Why has a Hollywood actor like George Clooney spoken out so loudly against this genocide, while the leader of the free world has kept relatively quiet?"

CHEAP BLOOD

June 7, 2011

A s I was doing research last week for a column on the Israeli-Palestinian conflict, I stumbled on a story in The New Republic titled "Darfur Is Getting Worse: Why Aren't the U.N. and U.S. Pressuring Khartoum to Reverse This Horrific Trend?"

According to Eric Reeves, a professor at Smith College and author of "A Long Day's Dying: Critical Moments in the Darfur Genocide," Darfur has become "all but invisible." As he writes: "With fewer and fewer human rights reports, news dispatches, or even candid accounts from U.N. leaders, events in the region have dropped almost fully out of international view."

This is the same region where, according to Jewish World Watch, 400,000 people have been killed and 3 million more have been displaced in the last decade. Sadly, Reeves says, the catastrophe there is deepening dramatically as they head into this season's "hunger gap," the dangerous rainy period beginning in October, when water-borne diseases become much more common.

Because of "increasing restrictions on travel imposed by the Khartoum regime," Reeves says, "hundreds of thousands of lives are at acute risk."

So, while human rights activists will be sailing their flotillas this month to protest Israel's partial and defensive blockade against a terrorist regime in Gaza, thousands of Darfurians will continue to suffer and die — quietly — because not enough people are screaming for the murderous regime in Khartoum to ease the strangling of its people.

And this fall, while the eyes of the world will be fixated on the Palestinians' diplomatic moves at the United Nations, don't expect to hear much about the hundreds of thousands of Darfurians whose misery will be compounded by water-borne diseases and the cruel blockade of their oppressors.

Even in President Barack Obama's speech of May 19, in which he used more than 5,000 words to discuss the ills of the Middle East and North Africa — including more than 1,000 words on the Israeli-Palestinian conflict — not one word was spoken about the genocidal suffering of Darfurians in Sudan.

Why is that? Is Sudan not "north" enough for the president — even though it borders Egypt and Libya and even Kenya, where Obama's father was born?

If Obama cares so much about the downtrodden, why is he giving so little public attention to the humanitarian disaster in Darfur?

Why has a Hollywood actor like George Clooney spoken out so loudly against this genocide, while the leader of the free world has kept relatively quiet?

As Reeves reminds us: "Darfur's ongoing catastrophe is poised to result in even greater human destruction and suffering. The reports are endless. So too, evidently, is the capacity of the international community to pretend that none of this is happening, or to ignore it, or to not care enough to act.

"The world has all the evidence needed to know that this is so, but it lacks the resolve to bring to bear on Khartoum the pressure that will change the regime's brutal ways."

It's a funny thing: When it comes to pressuring Israel, the world never seems to lack any resolve.

As far as pressuring Sudan, Reeves concludes that "the Obama administration should make clear that, unless Khartoum grants unfettered humanitarian access and freedom of movement for the U.N. peacekeeping mission, the regime will see no lifting of sanctions, no further discussion of removal from the list of terrorist-sponsoring nations, no further normalizing of relations, and robust U.S. opposition to debt relief for Khartoum at the World Bank and IMF [International Monetary Fund]."

Why couldn't Obama say those simple words in his May 19 speech?

What I find most disheartening about the Darfur crisis is that the facts are so clear. There's no torturous debate here about "two sides of the story." Like a passionate American politician once said: "The government of Sudan has pursued a policy of genocide in Darfur. Hundreds of thousands of men, women and children have been killed in Darfur, and the killing continues to this very day."

That passionate politician was candidate Barack Obama in 2008.

Three years and thousands of killings later, the tragedy continues. Where is Obama now? Sure, I know — he can't tackle every crisis that comes along. But if the president can harp about the plight of the Palestinians — by far the most coddled victim group in history — why can't he harp about a cause where 400,000 innocents have been slaughtered? If the "killing continues to this very day," doesn't that make the Darfurian cause at least as "urgent" as the Palestinian cause?

And where are all those human rights activists who've made a fetish out of bashing Israel but can't seem to get agitated at the notion of murderous African dictators drowning their people in misery?

Are Darfurian victims not "cool" enough because they don't throw rocks or look like Che Guevara? Are the bad guys not bad enough because they're not Jews or Israelis?

Imagine being one of those African victims and watching the international news one night. Imagine how it must feel to see that your genocide is being virtually ignored, while the Palestinian cause has become the darling mission of the world and a media and U.N. obsession.

How can you not conclude that Darfurian blood is cheap?

How can one ever call that "progressive"?

"In other words, the Arab definition of 'catastrophe' is that they failed to destroy the Jewish state at its birth."

NAKBA IS IN THE EYE OF THE BEHOLDER

May 17, 2011

While the world media was buzzing on May 15 about the violent Arab demonstrations marking the "Nakba" (catastrophe) of 1948, I was listening to a commencement address by Secretary of Energy Steven Chu at Pomona College in which he lamented, among other things, America's inability to reduce its addiction to oil. At one point, Chu spoke eloquently about a future in which electric cars would be mass-produced, and how this might ignite an environmental revolution that could "save the planet."

As he spoke, I thought of an article I had read on JPost that morning about an Israeli initiative to reduce global dependency on oil. The company Better Place unveiled the first electric car to be sold to the Israeli market — the Renault Fluence ZE. According to the report, "Israel will become, along with Denmark, the first country in which Better Place's rechargeable, zero-emission vehicles will be sold commercially."

I couldn't help connecting the dots. On the one hand, there was the "catastrophe" of Israel's creation in 1948 as expressed by Arab demonstrators, and, on the other hand, there was a miracle country with the potential to help "save the planet."

Which one is it, a catastrophe or a miracle?

It's easy to cop out and say we must recognize everyone's narrative. If the Palestinians see the birth of Israel and the subsequent displacement of Arabs as a "catastrophe," well, then, as Gideon Levy of Haaretz proposes, even Jewish schools in Israel must mark Nakba Day. As Levy wrote, "On that day it would be possible to tell our pupils that next to us lives a nation for whom our day of joy is their day of disaster, for which we and they are to blame."

Personally, I'm more aligned with Jeffrey Goldberg, who calls the Arab "disaster" of 1948 "largely self-inflicted because the Arabs rejected the U.N. partition plan for Palestine, attacked the just-born Jewish state and then managed to lose on the battlefield."

In other words, the Arab definition of "catastrophe" is that they failed to destroy the Jewish state at its birth.

Regardless, though, of how one sees the Nakba, it's clear that the Nakba mindset nurtures bitterness and resentment — elements that are hardly conducive to planting seeds of peace and reconciliation. How can an Arab student want to have a healthy and respectful relationship with his Jewish neighbors if he is encouraged to see that very Jewish presence as a mark of Arab failure — a mark of enduring Arab shame? And if he is encouraged to see this Jewish creation as something that must be corrected, or even reversed?

If you ask me, the real Nakba day for the Palestinians is the day Hamas created its official charter with hate-filled, anti-Semitic tracts like this one: "For our struggle against the Jews is extremely wide-ranging and grave, so much so that it will need all the loyal efforts we can wield, to be followed by further steps and reinforced by successive battalions from the multifarious Arab and Islamic world, until the enemies are defeated and Allah's victory prevails."

This Hamas "catastrophe" was made even more relevant recently with the reconciliation between Fatah and Hamas. As French philosopher Bernard-Henri Lévy lamented in The Huffington Post, prospects for peace have now "gone by the wayside with the rehabilitation of the only party concerned that is still proclaiming that 'the fulfillment of the promise' shall not come until 'the Muslims' have not only 'combated' but 'killed' all 'the Jews.' "

The plain, ugly truth right now is that there is no peace on the horizon. But many of us, including presidents, pundits and peaceniks, cannot accept that truth, so we ignore inconvenient facts or just spin them into glimmers of false hope. As Saul Bellow once wrote, "A great deal of intelligence can be invested in ignorance when the need for illusion is deep."

Beyond all this gloomy talk, perhaps the biggest disaster of all is the inability of the Arab world to see the Jewish state as anything but a cursed presence. Call me a cynic, but I don't think peace has a chance when Arabs still see the birth of Israel as a Nakba. In fact, I dream of the day when more Arabs will see the birth of Israel as a Fursa ("opportunity"). That would be the day Israeli Arabs discovered a messy and imperfect Jewish democracy that allowed them the freedom to speak up, and gave them rights and opportunities they could find nowhere else in the Middle East.

I even have an idea for who could lead this little movement: George Kerra, the Arab Israeli judge who sentenced the former president of Israel, Moshe Katsav, to seven years in jail for sexual aggression against a former female aide.

Think about that. A Middle Eastern country that is hated and threatened by its neighbors, forced to constantly fight for its life, manages to create a civil society where no one is above the law and where anyone can become a judge. Oh, and a society that still finds time to work on things like an electric car that could "save the planet."

You want to endorse the narrative of calling the birth of that nation a catastrophe? Don't count me in.

"Perhaps the rabbi understood that the scroll itself was the story – a symbol of how the Jewish people have survived despite impossible odds."

YOYA'S PROMISE

May 10, 2011

"Y ou must promise me that you will tell this story, what happened here," the rabbi said to the bar mitzvah boy, Joachim "Yoya" Joseph. They had just finished the ceremony in a small barrack in Bergen-Belsen, where they covered the windows so the Nazi guards would not see them. The rabbi, Simon Dasberg, a community rabbi from Holland, pressed a little Torah scroll in the young boy's hands as he spoke to him.

I probably won't make it out of here alive, the rabbi said to the boy. So take this Torah scroll; it will remind you to tell this story.

Nearly 60 years later, that little Torah scroll was sitting by Joseph's fireplace when someone asked what it was. The person asking was Col. Ilan Ramon, who would soon become the first Israeli astronaut and a Jewish hero. By some twist of fate, Joseph had become a space scientist and a colleague of Ramon's. When Ramon heard the story of the Torah scroll, he was "overwhelmed." He felt an urge to follow the rabbi's instructions — "you must promise me that you will tell this story."

The next day, Ramon mustered the strength to ask Joseph if he could take the Torah scroll with him into space. A few days later, in early January 2003, Ramon would take off as part of the U.S. Space Shuttle Columbia mission.

And he took with him Rabbi Dasberg's little Torah scroll from Bergen-Belsen.

On the morning of Feb. 1, as the shuttle was re-entering the Earth's atmosphere, it suffered a horrible malfunction and disintegrated somewhere above Texas. The tragedy stunned the world.

Meanwhile, soon after the tragedy, Dan Cohen, a documentary filmmaker living in Washington, D.C., saw a news clipping about the little Torah scroll and contacted its owner, Yoya Joseph.

When Joseph told him the story of the scroll — how he had smuggled it out of a concentration camp and eventually given it to Ramon — again it was as if Cohen was hearing Rabbi Dasberg's message directly: "You must promise me that you will tell this story."

Thus began Cohen's seven-year adventure to bring the story to the screen. Cohen was fascinated by this "little Torah that could," by the many twists of fate in the story, and, not least, by the incredible symbolism of an artifact of the Holocaust making it into space — as he describes it, "from the depths of hell to the heights of space."

Cohen's own journey culminated in Los Angeles last week, with the screening of his documentary film, "An Article of Hope," at the gala premiere of the Los Angeles Jewish Film Festival.

The selection of the film was made by Hilary Helstein, the festival's founder and driving force. It turns out that Helstein herself had been moved by Rabbi Dasberg's appeal to the bar mitzvah boy in Bergen-Belsen to "tell this story."

In fact, what I find most remarkable about this whole saga is that beyond the high drama of triumph and tragedy that the story represents, it is a little Dutch rabbi in a Nazi concentration camp who seems to drive the story: It was his idea to have a bar mitzvah ceremony, despite the dangers involved; to give a young Jewish boy secret lessons every morning at 4 a.m.; to smuggle the little Torah scroll into the camp for this very purpose; to figure out a way to smuggle in the boy's mother from another camp to attend the ceremony; and, finally, to put the Torah scroll into the boy's hands as a lifelong reminder to "tell the story."

It is as if the rabbi knew that one day the story of this little Torah scroll might make its way to prominent people, like a Jewish astronaut or professional storytellers in America.

The rabbi didn't settle for words and memories. He could have asked Joseph simply to "remember to tell this story," but instead, he added a ritual: Keep this Torah scroll with you at all times.

There's something very Jewish about backing up an idea with something concrete. We live for ideas and values that we can convey orally, but, ultimately, we're nothing without the written Book. The Book is our insurance policy, our timeless transmitter. Like President Shimon Peres says in the film, "Ilan Ramon didn't just carry the scroll into space, the scroll carried him."

Perhaps the rabbi understood that the scroll itself was the story — a symbol of how the Jewish people have survived despite impossible odds.

The film, which begins slowly, takes off the minute the scroll enters the picture. From then on, the story grabs you and doesn't let go. At the packed premiere at the Writers Guild Theater, there were very few dry eyes in the house.

I moderated a panel discussion after the screening, and as I listened to Cohen discuss his deep attachment to the making of the film, I felt a similar idea seeping into my own mind.

I imagined myself as the little bar mitzvah boy in Bergen-Belsen, and I could almost hear Rabbi Dasberg say: "You must promise me that you will tell this story."

As I left the theater, I could not imagine writing about anything else.

"We love to teach our kids that life is not about winning and losing but 'how you play the game.' That may be true when you're dealing with people of good faith."

THERE'S SOMETHING ABOUT WINNING

May 3, 2011

I 'll never forget sitting with a group of intellectuals several years ago, at the height of the messy war in Iraq, and discussing why President Bush and America had fallen so low in the esteem of the world. One great mind after another offered sophisticated analyses. My head was spinning.

Finally, someone piped up: "Everything would be different if Bush were winning the war."

At which point a distinguished professor from Israel said: "This is brilliant! Bush's real problem is that he's not winning!" I sat there, slightly stunned, thinking: How can something so complicated lend itself to such an easy insight?

I reflected on that insight the other night when President Obama announced the killing of Osama bin Laden after a nearly 10-year pursuit. Here was a president who had suffered relentless criticism for his handling of foreign affairs. And now, as Jeffrey Goldberg wrote on his blog: "Our President, in the blink of an eye, has gone from a hyper-criticized, seemingly-swamped possibly-one-term leader to an American hero, a commander-in-chief who calmly oversaw the killing of the greatest mass murderer in American history."

And why did he become a hero? Not because he made one of his inspiring speeches or announced a brilliant new policy.

He became a hero because he got a win. It's as simple — and as complicated — as that.

We love to teach our kids that life is not about winning and losing but "how you play the game." That may be true when you're dealing with people of good faith. But when you're dealing with people who are out for blood, it's a good idea to know how to win.

Naturally, Jews and Israel have always been juicy targets for people out for blood. So, how should one deal with such aggression?

I found a wonderful answer last week in a shoe store, of all places, on trendy St. Denis Street in downtown Montreal. The French Canadian owner of the store, who has been there for 25 years, decided last year to carry a woman's shoe line from Israel called Beautifeel. Well, wouldn't you know it, within a few months, a vicious boycott campaign was under way against the store, led by a popular local politician, Amir Khadir.

To give you an idea of the tone of their campaign, one of the boycotters' leaflets had an oversize image of a woman's shoe stomping on a pile of buried naked bodies — reminiscent of those horror shots of emaciated bodies you see in Holocaust documentaries. Written on the shoe was "Beautifeel. Made in Apartheid Israel." On top was the headline, in French, "Boycottons la boutique Le Marcheur" ("Let's boycott the boutique Le Marcheur").

Week after week, the boycotters recruited large and noisy crowds to hand out the leaflets and implore people not to enter Le Marcheur. Their mission was to pressure the owner, Yves Archambault, to stop carrying the Israeli shoe line so that the neighborhood would be "apartheid free." But Archambault refused, out of principle. It didn't seem right to him that he should be told how to run his business. His business suffered, but he held firm.

The story hardly ends there. The Jewish community in Montreal got wind of the boycott and went nuts. A "buycott" campaign was launched, and Jews from all over the city came to buy shoes at Le Marcheur. A woman bought a hundred pairs. Archambault became a local hero.

Meanwhile, creative minds went to work producing counter leaflets mocking the BDS (boycott, divestment and sanctions) movement as "Boycott Derangement Syndrome," explaining the discrimination and hypocrisy inherent in the movement. These leaflets gave people the Israeli side of the story. Archambault did his own research and found out that the Israeli shoe company (besides making great shoes!) hired women, minorities and Palestinians and treated their employees very well. The Quebec General Assembly drafted a unanimous resolution condemning the boycott and supporting the store.

And what happened to the initiator of the boycott, Amir Khadir? He went low-key and stopped coming to the demonstrations. Apparently, he concluded that the backlash might not be good for his political future.

I tell you this story not to remind you of the insidious global movement to demonize the Jewish state. That's old hat by now. I'm telling you this story because it's a tribute to the noble virtues of fighting back and winning.

Too often, we recoil at the idea of fighting. It leaves a bad taste in our mouth. We dread the thought of "lowering ourselves to the level of mudslinging." We prefer notions like "engagement" and "bridge building."

But the nasty boycotters of St. Denis Street who used Nazi imagery to malign an Israeli shoe company were not looking for engagement or bridge building. They were looking for blood — and a victory.

Faced with such aggression, how else to respond but to fight back?

Yes, in such cases, life is a zero sum game. One side wins, and the other side loses. The Jewish community of Montreal, with the support of a brave French Canadian shoe merchant, fought back ferociously and smartly against what it perceived as a grave injustice to the State of Israel. And, guess what — they won.

It's not as dramatic as taking down bin Laden, but we'll take it.

"This is a sure sign of the 'ifonlyitis' disease: The belief that everything is on our shoulders. It's all about us. We can achieve anything."

BRINGING SHALIT HOME

April 26, 2011

One of the most ironic obstacles to peace in the Middle East is what I call the Jewish disease of "ifonlyitis." This is the school of thought that says "if only" Israel would do this, or "if only" Israel would do that, then we finally might resolve the conflict. I suffer from the syndrome myself, and for that I blame my mother. She convinced me from a very young age that "if only" I put my mind to something, there's nothing I can't do.

Well, Mother, it turns out there's plenty I can't do, and one of those things is make my enemies like me.

I was thinking of this last week when I read about the plan to increase pressure on Prime Minister Benjamin Netanyahu to obtain the release of Gilad Shalit, the Israeli soldier held captive by Hamas since June 2006. According to reports, the plan in the Shalit camp now is to "take the gloves off" against Netanyahu. That might include politicizing the cause and having more disruptive demonstrations throughout the country.

In an editorial in Haaretz, Nehemia Strassler wrote that the Shalit family has to "wage a personal war against the prime minister" and be "much more militant." They must "organize mass protests and bring the country to a standstill. They must not give Netanyahu one moment of quiet."

Evidently, because Bibi has failed to convince Hamas to return Shalit in exchange for the release of almost 1,000 Palestinian prisoners, he's now the bad guy and must be punished. If you ever needed more proof of the Jewish instinct to blame ourselves for everything, this is it.

This is a sure sign of the "ifonlyitis" disease: The belief that everything is on our shoulders. It's all about us. We can achieve anything. If only we would release a few hundred more terrorists with Jewish blood on their hands, we might finally free Gilad Shalit.

If only we did this, or if only we did that.

There is a wonderful psychological benefit to this disease. It gives us the illusion that we are in control; that we can affect our situation, no matter how bad it might seem. It empowers us. And when we're in a hostile and unpredictable environment, we desperately need to feel we are in control of our destiny.

But we pay a heavy price for this illusion of control. First, it leads to tremendous tension and mutual animosity among Jews. Because we assume we are the ones who are always responsible for any situation, we end up constantly beating each other up.

Second, we get so busy beating each other up that we lose sight of the real obstacles to peace. To the Haaretz writer who is calling for a "war" against Netanyahu because Shalit is still not free, I want to scream: "Why on earth are you declaring war against Bibi? In case you forgot, he's not the one who kidnapped Shalit and is holding him hostage!"

What Jews need, it seems to me, is less hatred of one another and more hatred of evil. Any group that will target a guided missile at a children's school bus is evil. Any group that will codify the murder of Jews and destruction of Israel in its charter is evil. Those, my friends, are real obstacles to peace.

If we didn't have this obsession with blaming ourselves for everything, we might focus more of our energies against the real bad guys — and maybe even come up with some imaginative ways of getting what we want.

For example, instead of pressuring the Israeli government over Gilad

Shalit, why not transfer some of that pressure to the Palestinians?

A Syrian Jew who sat next to me at the first Seder this year had this idea: Take the names of the hundreds of Palestinian prisoners whom Israel has already offered to release and promote those throughout the Palestinian territories. Drop millions of leaflets with their names and pictures. Promote them on the Internet and social networks. Buy ads in Palestinian newspapers. Film some prisoners pleading for their freedom and run the clips on Al Jazeera.

In other words, put the real pressure on Hamas, not on Bibi. Humiliate Hamas for refusing to obtain the release of its own Palestinian brothers. Have them answer to the hundreds of Palestinian families who would love nothing more than to see their own Gilad Shalits returned home. Expose Hamas for turning its back on its own people.

Think that wouldn't be more effective than starting a "personal war" against the Israeli prime minister?

It's ridiculous to keep beating Bibi up over Gilad Shalit. His offer to release hundreds of prisoners is already risky — going beyond it would be reckless and irresponsible. He's done his part. Now we must do ours.

Just like the global movement to free Nathan Sharansky focused on pressuring the Soviet Union, the global movement to free Gilad Shalit must focus on pressuring the Palestinians. Ideally, we ought to find someone with international credibility who could spearhead this effort — someone highly motivated to do something special for Israel and the Jewish people.

In fact, I have a name in mind: Richard Goldstone.

Now "if only" I can convince him to go after the bad guys.

"Ironically, Passover, the unique Jewish story, has fallen all over itself to dull its Jewish uniqueness. The rationale for this is proper and utterly predictable."

A SEDER FOR BROKEN JEWS

April 19, 2011

The big fashion of recent times has been to rewrite or repackage the Passover haggadah to fit our individual tastes. If you're vegetarian, there is the "Haggadah for the Liberated Lamb"; if you're interested in Buddhism, there is the "Haggadah for Jews & Buddhists: A Passover Ritual"; if your thing is spiritual traditions, there is "The Santa Cruz Haggadah: A Passover Haggadah, Coloring Book, and Journal for the Evolving Consciousness"; for all you social justice lovers, there is Arthur Waskow's "Freedom Seder: A New Haggadah for Passover"; if you are gay, you can try "Like an Orange on a Seder Plate: Our Lesbian Haggadah"; and if you don't believe in God, don't worry, you can get "The Liberated Haggadah: A Passover Celebration for Cultural, Secular and Humanistic Jews."

There are literally hundreds of others, but you get the point — one of the modern freedoms we celebrate at Passover is the freedom to create our own haggadah. This is so wonderfully American — a craving to inject our personal identities into everything. It's as if Passover were a time to break down our collective Jewish identity into individual morsels of sub-identities that we can feel more comfortable with.

The Master Story of the Jews, then, becomes the Master Story of Me. I celebrate not the story of my people, but how I have adapted that story to fit my own story, my own modern identity.

What does this say about Jewish identity in the first place? Is it not enough to carry the day for so many American Jews — or is it too much?

Leon Wieseltier, in his book "Against Identity," writes, "I am always at a disadvantage toward my own tradition. I am not only quickened by my intimacy with what I have been given, I am also dulled by it. I lack the wakefulness of the stranger. I should conduct myself toward the tradition to which I have fallen heir like an actor who has played a scene poorly: I should go out and come in again."

Too many American Jews have gone out but have not come in again. They haven't come in because they see no reason to. For 364 days a year, they live out their chosen identities, identities that were chosen to carry few burdens or complications.

Then comes seder night, the night of their ancestors, when they come face-to-face with the ancient story of their people, and, somehow, it feels a little weird — a little too close for comfort. It may be hazy, mythical and distant, but it can't easily be dismissed. This is, after all, the story that nourished their bubbes and zaydes going back many centuries.

It's a spiritual showdown: Who shall surrender? Shall I become the story or shall the story become me? Shall I become my grandparents or shall they become me?

It's not an easy call. As Wieseltier writes, "Identity thrives on facts: you are the child of this man and this woman, this neighborhood, this town, this nation, this faith, this country. But there is one fact to which identity is oblivious, and that is the fact of individuation: you are nobody else and nobody else is you."

Maybe this helps explain the mysterious power of Jewish identity — we are a family with the seed of individuation: We are nobody else, and nobody else is us.

And yet, in this great American nation that has smothered us with acceptance, Jewish identity has easily morphed into: We are everybody, and everybody is us.

Ironically, Passover, the unique Jewish story, has fallen all over itself to dull its Jewish uniqueness. The rationale for this is proper and utterly predictable: By making it more universal, or more personally relevant, we make it more Jewish. This truism is now a modern sacred cow.

But it's a truism that can take us very far from the womb, and it's one that doesn't get me in the kishkes. It's a little too perfect, a little too correct. Why can't Passover become a little more Jewish-Jewish? A time when we can look inward rather than outward; a time to assess how we are doing as a family; when we can recount our master story and use it to bring us closer together.

Next year, someone ought to create a Haggadah of Broken Jews. This one would celebrate the incredible variety of our people from across time and cultures and offer interpretations from as many different sources as possible. Thankfully, the haggadah is long enough to allow for a very diverse list of Jewish thinkers, ideas and traditions that would enrich the evening with the glow of peoplehood.

In addition to all the symbols of the evening, I would also add an empty chair. This empty chair would be there to remind us of the Jew or Jews we don't talk to. As long as that chair stays there, empty, we will never forget that we are still a broken people, still working to fulfill the Passover ideal of uniting for a common destiny.

And for those of you who would prefer to express your fondness for Buddhism, social justice or vegetarianism on seder night — hey, you have the rest of the year. Give one night for your people.

Happy Jewish Passover.

"If I were Bibi, I would dust off a peace plan, call a press conference, and tell Abbas simply and clearly: 'Sign here and the conflict is over.'"

BIBI NEEDS A PLAN, FAST

April 12, 2011

I had a lively debate with the founder of J Street, Jeremy Ben-Ami, April 11 at Temple Israel of Hollywood, and as much as we disagreed sharply on many issues relative to Israel, there was one item on which we were in complete agreement: The Palestinians' steady march toward unilateral recognition of a Palestinian state at the United Nations in September is a disaster-in-waiting for Israel.

We disagreed on what Israel should do: Ben-Ami thinks Israel should try to entice the Palestinians back to the peace table with another temporary settlement freeze, while I think the United States should pressure the Palestinians to come to the peace table without preconditions.

If that approach fails, however, Israel must do something, and do it fast.

Before Israel can figure out what that "something" is, it must admit to itself that it has lost the battle of the narrative. Right now, Israel is seen, almost universally, as the main obstacle to peace. You can cry foul all you want about this, but it won't change the reality. From the moment two years ago that President Obama elevated the settlements as the main impediment to peace, the die was cast.

Israel has been scrambling ever since, but it's been an impossible battle. No amount of clever diplomacy or lobbying could undo the lethal vise that Israel is in — not even last year's partial settlement freeze.

Simply put, the Palestinians have hidden behind the United States' initial demand for a settlement freeze to stay away from peace talks, while developing their enormous international support to do an end run around Israel and further isolate the Jewish state.

By repeating their U.S.-sponsored mantra — "We will not negotiate until Israel freezes all settlement activity" — the Palestinians have managed to camouflage the real obstacles to peace. To name just one, there is the obvious obstacle that the Palestinian Authority (PA), which governs the West Bank and could still engage in peace talks, has absolutely no control over the terrorist Hamas regime in Gaza.

In fact, one of the absurd aspects of this peace process is that Israel is acting like the buyer when it should be acting like the seller. If peace is the "product," then Israel owns it and should be selling it. Because it can control its army, it can deliver peace. Who can say with a straight face that the PA will be able to control its "army" (including Hamas) and hence be able to deliver peace?

Another obstacle is the fact that the PA has never prepared its people for a compromise on the sacred "right of return." Sure, it may have made private statements to Ehud Olmert a couple of years ago suggesting flexibility on borders and Jerusalem, but the analyses that I have seen of the "Palestine Papers" suggest that they are far from compromise on the issue of the right of return. And that is a deal killer.

But it is the bright glare of the settlement issue that has created the perception that Israel is the major obstacle to peace. It may not be fair, but it is what it is.

What should Israel do now?

The first thing is not to expect the Palestinians to return anytime soon to the negotiating table. They won't. They've got their eyes fixed on the U.N. and the world community, where they are treated like kings and never have to compromise. They want a lot more than what Israel could offer, and they think the U.N. will give it to them.

The second thing is to stop arguing. We've lost the argument. We can make cogent arguments until we're blue in the face, but it won't help.

The only way for Israel to regain the initiative is with real, dramatic action.

If I were Bibi, I would dust off a peace plan, call a press conference, and tell Abbas simply and clearly: "Sign here and the conflict is over."

Which peace plan? The plan that's got one of the world's most credible names on it: The Clinton Parameters. Bibi might make a few security-related adjustments to reflect new realities, but the thrust of the plan should be unchanged.

Will Abbas sign it? Let me put it this way: The Jewish Journal will become the voice of right-wing fanatics before Abbas signs this peace plan. Why? Because he can't. The Clinton plan is his nightmare. It forces him to compromise on too many things, including the right of return. It gives him a lot less than he has already rejected.

Compared to the Rolls-Royce he is about to be handed by the U.N., the Clinton plan is a Yugo that needs repairs. It's dead on arrival.

Israel should present the plan not because it believes the PA will sign it, but because Israel desperately needs to present a credible alternative to the unilateral recognition of a Palestinian state at the U.N., a diplomatic disaster that Ehud Barak said would bring a "tsunami" of further pressure and isolation on the Jewish state.

If Palestinians say no to the Clinton plan, they then automatically become the "major obstacle" to peace.

At the very least, this might shock them back to the negotiating table.

"Surely you must have anticipated the vermin that would rain on the Jewish state if a Zionist jurist formally accused it of targeting innocent civilians."

DEAR MR. GOLDSTONE:
SIX MONTHS UNTIL KOL NIDRE

April 4, 2011

Dear Mr. Goldstone:

You really screwed up. You screwed up so badly that Jeffrey Goldberg of The Atlantic says you contributed, more than any other individual, to the delegitimization and demonization of the Jewish state.

The deliberate killing of innocent civilians is the equivalent of murder. As far as accusations go, that's about as low as you can go. Your report accused Israel of a lot of things, but that accusation was the most lethal: targeting innocent civilians.

Now you write that you were wrong. Israel is not the war criminal she was made out to be. It was Hamas that targeted innocent civilians, not Israel. Well, like Goldberg says, "It is somewhat difficult to retract a blood libel, once it has been broadcast across the world."

Remember, this was no ordinary blood libel. This was an official indictment bearing the stamp of approval of the closest thing we have to a global legislative body — the United Nations. Thanks to this stamp of approval, Israel's enemies have feasted on Israel's good name like vultures on a carcass.

I'm sure you've noticed the global campaign to delegitimize Israel, as well as the flourishing BDS (boycott, divestment and sanctions) movement that is turning Israel into a pariah state. Sadly, much of the ammunition for these movements has come from the Goldstone report — the same report you now have repudiated with a phrase that might go down in Jewish infamy: "Civilians were not intentionally targeted as a matter of policy."

I wonder what went through your mind as you wrote those words: "Why did I rush to judgment? Should I have paid more attention to the hundreds of thousands of Israeli leaflets and phone calls that warned civilians, and to the preliminary Israel Defense Forces reports and other publicly available information that contradicted our conclusions? Should I have put Israel's behavior in the proper context of defending its people after years of Hamas rockets? Should I have been more skeptical of sources I knew were unreliable?"

A friend told me over Shabbat that I should cut you some slack because you had the courage to eat your words in public after getting "new information." That's fine, but another friend told me a parable that made him somewhat less forgiving.

It's the story of a man who goes to his rabbi to ask for forgiveness because he spread false rumors about him. The rabbi instructs him to take a feathered pillow and a knife, go to a nearby forest and slice open the pillow. When the man returned, the rabbi said to him, "Now go try to retrieve all those feathers."

Now go try, Mr. Goldstone, to "retrieve" all the damage your report inflicted on Israel. Go to every television and radio station, to every newspaper and magazine, to every Web site and blogger, to every Jew and non-Jew on the planet who inhaled your dark accusations against Israel, and try to take those accusations back. Try telling them you didn't mean it.

Surely you must have known that so many past accusations of Israeli "massacres" have been proved false (see Jenin). And as an international jurist who is familiar with the phenomenon of anti-Israel bias, surely you must have anticipated the vermin that would rain on the Jewish state if a Zionist jurist formally accused it of targeting innocent civilians.

I wouldn't be surprised if you've had more than a few sleepless nights since then. Why? Because I do believe there is a piece of your heart that loves Israel, that believes in Israel and that now cries for Israel because of the damage you have inflicted upon her.

While you can never undo that damage, there is still something you can undo: the report itself. Given your deep knowledge of international law, with all its arcane rules and procedures, if anyone can formally retract the report or officially amend it, it is you.

It won't be easy. You will be going up against the many enemies of Israel, those who dream of turning the Jewish state into an illegal enterprise, those for whom the Goldstone report is the gift that keeps on giving — their little gold mine rich with never-ending ammunition against the hated Zionist entity. They won't let you take away their gold mine that easily.

But I have confidence you can do it. I have seen how you can be dogged and relentless in front of intense opposition. I have seen how when you put your mind to something, nothing can stop you, not even your own people. I have seen you go the distance.

Now go the distance on this one, Mr. Goldstone. Make this your cause. Put the Goldstone report where it belongs, in the delete button of history. You can replace it, amend it, retract it or do whatever you feel will correct it. You will not undo the damage, but you might at least stanch some of the bleeding — not just in Israel's name, but perhaps in yours, as well.

Kol Nidre is still six months away, but you don't have to wait that long.

"Several years ago, Ross said something to me at a charity event that stuck with me: His biggest regret was that they didn't enforce the anti-incitement clause in the Oslo agreement."

OBAMA PLANTED SEEDS OF FAILURE

March 30, 2011

A couple of years ago, I wrote a public letter to President Obama applauding his commitment to peace in the Middle East, but warning that he should be prepared to fail. My reasoning was that he was following Albert Einstein's definition of insanity: doing the same thing over and over again and hoping for a different result.

In critiquing his approach, I used the metaphor of trying to plant a flower into desert sand. No matter how hard you try to force it, if the earth isn't right, nothing will grow.

This flower — a sapling would be a more apt metaphor — represents peace between the Israelis and the Palestinians. For nearly two decades, this little tree has been paraded around the world as the "key to peace in the Middle East." Accordingly, no issue has captivated globetrotting diplomats quite like this one.

Among all diplomats, perhaps the one who has spent the most time on this issue has been Dennis Ross, the point man on the peace process for three U.S. presidents, including the current administration.

Several years ago, Ross said something to me at a charity event that stuck with me: His biggest regret was that they didn't enforce the anti-incitement clause in the Oslo agreement.

Ross was revealing a painful truth about the peace process — you can't have peace without education. You can haggle over borders all day long, but if the people living within those borders are poisoned with hate and are not prepared for compromise, no leader will sign on to an "end of conflict" agreement.

You can make a good case that, had the Palestinian Authority spent the last two decades selling peace to its people, they'd have their own state by now and we'd be talking today about common projects, not Qassam rockets.

But of course they didn't sell peace. Instead, they sold the well-worn script of Arab dictators who need to build street cred with the masses: Demonize the Jews and the Zionist entity. Is it any wonder that Palestinian leaders, from Arafat to Abbas, have found it so difficult to say yes to Israeli peace offers? How could they compromise with an enemy they helped to demonize?

What would they say to their people? Sorry, we lied to you — the Jews really do have a claim to this land? It's true, they've had a presence in Jerusalem for more than 3,000 years? If Israel is willing to withdraw settlements for the sake of peace, we should also be willing to compromise on the right of return? Let's be nice with them so they will help us create a great country?

What is so shocking about those simple words is that we have never heard them spoken by any Palestinian leader, in English or in Arabic.

Yet those words were the crucial missing ingredients to nourish the tree of peace. They needed to be spoken not occasionally at interfaith meetings, but consistently and persuasively in Palestinian schools, media, summer camps and mosques.

But who ever dared pressure Palestinian leaders to speak those words? Peace groups? A global community that kept pouring billions into Palestinian coffers while reinforcing their narrative of exclusive victimhood? The United States, which never gave Palestinians any incentive to stop glorifying terrorism and start teaching peace?

When Obama the peacemaker finally had his chance, instead of promoting peace, he promoted the tired old trope of putting pressure on Israel to make more unilateral concessions.

Instead of launching, for example, a breakthrough peace-education campaign to convey to Palestinians that peace was worth compromising on the right of return, and to Israelis that peace would not mean suicide, he came up with a new excuse for Palestinians to stay away from peace talks: A Jewish construction freeze as a precondition to those talks.

By the time he realized his blunder, it was too late. He had already lost both sides. As Rabbi Donniel Hartman politely suggested last week in a "Letter to Obama," Israeli society "doesn't fully trust you yet."

Ironically, neither do the Palestinians, who, given no incentive by the United States to negotiate or compromise, simply flew off to make their own deal with the world.

Obama planted seeds all right, but instead of seeds of peace, they were seeds of failure.

"Let's compare those regimes with Israel's democracy, and let's see who's apartheid and who's not."

MURDERING ISRAEL'S NAME

March 23, 2011

While five Israeli Jews were being murdered in Itamar last week, something else was being murdered on college campuses across America: Israel's name.

This murder rampage is called Israel Apartheid Week.

There are few things worse for a country today than being labeled apartheid. This insult has it all: racism, decades of violent and racist oppression, international boycotts, even a global hero (Nelson Mandela) who conquered the demon.

No wonder the accusation has done so much damage to Israel. As Natalie Menaged, a pro-Israel activist, wrote recently in the Jerusalem Post: "Passing through many North American campuses this month — from New York and Boston to Chicago and Los Angeles — students are likely to draw the conclusion that Israel is a brutally oppressive regime, worthy of global boycotts and sanctions."

In fact, if there is one word that has fueled the global campaign to delegitimize Israel, and the ensuing BDS (boycott, divestment and sanctions) movement, you can be sure it is the dirty word apartheid.

Even groups like J Street, who are not known for their passionate defense of Israeli policies, have gone on record against this racist accusation.

And yet, despite the obvious slander, the "Israel is apartheid" movement grows stronger every year.

What can Israel do to defend itself?

One approach would be to go positive, like many pro-Israel activists did this year, by playing up messages like Israel's desire for peace and its history of making compromises for peace.

This approach is noble, but it is not enough.

It is not enough because the forces that hurl extremist accusations like "Israel is apartheid" are not looking for peace. They claim that all of Israel is apartheid and worthy of boycotts. Their aim is not to engage in debate but to destroy Israel's name.

And let's face it: They're winning.

They have lodged a racist accusation in people's heads that can't be dislodged with feel-good language. The only way to get at this poison is with a specific and powerful antidote.

In other words, Israel must develop a PR message that will destroy the enemy's accusation while reclaiming the higher ground.

Here's my candidate: "Israel is the ONLY country in the Middle East that is NOT apartheid."

Now imagine if Israel took this PR message and made it the focus of a global campaign on banners, Facebook pages, billboards, print ads, T-shirts, YouTube clips, etc. Who would be on the defensive then?

Unfair, you say? Not accurate? My answer: It's certainly a lot more fair and accurate than "Israel is apartheid" — but if you disagree, well, then, let's debate!

With the widespread revolts going on right now in the Middle East against decades of oppression, the world could use a debate comparing the democratic policies of Israel with those of her neighbors.

As Arsen Ostrovsky, an attorney for human rights and international law, writes: "The real apartheid today is in places such as Saudi Arabia, where the government totally forbids the public practice of non-Muslim religions, the presence of a Bible there, officially labels both Christians and Jews 'unbelievers' and cautions Muslims not to befriend Christians or Jews."

He goes on: "If Israel were an apartheid State, people like Arab Israeli Salim Jurban would not have been elected to Israel's Supreme Court ... and there would not be five different Arab parties and 14 Arab Israeli members of Knesset, some of whom are the most outspoken and harshest critics of Israel."

But what about the suffering of Palestinians, you ask? In a recent article in the Jerusalem Post ("Where Is the Outcry Against Arab Apartheid?"), Palestinian journalist Khaled Abu Tomaeh reported on the "hundreds of thousands of Palestinians who live in impoverished refugee camps in Lebanon and who are the victims of an apartheid system that denies them access to work, education and medical care."

Tomaeh also reported on the 180,000 Palestinians from Gaza and the West Bank, who, in the past year alone, were welcomed into Israel to receive some of the finest medical care in the world, whether they could afford it or not. I can think of a few hundred million Arabs in the Middle East who wouldn't mind this kind of service.

So, yes, let's debate. Let's hear Israel's apartheid accusers defend the apartheid abuses in Lebanon, Syria, Saudi Arabia, Egypt, Iran, Turkey, Yemen, Jordan and other Middle East countries — where, as Ostrovsky notes, "people are being jailed, tortured and often killed fighting for their human rights."

Let's compare those regimes with Israel's democracy, and let's see who's apartheid and who's not.

The truth is, when you look at the Middle East, the more liberal you are, the more you should defend Israel. At the very least, you should push back against the absurdly unfair apartheid slander. Israel might have an imperfect democracy with its share of flaws and inequities, but it hardly merits the vicious and unjust apartheid libel — a libel that even leftist groups agree goes way beyond the dispute with the Palestinians.

If you call yourself pro-Israel, you must fight this injustice.

"These are the heroes of Palestinian society – not Abraham Lincolns and Albert Einsteins and Martin Luther Kings, but murderers who crave the spilling of Jewish blood."

BEHIND THE ITAMAR MURDERS

March 13, 2011

It is fashionable when talking about the "peace process" to focus on hope—to try to nurture the moderate elements among our "peace partners" and constantly inject good faith and good will to keep the process moving "forward."

Because I crave peace by nature, I've always had some sympathy for this approach, which is why I have many friends on the left and why I occasionally take a break from my hard-nosed realism to indulge in more dreamlike and wishful prose.

This is not one of those times.

When I saw the horrifying pictures of the Jewish family members in Itamar who were stabbed to death in their own home— Udi and Ruth Fogel (36 and 35 years old), their children Yoav (11), Elad (4) and Hadas, their 3-month-old daughter— I thought of recent reports on the glorification of terrorism in Palestinian society.

It was impossible not to connect the dots.

In the reports, from Palestinian Media Watch, I learned that Dalal Mughrabi, the terrorist who, in 1978, was responsible for the most lethal attack against Israel, is now immortalized by having the following named for her: two elementary schools, a kindergarten, a computer center, summer camps, football tournaments, a community center, a sports team, a public square, a street, an election course, an adult education course, a university club, a dance troupe, a military unit, a dormitory in a youth center, a TV quiz team and a graduation ceremony.

I also learned that today, a Palestinian child can walk to school along a street named after the terrorist Abu Jihad, who planned a bus hijacking that killed 37, spend the day in a school named after Ahmad Yassin, the man who founded Hamas, play soccer in the afternoon in a tournament honoring terrorist Abd Al-Basset Odeh, who killed 31, and end his day at a youth center named after Abu Iyad, who was responsible for killing 11 Israeli Olympic athletes in Munich.

These are the heroes of Palestinian society—not Abraham Lincolns and Albert Einsteins and Martin Luther Kings, but murderers who crave the spilling of Jewish blood.

Before you rush to defend our "new and improved" Palestinian "peace partners," note that it was Palestinian Authority (PA) President Mahmoud Abbas who funded a computer center named after Dalal Mughrabi in 2009, and who supported the naming of the square in her honor in 2010.

"Of course, we want to name a square after her," he said to Al-Hayat Al-Jadida on Jan.17, 2010.

And who sponsored a sporting event named after one of the most prominent terrorist of all, Abu Jihad, in May 2010? None other than PA Prime Minister Salam Fayyad, the man who is building the "new" Palestine.

Just last year, Mahmoud Al-Aloui, a member of the Fatah Central Committee, said in an interview in Al-Hayat Al Jadida: "It is our right and our duty to take pride in all of the Shahids (martyrs), and it is our duty to convey this message in the most direct manner to the generations to come."

He wasn't kidding. Only a month ago, PA President Abbas awarded $2,000 to the family of a terrorist who attacked two Israeli soldiers in December.

And the very day before the Itamar murders, PA presidential advisor Sabri Saidam delivered a speech reported in Al Ayyam, in which he emphasized that "the weapons must be turned towards the main enemy [Israel] and internal differences of opinion must be set aside."

This glorification of Jew-hatred and murder in the name of martyrdom—which marinates all strata of Palestinian society—is happening under the watchful eyes of our Palestinian "peace partners," who have convinced most of the world, and many Israel supporters, that the real obstacle to peace is not Palestinian incitement to murder but Jewish building of apartments in East Jerusalem.

Even if you're a passionate peacenik, you have to admit that this is a joke. What does Jewish construction have to do with a Jew-hatred that has been burned into Arab hearts since before the first settlement or even Israel ever existed?

What else but Jew-hatred can explain the consistent refusal by Palestinian leaders to recognize a Jewish state and prepare their people for the inevitable compromises that peace with Jews will require?

As Sari Nusseibeh once said, "How can we Palestinians expect Israel to think we want co-existence when our position on the refugee issue has been tantamount to a call for Israel's destruction?"

So, here's my message to my friends in the peace camp. You've done an amazing job of telling the world that a peace agreement with the Palestinians is really, really important, and that Israel is primarily responsible for the absence of this agreement.

In fact, you've done such an amazing job of blaming Israel that my friend Gary Rosenblatt, editor of the Jewish Week in New York, wrote last week that Israel has become a "source of embarrassment" for many American Jews. Imagine that.

Well, now you have a chance to make amends and bring some balance to your message.

In honor of the children who were stabbed to death in Itamar, you can release this statement to the world: "It is really, really important, for the sake of peace, that Palestinian leaders eliminate the glorification of terrorism and Jew-hatred that permeates their society, and begin immediately to teach the benefits and compromises of peaceful co-existence with a Jewish state."

Who's brave enough in the peace camp to sign their name to that statement?

"For my money, though, the most flagrant demonstration of U.N. hypocrisy is how they have ignored the plight of ... Palestinians. Yes, Palestinians."

A U.N. RESOLUTION AGAINST HYPOCRISY

March 9, 2011

W riting a column protesting the hypocrisy of the United Nations is not really fair. It's like a turkey shoot. The evidence is so overwhelming that the U.N. is viciously biased against Israel — and ridiculously biased in favor of the Palestinians — that you're tempted to just move on to a less depressing subject.

But the consequences of these biases are real. Last month, for example, I was reminded at a Jewish World Watch (JWW) event of the genocidal horrors that continue to befall so many millions of Africans, and then, just a few weeks later, I watched the U.N. be all-consumed with yet another resolution against Israel.

According to JWW, the first genocide of the 21st century, in Sudan's Darfur region, has killed up to 400,000 people, and 3 million more have been displaced. If you think that's bad, since 1998, 5.4 million civilians in Congo have been killed by war-related violence, hunger and disease, and 45,000 more continue to die every month. Hundreds of thousands of women and girls have been raped, and 2 million people have been displaced.

Have you seen any emergency sessions and U.N. Security Council resolutions defending these victims and condemning these atrocities? Of course not.

Meanwhile, if you're a Palestinian whose home has been displaced by a Jew in East Jerusalem — with the legal backing of the Israeli Supreme Court, no less — you can expect an outpouring of international support with a ready-made stage for weekly protests and top-level U.N. attention.

My point here is not to overplay or underplay the rights of any group, but to highlight hypocrisy — criminally negligent hypocrisy from an international organization whose charter obligates it to defend the rights and dignity of all human beings.

According to the Anti-Defamation League, from 2009-2010, the U.N. General Assembly passed 22 resolutions that were "one-sided or blatantly anti-Israel," and of their 10 emergency sessions, six were about Israel. No emergency sessions were held on the Rwandan genocide, ethnic cleansing in the former Yugoslavia or the two decades of atrocities in Sudan. That's right, none.

And if you want to rail against the "Palestinian occupation," don't go to Tibet, where, according to various estimates, as many as 1.2 million Tibetans have died due to the Chinese occupation. Now, when's the last time the U.N. took a break from Israel bashing to pass a resolution condemning the "Tibetan occupation"? How about never?

Like I said, a turkey shoot.

For my money, though, the most flagrant demonstration of U.N. hypocrisy is how they have ignored the plight of ... Palestinians. Yes, Palestinians.

I'm talking about the millions of Palestinians who live in countries that have nothing to do with Jews or Israel. A country like, say, Lebanon.

This is what Mudar Zahran, a Palestinian refugee who fled Jordan and was granted asylum in the U.K., wrote last year in The Jerusalem Post:

"Lebanon, a country with some of the most hostile forces to Israel, has been holing up Palestinians inside camps for almost 30 years. Those camps do not have any foundations of livelihood or even sanitation."

Zahran writes that the "Lebanon atrocities toward the Palestinians have been tolerated by the international community, not only by the media," and that "many other Arab countries are no different than Lebanon in their ill-treatment and discrimination against the Palestinians."

When's the last time we heard of a Goldstone Report or a U.N. resolution in support of the poor, oppressed Palestinians who live in Arab lands? That's right, never.

The U.N. is the Picasso of hypocrisy. For that honor, I'd love to see a brave member introduce at their next general session a Resolution Against Hypocrisy, complete with an independent watchdog group that would report on violations like misplaced priorities, double standards, disproportionate criticism and just plain discrimination.

If they have time, they could also report on the slew of NGOs that claim to fight for Palestinian rights, but who completely ignore the millions of oppressed Palestinians who don't live inside or next to Israel.

This would be one busy watchdog group, especially if they report on the mind-bending hypocrisy of liberal groups pushing for boycotts against Israel while genocidal murderers and oppressors are let off the hook.

Of course, it'll take a while to push through this resolution. But for the women and little girls being raped and murdered every day in the dark corners of Africa, or the millions of Arabs across the Middle East whose decades-long suffering has nothing to do with Jews or Israel, or the many millions of other oppressed people around the globe whose daily torture is worlds away from the glamorous press lounge at the American Colony Hotel in East Jerusalem, it won't be a moment too soon.

Maybe President Obama can introduce the resolution on his next trip to Darfur, with a rape victim standing next to him.

"I expect more from open-minded liberals who claim to care for the 'other side.' For one thing, I expect they would also care for the other side of an argument."

J STREET NEEDS ANOTHER LANE

March 1, 2011

I was watching the J Street convention on its Web site, and it reminded me a little of those underground meetings among religious settlers in the West Bank. That is, a constant flow of red meat served to the fervent and the like-minded.

In the case of J Street, this red meat can be boiled down to this: It is really, really, really, really important that Israel reach a peace agreement with the Palestinians.

One fervent speaker after another came down from the mountaintop to convince an already convinced audience of how really important this goal is. Whether it was Peter Beinart fearing for Israel's democratic future, or Rabbi David Saperstein appealing to our highest Jewish values, or Sara Benninga finding her meaning in life by leading weekly demonstrations at Sheikh Jarrah, the theme was the same: Israel must make peace and end the occupation as soon as possible.

And who's the bad guy in all of this? Take a guess. With the J Street crowd, the underlying assumption is always that the major obstacle to peace is Israel. Palestinian obstacles to peace? They're as likely to be mentioned at a J Street convention as Avigdor Liberman is of being invited.

Sometimes I wonder what it must feel like after three days of one of these J Street smugfests. How do you go from feeling absolutely certain that you are right to feeling even more certain that you are right?

I remember when Rabbi Michael Lerner of Tikkun invited me to speak several years ago at one of its peace conventions in New York City. I was glad that he did, because it gave me a chance to ask a few hundred peaceniks a question they likely rarely hear: "When is the last time any of you woke up in the morning and asked yourself: 'What if I'm wrong?' "

No one raised their hand.

Yes, compassion is a great Jewish virtue, I told them, but so is humility. I confessed that, initially, I didn't believe in the Oslo peace process (because I didn't trust Arafat), but I asked myself, "What if I'm wrong?" and I ended up going along with it. So, I suggested, "What would happen if you all asked yourselves that same question?"

When I look at J Street now, I see some obviously good intentions ("We want peace!"), but not much humility. What comes across more than anything is an orgy of ideological self-confirmation toward pressuring Israel.

That's disappointing. I expect more from open-minded liberals who claim to care for the "other side." For one thing, I expect they would also care for the other side of an argument.

Have they studied, for example, the Palestinian Authority's global campaign to undermine and demonize Israel and the corrosive effect this has had on the peace process? As a "pro-Israel" group, what kind of public pressure have they brought to bear on the Palestinians to end their glorification of terror and indoctrination of Jew-hatred that has made so many Jews reluctant to take more risks for peace?

Where was their public campaign to pressure the Palestinians to return to the peace table during the first nine months of a 10-month Israeli settlement freeze the Obama administration lauded as "unprecedented"?

To balance their countless speakers who advocate putting more pressure on Israel, why haven't they included speakers like Itamar Marcus of Palestinian Media Watch, who has documented the continued anti-Semitic incitement in official Palestinian media, or an award-winning Mideast journalist like Khaled Abu Toameh, who makes a powerful case that the Palestinian Authority's primary interest is not to make peace with Israel — but to delegitimize the Jewish state?

If the goal is to bring together two sides, isn't it important to scrutinize both sides?

Why doesn't J Street bring in experts to explain the danger of Hamas taking over a Palestinian West Bank and pointing 10,000 rockets at Israel's nuclear installations, potentially creating a catastrophic meltdown in the Jewish state? Talk about fearing for a country's democratic character.

J Street's relentless focus on pressuring Israel isn't only unfair, it's also remarkably ineffective. A couple of years ago, Palestinian and Israeli leaders were negotiating directly as a matter of course. Now, in the face of the enormous and single-minded global pressure on Israel, Palestinians are negotiating in international forums on how best to demonize Israel. They won't even consider talking to Israel until it commits to freezing all construction in disputed territory, including, I presume, freezing any renovation of the restrooms at the Western Wall.

We've seen that the greater the pressure on Israel, the faster the cockier-than-ever Palestinians have run away from the peace table. J Street's reaction to all this is to bring 2,000 people together in Washington, D.C., to put even more pressure on Israel and urge the Obama administration to do the same.

In other words, after two years of generating bumper-to-bumper traffic on the failed road called "let's pressure Israel," J Street has decided that the best thing to do is to attract even more traffic to that road.

Maybe they ought to consider adding another lane to their congested highway and calling it "Let's pressure the Palestinians to stop undermining Israel and return immediately to the peace table."

In Los Angeles, we would call that the carpool lane.

"Think of how infinitely proud and happy our God would be to see His Muslim and Jewish children end their conflicts and live in harmony."

A KING'S SPEECH

February 22, 2011

If I were advising the president or prime minister of Israel, I would suggest he go on Al Jazeera this week and deliver this message to the people of the Middle East:

Dear Neighbors:

What is happening right now in our region is historic. You, the great people of the Middle East, are rewriting history. You are rising up and saying, "Enough! Enough with oppression, enough with humiliation. We want opportunity, freedom and human rights." Young and old, men and women, religious and secular, you have risen up as one and demanded a better future.

We, the people of Israel, want to be part of that better future.

It is not a coincidence that we are descendants of the same father, Abraham. Although we might be in conflict now, this was not always the case. We had our golden eras when we cooperated and respected each other like the biblical cousins that we are. We cherish to this day stories of the great Jewish and Muslim philosophers engaging each other in search of higher truths.

One of those higher truths is that we have so much in common as children of the same God and as members of the human race. We all want to laugh, provide for our families, lead meaningful lives, fall in love and be happy. Those are not Jewish or Muslim or Christian ideals — they are human ones, and they can bring us together.

Think of how infinitely proud and happy our God would be to see His Muslim and Jewish children end their conflicts and live in harmony.

Yes, Israel has made its share of mistakes. The challenges we face have humbled us. In truth, it hasn't been easy to build a nation while constantly having to defend ourselves. Sometimes, this has brought out the worst in us and made us look like we care only about our own security. We deeply regret the displacement of so many people that occurred in 1948, when we had to defend ourselves against invading armies after the Arab rejection of U.N. Resolution 181, which partitioned the land for two states.

We're human. It does hurt to feel unwelcomed in a neighborhood we have called home for 3,000 years.

We have made peace with two of our neighbors, but that is not enough. We have made further offers and even evacuated settlements, but to no avail. Because our Palestinian neighbors are deeply divided between Gaza and the West Bank, we fear we don't have the strong partner we need to make a deal — and that further evacuations might lead to more violence against us.

Despite our fears, we still yearn for peace. But it is not enough to just meet and "negotiate directly." If both sides don't bring to the table good faith and a willingness to compromise, our hopes will only be false hopes.

The fact that our Palestinian neighbors refused to negotiate last year for the first nine months of our 10-month settlement freeze was not a sign of good faith. Neither are their efforts to undermine us in international forums. Israel has already demonstrated its ability to make painful compromises in all areas, including settlements. Now is not the time for either side to demand preconditions that belong to the negotiating table. Now is the time to sit down in good faith and try to resolve our differences. We say to our Palestinian neighbors: We are ready to begin tomorrow morning. Are you?

We bring the same message to all our neighbors of the Middle East: We are ready to meet tomorrow morning to begin the journey of reconciliation. We dream not only of peace but of a future in which we would all enjoy the fruits of peace. We dream of the day when delegations from Yemen, Libya, Bahrain, Tunisia, Algeria, Egypt, Lebanon and others will visit Israel and see that we are not the enemy, but a friend-in-waiting.

We can cooperate in trade, commerce and culture. We can share our technological and medical innovations to improve quality of life. We can enjoy each other's movies, poems, stories, music and food. Our rabbis can talk about God with your imams. In short, we can create a new golden era of mutual respect and cooperation.

We might disagree, even on some important things, but one of the great human values is not to allow disagreements to turn into animosity and violence.

Beyond our own disagreements, we see too much pain today on the faces of the millions of Arabs rising up throughout the Middle East. We urge all leaders to honor their people by trusting that freedom, dignity and human rights will lead to a better future.

Israel would love nothing more than to have free and democratic neighbors, and we want to be your partner in this momentous endeavor. Cynics will claim that this partnership is impossible — that you have been taught only to hate Jews and Israel, and that it will take a hundred years, if not more, before we can reconnect as the children of Abraham.

Maybe so, but I have no doubt that if our patriarch Abraham were alive today, he would hold our hands and bless us. He would bless us that we should find the strength to transcend our animosities and embark on our journey of reconciliation.

And he would remind us that Allah is with us, watching, hoping we will succeed.

Shalom and As-Salamu Alaykum.

"If the world is really serious about responding to the revolution of Tahrir Square, then the real urgency is to stop ignoring the 99 percent of Arab victims not named Palestinians."

THE 22-STATE SOLUTION

February 16, 2011

H as the world ever witnessed such a radical and overnight transformation of one country? Have we ever seen a nation, in 18 short days, go from a place that represents darkness to one that represents hope, renewal and liberation?

I'm not talking about Egypt; I'm talking about Israel.

In the branding business, we have this thing called "truth transformation." In a nutshell, it says that if your brand has "issues," you can fix them only by finding a deep and meaningful truth. A legendary example is Pepsi, which made great headway against Coke by showing that "in a blind taste test, more people prefer the taste of Pepsi."

Well, it turns out that in a blind taste test, more Arabs prefer the taste of Israel.

I'm not sure people realize yet the extraordinary nature of this transformation. Israel, the most maligned, boycotted and condemned country on the planet, the nation held perennially responsible for the frustrations of millions of Arabs across the Middle East, turns out to have what those frustrated Arabs are now clamoring for: freedom, human rights and a system that protects those rights.

Overnight, this brave and besieged little country has gone from demon to model — from being the curse of the Middle East to its potential cure. We may not see such a radical shift of perception again in our lifetimes.

And yet, hardly anyone is talking about it. I see two reasons. First, the hero country that ought to be promoting this transformation, Israel, is focused more on immediate security than on exporting its democratic gold to its neighbors. This is not unreasonable. Israel already has serious threats on its doorsteps — like Hamas and Hezbollah — and its deep wish is that the chaos of newfound freedom in Egypt will not result in a new security threat.

Second, and more important, the global forces that have worked for years to undermine Israel are now suddenly on the defensive, and they're desperate to keep you focused on "big, bad Israel." They can see the writing on the wall. The edifice that took them decades to build — making Israel global enemy No. 1 and the Palestinians the world's glamour victims — is now in real danger of crumbling.

Just look at the facts. There are 330 million Arabs in the Middle East region who, according to Freedom House, live in countries considered "not free." While those Arabs languished for decades in misery and oppression, where do you think the world concentrated its attention and its billions in aid? That's right, on the Palestinian Arabs who represent less than 1 percent of that total.

And what did the world get in return? A split group of permanent victims who teach the hatred of Israel while refusing to make any real concessions for peace. Talk about a crummy deal.

That's why I wouldn't want to be with the Palestinian PR machine right now. They worked so hard to pull a Houdini and convince the world that Israel is the scourge of humanity and Palestinians the world's biggest victims, and now look — millions of competing Arab victims come to Tahrir Square and steal the attention.

From now on, anyone who pushes for a boycott of Israel can and should be denounced as a hypocrite who couldn't care less about Arab victims not connected with Israel. And good luck to anyone trying to claim with a straight face that pressuring Israel on the Israeli-Palestinian conflict should remain the central mission of the world — not when millions of other Arab victims who have lived for so long under the "occupation" of brutal dictators are finally getting their voices heard.

And not when those Arab voices are craving the very freedom and human rights that Israel, with all its warts and imperfections, already offers.

It is also laughable now for peace-process junkies to claim that a three-state solution (Israel, Palestine and Hamastan) is "more urgent than ever," and would help fix other Middle Eastern problems, like the threat of a nuclear Iran or bringing human rights to the Arab world.

Israel can surely keep chasing the dream of peace with Hamas and the Palestinians, which would be wonderful if it ever happened. But if the world is really serious about responding to the revolution of Tahrir Square, then the real urgency is to stop ignoring the 99 percent of Arab victims not named Palestinians.

In other words, instead of the narrow-minded "two-state solution" mantra that is repeated ad nauseam, the future of the Middle East should revolve around a more just and inclusive "22-state solution," whereby the nations of the region would gradually be exposed to the liberating and dignifying values of democracy. Maybe the United Nations, instead of issuing another condemnation of Israel, can send a mission to the Jewish state to pick up some pointers on how they might introduce democratic institutions and economic prosperity to the rest of the Middle East.

I'm not holding my breath. The industry of maligning Israel is a deeply popular one, and the obsession with Palestinian victimhood is a global phenomenon. Still, the wrenching process of "truth transformation" has begun. The fact that the freest Arabs in the Middle East live in Israel is a truth that Israel's enemies cannot bear. In the post-Tahrir Square era, more and more Arabs will come to see that Israel was never the enemy — but a model to aspire to.

Once the shock of that truth wears off, we'll see how many will taste it.

"Imagine if those Israel bashers, during all the years they put Israel under their critical and hypocritical microscope, had taken Israel's imperfect democratic experiment and said to the Arab world: Why don't you try to emulate the Jews?"

ISRAEL NEVER LOOKED SO GOOD

February 2, 2011

They all warned us. The geniuses at Peace Now. The brilliant diplomats. The think tanks. Even the Arab dictators warned us. For decades now, they have been warning us that if you want "peace in the Middle East," just fix the Palestinian problem. A recent variation on this theme has been: Just get the Jews in the West Bank and East Jerusalem to "freeze" their construction, and then, finally, Palestinian leaders might come to the table and peace might break out.

And what would happen if peace would break out between Jews and Palestinians? Would all those furious Arabs now demonstrating on the streets of Cairo and across the Middle East feel any better? Would they feel less oppressed?

What bloody nonsense.

Has there ever been a greater abuse of the English language in international diplomacy than calling the Israeli-Palestinian conflict the "Middle East peace process?" As if there were only two countries in the Middle East.

Even if you absolutely believe in the imperative of creating a Palestinian state, you can't tell me that the single-minded and global obsession with the Israeli-Palestinian conflict at the expense of the enormous ills in the rest of the Middle East hasn't been idiotic, if not criminally negligent.

While tens of millions of Arabs have been suffering for decades from brutal oppression, while gays have been tortured and writers jailed and women humiliated and dissidents killed, the world — yes, the world — has obsessed with the Israeli-Palestinian conflict.

As if Palestinians — the same coddled victims on whom the world has spent billions and who have rejected one peace offer after another — were the only victims in the Middle East.

As if the Israeli-Palestinian conflict has anything to do with the 1,000-year-old bloody conflict between Sunni and Shiite Muslims, or the desire of brutal Arab dictators to stay in power, or the desire of Islamist radicals to bring back the Caliphate, or the economic despair of millions, or simply the absence of free speech or basic human rights throughout the Arab world.

While self-righteous Israel bashers have scrutinized every flaw in Israel's democracy — some waxing hysterical that the Jewish democratic experiment in the world's nastiest neighborhood has turned into an embarrassment — they kept their big mouths shut about the oppression of millions of Arabs throughout the Middle East.

They cried foul if Israeli Arabs — who have infinitely more rights and freedoms than any Arabs in the Middle East — had their rights compromised in any way. But if a poet was jailed in Jordan or a gay man was tortured in Egypt or a woman was stoned in Syria, all we heard was screaming silence.

Think of the ridiculous amount of media ink and diplomatic attention that has been poured onto the Israel-Palestinian conflict over the years, while much of the Arab world was suffering and smoldering, and tell me this is not criminal negligence. Do you ever recall seeing a U.N. resolution or an international conference in support of Middle Eastern Arabs not named Palestinians?

Of course, now that the Arab volcano has finally erupted, all those chronic Israel bashers have suddenly discovered a new cause: Freedom for the poor oppressed Arabs of the Middle East!

Imagine if those Israel bashers, during all the years they put Israel under their critical and hypocritical microscope, had taken Israel's imperfect democratic experiment and said to the Arab world: Why don't you try to emulate the Jews?

Why don't you give equal rights to your women and gays, just like Israel does?

Why don't you give your people the same freedom of speech, freedom of religion and freedom to vote that Israel gives its people? And offer them the economic opportunities they would get in Israel? Why don't you treat your Jewish citizens the same way Israel treats its Arab citizens?

Why don't you study how Israel has struggled to balance religion with democracy — a very difficult but not insurmountable task?

Why don't you teach your people that Jews are not the sons of dogs, but a noble, ancient people with a 3,000-year connection to the land of Israel?

Yes, imagine if Israel bashers had spent a fraction of their energy fighting the lies of Arab dictators and defending the rights of millions of oppressed Arabs. Imagine if President Obama had taken 1 percent of the time he has harped on Jewish settlements to defend the democratic rights of Egyptian Arabs — which he is suddenly doing now that the volcano has erupted.

Maybe it's just easier to beat up on a free and open society like Israel.

Well, now that the cesspool of human oppression in the Arab world has been opened for all to see, how bad is Israel's democracy looking? Don't you wish the Arab world had a modicum of Israel's civil society? And that it was as stable and reliable and free and open as Israel?

You can preach to me all you want about the great Jewish tradition of self-criticism — which I believe in — but right now, when I see poor Arab souls being killed for protesting on the street, and the looming threat that one Egyptian Pharaoh may be replaced by an even more oppressive one, I've never felt more proud of being a supporter of the Jewish state.

"As long as the world believes the Palestinian narrative that this is stolen land, Israel's painful land concessions have no perceived value. This is one reason negotiations have gone nowhere."

ISRAEL SHOULD STOP HIDING AT THE U.N.

January 19, 2011

W hy is Israel hiding while its Palestinian "peace partners" are accusing the Jewish state of engaging in an illegal enterprise? In case you missed it, the Palestinian Authority is planning to introduce a resolution to the United Nations Security Council this week declaring all Jewish settlements "illegal." It's not enough that most of the world already believes this; the Palestinians are feeling so confident these days, they've decided to push their luck and intensify their campaign to malign Israel.

Israel, no doubt expecting that the United States will veto the measure, has responded by burying its head in the sand. This is a big mistake.

For one thing, hiding reinforces the image of guilt. Israel already looks super-guilty on the issue of settlements. Keeping quiet suggests to the world that Israel essentially agrees with the accusations.

But beyond the need to play defense, this resolution offers, I believe, a chance for Israel to win a rare public relations victory on a global stage. Israel can use the U.N. forum to turn the tables on the Palestinians and present to the world a message it never hears.

It can actually push back on the issue of the legality of settlements.

You're probably thinking: How can anyone in his right mind challenge the accepted truism that the Jewish settlements are illegal? And even if Israel could successfully make a case that the settlements are not illegal, so what? How could that contribute to the peace process or the two-state solution?

The sharpest answer I've heard on this point came from Talia Shulman Gold, the local representative of CAMERA, a watchdog organization that fights anti-Israel bias in the media. Because I sit on its board of advisers, I recently hosted a small gathering at my home. That night, after Shulman Gold made the case that any discussion of the legality of settlements must include the resolution of the League of Nations in San Remo in 1922, I asked her that very question: "So what? Even if you're right, how will this help move us forward?"

"Israel must show the world that it is not a thief," she answered. "Even if Israel ends up giving up the West Bank, it must show that it is doing it for peace — not because it is returning stolen land. As long as the world believes the Palestinian narrative that this is stolen land, Israel's painful land concessions have no perceived value. This is one reason negotiations have gone nowhere."

What I liked about her answer is that it opens up conversation, instead of slamming the door shut. My eyes glaze over when I hear arguments from some of my friends on the religious right, such as, "We can't give back the land because God gave it to us!" This might well be true, but it doesn't make for great conversation. It makes everything black and white.

One point Shulman Gold tried to bring home the other night is that the legality of Jewish settlements is anything but black and white. If you're interested in this subject, I suggest you Google Middle East scholar Eli E. Hertz and go to his Myths and Facts Web site (mythsandfacts.com), in particular the section on "Mandate for Palestine." He describes this mandate as "an historical League of Nations document [that] laid down the Jewish legal right to settle anywhere in western Palestine, between the Jordan River and the Mediterranean Sea, an entitlement unaltered in international law."

According to Hertz, this was not "a naïve vision briefly embraced by the international community," but, rather, a unanimous declaration by the entire League of Nations (51 countries) on July 24, 1922, which he quotes: "Whereas recognition has been given to the historical connection of the Jewish people with Palestine and to the grounds for reconstituting their national home in that country."

Hertz, as well as many others, makes a case that the League of Nations agreement was legally "inherited" by the United Nations, that it has never been revoked and that it is still legally binding according to international law. Subsequent U.N. resolutions, they argue, even the one establishing the State of Israel, did not override the League of Nations agreement and never established the illegality of Jewish settlements. They also punch holes in the strongest argument against their case, article 49 of the Fourth Geneva convention.

My point here is not to sway you one way or the other on the legality of Jewish settlements. It's simply to suggest that this issue is a lot more complicated than the Palestinian public relations machine alleges and to suggest that Israel should not be afraid to stand up at the United Nations this week and face this P.R. monster head on.

Israel should make a bold and compelling case based on international law that it doesn't believe the settlements are illegal, and then tell the world the following: "For years, Israel has offered to evacuate Jewish settlements for the sake of peace. We have done so not because we think the settlements are illegal, but because we value peace so highly.

"Unfortunately, because so many of our past offers and gestures have been rewarded by terror, rejection and bad faith, the mood among many of our people today is guided by extreme caution and mistrust.

"The resolution advanced by our Palestinian neighbors this week is another example of a needless and poisonous gesture — one that inevitably will breed even more mistrust and take us even further away from peace and reconciliation."

"Every mitzvah is a gift box of personal meaning. The real gift we get when we do the mitzvah is that we can start to own it. It becomes ours, not only God's. There's nothing like a sense of personal ownership to deepen your attachment."

WHY DO JEWISH?

January 11, 2011

C an Orthodox Jews learn something fundamental from unaffiliated Jews? That is, can Jews who practice Torah rituals learn something from Jews who practice virtually none? This question was on my mind recently as I attended two events representing the polar opposites of Jewish life.

The first was the annual West Coast convention of the Orthodox Union, where the theme this year was "Keeping Our Values for the Next Generation." I attended several of the events and moderated a closing panel on "Values for Our Future." While the overall theme was values, the underlying mission of the convention was how to strengthen the Orthodox movement, and, in particular, how to keep the next generation from straying from the Modern Orthodox derech (path).

In the same way that the broader community constantly talks about "Jewish continuity," the Orthodox community is also very busy these days with "Orthodox continuity."

This idea of Jewish continuity played a big part of the second event I attended, "Funding Your Passions: A Breakfast With Harold Grinspoon." Grinspoon, a renowned philanthropist, talked about many things, but one subject in particular put a twinkle in his eyes: The PJ Library, a 5-year-old initiative that has already distributed more than 2 million children's books to thousands of Jewish families across North America. For many of these families, who are unaffiliated, these colorful and engaging bedtime books have become their major connection to the Jewish tradition and their entrance to the Jewish community.

What I found remarkable about the books is that while they are fun to read, they don't dumb down Judaism. One of my favorites is "The Only One Club," a charming and intelligent primer on one of the philosophical dilemmas of modern Jewish life — how to balance the particularity of the Jewish tradition with the universality of humanism.

It is books like "The Only One Club" that made me think of how programs for unaffiliated Jews might help programs for Orthodox Jews. The Orthodox community spends a lot of time on the who, what, where, when and how of Jewish rituals, but not as much, it seems to me, on the "why." We study Torah commandments from all angles, but rarely will we ask: "Why should I do this in the first place?"

"Because God and our Sages said so" and "because our ancestors did so" are easy and powerful answers, but they are not the only ones. For the Orthodox community to thrive, it will need to open up to the kind of "why" questions outreach groups like the PJ Library routinely ask: "Why is Judaism good for me? Why do I need it? Why is it meaningful?"

These are not the kinds of questions my grandparents asked in their cozy Orthodox neighborhoods of Casablanca, but they are questions that are sneaking up on the Orthodox world and in our Modern Orthodox shtetls like Pico-Robertson.

While outreach to the unaffiliated deals more with identity — "Why be Jewish?" —outreach to the Orthodox must deal more with activity — "Why do Jewish?" Both questions are fundamental. They both 'fess up to the reality that in today's world of nonstop distractions, we can't assume that Judaism of any denomination will simply sell itself.

The good news is that if we use our imaginations, we can come up with great answers. One answer I give to my kids for "Why do Jewish?" is that a mitzvah is not something that boxes you in, but rather, a gift box from God.

Open the mitzvah box and create your own personal meaning. For example, kissing the mezuzah reminds me to show love to my friends and family. Separating meat from milk reminds me to separate work from play. Making a blessing on food reminds me to show gratitude and help the hungry and less fortunate. Putting on tefillin reminds me that God is a filter between me and negative forces. Lighting Shabbat candles reminds me that I must aspire to be a shining candle in the world.

At Passover time, cleaning out the chametz from my house reminds me not to meddle with my neighbor's chametz; in other words, not to do lashon harah. The possibilities are endless.

Every mitzvah is a gift box of personal meaning. The real gift we get when we do the mitzvah is that we start to own it. It becomes ours, not only God's. There's nothing like a sense of personal ownership to deepen your attachment.

This is what I learned from a program like PJ Library that is geared to non-Orthodox and unaffiliated Jews. It's always a good idea to start at the beginning and ask, "why?" It's a question that works for everyone — either as an entry door for the beginner or as a source of personal renewal for the observant. It's the kind of no-nonsense approach that can only bring out the best in us.

Jewish leaders of all denominations shouldn't be afraid to "sell" Judaism. Even an Orthodox convention can permit itself to show how Torah rituals can help make Jews better and happier people.

Seriously. If Coke Zero can sell happiness and a bank can sell meaning of life, why can't we?

"The extraordinary thing about Eva's message is that even as she talked about death, murder and pain, she always ended up in the same place – with an intense love of life. She left Holocaust theory to the intellectuals. Her specialty was living."

SO LONG, EVA

January 5, 2011

It's not easy to handle death. It's so naked and finite. No matter how much we talk about the spiritual journey to the next world, about legacies that never die, about a life well lived, there's really no consolation for the pain of missing someone — really, really missing someone.

I will miss Eva Brown, a Holocaust survivor who passed away last week at the age of 83 after a three-year fight with cancer.

What I will miss most is the sparkle in her eyes. She seemed to always have it — when she first told me about her cancer; when she'd listen to me complain about stuff in my own life; when someone would let her down; when things were really good or when things were really bad.

She even had it a couple of weeks ago, when I brought my kids to see her one last time to say good-bye. I had a premonition it would be the last time, because my friend Marci Spitzer had left me a message that "Eva would like to see you very soon." When I got to Eva's house in West Hollywood that Sunday afternoon — where we'd once been neighbors and where she had lived for nearly 60 years — Eva told me the doctors had said her long battle was over. By now, her two surviving daughters and her granddaughter were there with her around the clock. She was taking painkillers. It was just a question of time.

But she still had the sparkle in her eyes, the sparkle that said, "I'm still here."

She mentioned that for the past few days she had been having visions of her father and husband walking through her room. They were the two men closest to her. She lost 59 members of her family in the Holocaust, but her father, a prominent rabbi, miraculously survived. They had moved to America after the war, and she never lost her attachment to him. She spent many hours at our Shabbat table telling us stories of what it was like to grow up as the daughter of the chief rabbi of a little town in Hungary when there was plenty of love but no running water.

She had a 50-year love affair with her husband, Ernie, who passed away about 10 years ago. But they had different outlooks on life. Her husband could never get over the pain of the Holocaust and the bitterness in his heart. She once shared with me that on his deathbed, he confessed to her that he regretted having been bitter most of his life.

Eva, somehow, managed to avoid bitterness. At the age of 16, she was sent to 10 concentration camps in just one year. Her signature story, captured at the beginning of Thomas Fields-Meyer's book, "If You Save One Life," describes her encounter with an American soldier, who rescued her from a long death march. He asked her, in Yiddish, "Who did this to you?" and she didn't have it in her heart to point her finger at a German soldier. She believed in justice, but not revenge. She also believed, as her father taught her, that every life was worth saving — hence the title of the book.

This ability to be positive and look to the future was almost inexplicable, because she spent so much of her time talking about the pain of her past. For many years now, she has been part of the family at the Museum of Tolerance, where she has spoken regularly to various groups about her Holocaust experience. The last few years, as if she could sense the clock ticking, she increased her appearances at schools, churches and colleges. El Camino College in Torrance even set up the Eva Brown Peace and Tolerance Educational Center in her honor.

I attended many of her talks. The extraordinary thing about Eva's message is that even as she talked about death, murder and pain, she always ended up in the same place — with an intense love of life. She left Holocaust theory to the intellectuals. Her specialty was living.

It was as if her years in the pits of darkness had led this tiny woman to reveal herself as an evangelist for the celebration of life. She saw this as a very Jewish thing — savoring every breath of life that God gave her. She loved going out. When I would take her as my "date" to the Maimonides Academy trustees dinner, she'd put on a nice dress and perfume and would ask to go in the sports car, even if she had trouble getting in.

Her sparkle attracted a "circle of love" from Jewish women in the community, among them Sara Aftergood, Lesley Wolman, Marci Spitzer and Kathy Barnhard, who constantly brought her the soup she so loved and invited her for Shabbat and holiday meals. When Rabbi Shawn Fields-Meyer visited her a few days before she died, Eva didn't want soup — she wanted to hear the song, "Eshet Chayil." She soaked up pleasure until the very end.

One of those pleasures was taking pictures. Her house was full of them.

On that last Sunday when my kids and I went to say good-bye, after we all shared kisses and sweet words, she asked me in a weak voice: "Can we take a picture?"

We took a couple of great shots with the kids. If you look carefully, you can still see that little sparkle in her eyes.

"Facebook is like a never-ending virtual cocktail party full of people you know, used to know or would like to know, with one irresistible advantage over a real party: you can eavesdrop on all the happenings while still in your pajamas."

FACEBOOK BLUES

December 22, 2010

Besides the mandatory Belgian chocolate pretzel challah from Got Kosher?, I always try to bring a little food for thought for my kids to our Friday night Shabbat table — either an interesting story or dvar Torah or an experience I had that week. Last Friday, I decided to bring something I'd read in Tablet magazine on the modern-day obsession with Facebook:

"What computers can do is think in code, a series of simple, mathematical statements. Human beings, on the other hand, can imagine and dream, hope and despair, hate and love with all their hearts. When they meet — truly meet, face to face and at leisure — with their friends — true friends, not an assortment of barely recognizable acquaintances living on the periphery of an enormous virtual network — they are capable of subtle wonders. If, instead, they opt for convenience, if they reduce their thoughts to brief posts, if they don't bother finding out who they really are outside the bounds of their Facebook profiles, they're doomed to wither into a virtual oblivion."

It wasn't a paragraph; it was a punch to the stomach. The writer, Liel Leibovitz, was doing a wicked riff on the Facebook Generation, which he believes is mired in a "thick but meaningless pile of likes and dislikes" and getting more and more disconnected from what really matters in life.

This is serious food for thought: Does Facebook disconnect us from real life, and if so, how?

I got one answer on Friday night. While I was reading the quote, my oldest daughter, Tova, a freshman at the UCLA School of Fine Arts, interrupted me: "Oh, my God, I can't believe you're reading this," she said. "I just disconnected myself from Facebook."

It turns out Tova was getting exhausted by the idea of having 935 "friends," when in reality she has less than a dozen. But, more importantly, she just felt the whole experience was becoming empty and frivolous — that she wasn't being very nourished by Facebook.

Yet there are 600 million people around the globe who apparently feel differently. How do we explain this phenomenon? Is it simply that people crave human contact? That we are fascinated by other people — what they look like, what they do, what they think, what they like, who they know? That in a chaotic world, we need the perceived safety of belonging to a group?

It's certainly all that. Facebook is like a never-ending virtual cocktail party full of people you know, used to know or would like to know, with one irresistible advantage over a real party: you can eavesdrop on all the happenings while still in your pajamas.

It would be unfair to undervalue this experience. Facebook helps you reconnect with old friends (and old flames, but that's a whole other story); share ideas, photos, movies, songs, videos, jokes, musings and articles; promote your work, causes and events; join movements; and so on. But beyond its utilitarian value, the real problem for those seeking human connection is that everything happens on a digital screen. This plays to our laziness. It's so convenient to hang out at this "virtual" party that it can easily become a substitute for the real thing.

Worse, though, is that it also plays to our narcissism. Once you start posting personal statuses like, "I think I'll make soup now" or "I can't believe I have another headache," you know you're approaching the status of self-worship.

Ultimately, as I see it, it all comes back to the digital screen. You can "like" to paint or hang glide or read poetry or engage in deep conversation, but while you're on Facebook, you're actually not doing any of those things. You can crave human contact, but how human is the contact? You can create a profile that makes you look great, but how great do you feel inside?

You can be networking all day long — but are you living?

In a recent piece in Time Out New York, writer Sharon Steel exhorted her fellow New Yorkers to lessen their obsession with social networks: "Just keep in mind that anyone anywhere can thumbs-up a YouTube video of the Rufus Wainwright concert at Carnegie Hall, retweet a pic of the red-quinoa salad from Octavia's Porch or comment on how insane the Panda-sonic party looks. But you, lucky New Yorker, can actually go."

No matter where we are, we can "actually go" to experience what Leibovitz calls the "subtle wonders" of the nonvirtual life, whether that would be walking barefoot on a beach or having a passionate conversation over lunch with a friend. Can a computer geek who designs "social network" algorithms ever replace those experiences for us?

As I was reading Leibovitz's quote to my children last Friday night, it struck me that I was living, right there and then, an antidote to the Facebook experience. It was the Shabbat table, with its slow, unhurried pace, when everyone dresses nicely and everything is real — from the candles, the blessings, the singing and the chocolate challah to the safety of family and the stories that are allowed to extend beyond a few sound bites.

It also struck me that Facebook might be the most misleading name in the history of marketing. For all its virtual wonders, it comes with neither a face nor a book.

"Israel should fess up that it doesn't have the power to turn enemies into peacemakers. If such honesty spares us the pathetic spectace of grown men pretending to make peace, that alone would be a miracle."

CAN WE EVER ADMIT FAILURE?

December 15, 2010

The State of Israel was built on the very Jewish idea of taking personal responsibility. It was built not by whiners but by Jews for whom no miracle was impossible — whether that meant defending against an Arab invasion or turning a desert into lush fields of agriculture. Throughout its young history, this can-do attitude has been the life force behind Israel's military success as well as its economic and cultural renaissance.

There is one area, however, where Israel's can-do attitude has been a big failure, and that is in making peace with the Palestinians.

Success in business is clear — you create a product or service that people want to buy. But with the business of making peace, history has shown that it's far from clear whether Israel has a product the Palestinians want to buy. This has thrown Israel's macho swagger for a loop: If we can make or sell pretty much anything, why can't we make peace with the Palestinians?

Because Israel's can-do reputation is so strong, the country has been under enormous pressure over the years, internally and externally, to "do something" to bring peace. More often than not, Israel has been too embarrassed to admit that "we can't solve this one," that the parties are too far apart, that peace, no matter how desirable, is simply not in the cards at the moment.

But what if, in fact, this is the truth? What if there is nothing Israel can offer the Palestinians to get them to accept and deliver a durable peace with a Jewish state? What if the ugly, unbearable truth is that Israel can evacuate 300,000 Jews from the West Bank tomorrow and give up half of Jerusalem and that this would still not bring peace — and might even bring more war?

How does a macho country admit failure?

I got a glimpse of Israel's dilemma the other morning at the Museum of Tolerance (MOT), where Yuli Edelstein, Israel's Minister of Public Affairs and the Diaspora, was giving a briefing to the museum's board of directors and other community leaders. After Edelstein's candid but balanced assessment of Israel's situation, the MOT's dean and founder, Rabbi Marvin Hier, said something so simple and stark that it seemed to stun the room.

"What two-state solution are they talking about?" he asked. "It's a three-state solution: Israel, the Palestinians, and Hamas in Gaza. What do we do about Gaza?" Hier's point was that even if Israel can achieve the impossible and make a deal with Abbas in the West Bank, a mortal enemy remains at its doorstep in Gaza. How do you convince a terrorist neighbor to cancel its charter calling for your destruction? How do you make them stop hating you? Apparently, not even Israel's ingenuity can crack this code.

Lord Jonathan Sacks, chief rabbi of the UK, seems to understand the conflict behind the conflict. In response to a Jewish community leader's recent admonition of Prime Minister Benjamin Netanyahu for lacking "the courage to move the peace process forward," Sacks wrote that the debate is "deflecting us from the real issue," which is that Israel's enemies — Hamas, Hezbollah and Iran — refuse to recognize its existence as a matter of religious principle. And as long as this is the case, he says, "There can be no peace, merely a series of staging posts on the way to a war that will not end until there is no Jewish state at all."

This is scary stuff. It suggests that even if we had the leaders of J Street or Peace Now negotiating for Israel, there would still be no peace. How painful is that?

The way I see it, Israel has one option left: Stop the swagger and start speaking the truth. The Palestinian demand for a "right of return" is a deal-killer. So is a return to nondefensible borders, and so is the presence of a terrorist state in Gaza.

Instead of looking so macho and responsible, Israel should just be candid. Netanyahu had no business calling Abbas his "peace partner" after the wily Abbas dragged his feet for nine months during Israel's 10-month settlement freeze. He should have said, bluntly: "This is not the behavior of a peace partner." By looking so darn optimistic while the other side looked so darn pessimistic, Bibi ended up looking so darn guilty.

The fact that peace is immensely desirable has nothing to do with the reality that it is immensely unobtainable. If anything, the more Israel has shown its desire, the more the price has gone up. The Palestinians have said "no, no, no, no" to every peace offer Israel has ever put on the table. Seriously: What are the chances that Abbas will receive a better offer from Bibi than the generous one he rejected from Olmert two years ago? With Hamas breathing down his neck, how likely is it that Abbas can even deliver on a peace deal?

Let's stop faking it. The status quo may be untenable, but a fake peace process makes it even worse. There's no deal at the moment. That's the annoying truth.

Admitting this truth may not be macho or practical, but at least it's honest. Israel should fess up that it doesn't have the power to turn enemies into peacemakers. If such honesty spares us the pathetic spectacle of grown men pretending to make peace, that alone would be a miracle.

"Donniel Hartman can't stand anything easy and quick; he might have lasted 30 seconds in an ad agency. He thinks in long form."

LONELY MAN OF THOUGHT

November 10, 2010

T he elderly man was hunched over, walking slowly with the help of a cane toward a small stage where a table, chair and microphone awaited him. The medium-size conference hall was utterly silent despite being packed with people, most of whom knew him well, some of them wondering, perhaps, whether he would make it up the steps to the stage. I was one of those people, sitting in the back. I had waited years for this moment — the chance to be in Jerusalem at the Shalom Hartman Institute and listen to the words of its founder, Rabbi David Hartman.

He owned the room for three hours, doing a verbal jazz session that blended philosophical rants and challenges to Orthodox dogmas, talmudic insights and silly recollections of his childhood in Montreal. I scribbled furiously, filling a whole notebook with the rabbi's rebellious musings. There was one thing he said, however, that stood out and that I couldn't get out of my mind:

"I'm not my son," Rabbi Hartman said, "and my son is not me."

Hartman was talking about his disagreements with men he felt very close to: his teacher and mentor Rabbi Joseph Soloveitchik, the founder and guiding light of the Modern Orthodox movement; and the great Maimonides, about whom Hartman has written extensively. He was telling us that you can love and admire someone but still disagree with that person

— that being a follower doesn't mean being a blind follower.

And that includes the relationship between father and son.

Two years later, that son, Rabbi Donniel Hartman, the man who has taken the institute to the next level and made it an intellectual force in the Jewish world, was sitting in my living room and sharing his own philosophical musings. He was on a U.S. visit to drum up support for the many initiatives of the institute, which is a combination think tank, nerve center and study retreat for all things deep and Jewish.

Donniel Hartman can't stand anything easy and quick; he might have lasted 30 seconds in an ad agency. He thinks in long form. His latest mastermind, called the Israel Engagement Project, includes a DVD set that features some of the top Zionist thinkers in Israel engaging the complex subject of Israel and Jewish values. He hopes it will become the basis for a national conversation in the American Jewish community.

If you have a short attention span, watch out: The DVD set is 15 hours long.

Donniel Hartman embodies things that are usually perceived as mutually exclusive: a charismatic speaker who shies away from sound bites; an Orthodox rabbi who legitimizes other branches of Judaism; a fervent Zionist who is deeply liberal; a centrist with passion; a theorist who is pragmatic; a thinker who can act.

A friend of his once remarked that "he lives at the meeting point of conflict."

He's the only liberal I know who has actually called for an "end to Charedi bashing," which he did in a recent op-ed on Ynet. He's pragmatic enough to recognize that the Charedim have become "central players in Israel's social and political environment," while also high-minded enough to see that the Zionist majority must not cede the ideological high ground in the debate, lest you "undermine your own position and make it impossible to have any impact on those with whom you are arguing."

This ability to embrace different polarities has been a key part of the Hartman Institute's success. When I was there for a study program two summers ago, I saw lay and rabbinic leaders from all denominations mingling together. It's true, they were all of the "open-minded" variety, but that's precisely the point of the institute — to nurture and grow this so-called "segment of the open-minded."

This is one the great ironies of the Hartman Institute. They promote the kind of thinking that encourages you to go off and think for yourself. They are rebels against dogma, enemies of the status quo. They may be as Torah observant as any Orthodox Jew, but within this Torah context, they are agitators.

Before he left my house, I had to ask Donniel if he ever "broke" with his famous father on any issue. He came up with two issues on which they've had some disagreements: the "validity of secular Judaism" and "Can there be a Judaism without God?" Donniel is more of a pure pluralist than his father, and he puts a greater value on what he calls a "Judaism of belonging to a people," whether one believes in God or not.

The root of all these disagreements — this family tradition of "thinking for oneself" — originates at the Hartman dinner table. Growing up, they were all encouraged to challenge the status quo. In fact, Donniel's sister, Tova, is one of the founders of the egalitarian Shira Hadasha minyan in Jerusalem.

Donniel recalls that his father's favorite question was: "What do you think?"

He remembers one of the first times he heard the question. As soon as he started answering, "Rashi says ...," his father interrupted him.

"I didn't ask you what Rashi said," the father told him. "I asked you what you think."

"Stewart will get up at a rally in front of thousands of followers and rail against 'the country's 24-hour politico-pundit-perpetual-panic-conflictinator.' Sheleg will talk to a small group and quietly say things like, 'In the media, radicals get all the attention.'"

JON STEWART, MEET BAMBI

November 3, 2010

The last name I expected to come up at our Shabbat table last week was Jon Stewart. I was hosting a serious, soft-spoken public intellectual from Israel, Bambi Sheleg — who was in town on a speaking tour — and her words to my Shabbat guests were anything but funny and ironic.

Since she launched her bimonthly magazine Eretz Acheret (A Different Place) 10 years ago, Sheleg has made quiet waves in the Jewish state. Her magazine doesn't go for easy drama or sexy opinion. It tackles complicated issues dealing with social, cultural and spiritual developments in Israel and among the Jewish people.

I can't imagine Sheleg doing a "Daily Show" in Israel with the snarky and hysterical ridicule that has made Jon Stewart famous.

Yet there she was, at our lunch, extolling the virtues of Stewart. In particular, she was responding to what she saw as his call for "sanity" in dialogue and public discourse.

Everything about Sheleg screams sanity. I met her in Jerusalem last summer, and for three hours she mesmerized me with her seriousness. She cares deeply about the issues that affect Israel. She is originally from the world of religious Zionists, but over the years she has become a lot less ideological and a lot more introspective. She preaches humility over ideology.

Around the time of the Gaza disengagement, she wrote a controversial piece that got her in trouble with her religious Zionist brethren, because she talked of the mistakes they made, and how, in their zeal to settle the land, they ignored other important issues and "disengaged" from much of Israeli society.

It was vintage Sheleg. Take on your own, but do it from a place of love and intelligence.

She hates to win arguments.

Her ideology has become civilized debate. Her magazine has given a voice to Israelis from all walks of life, from Charedim, settlers, Ethiopian and Russian immigrants to Tel Aviv artists, women, academics, impoverished Israelis and the Israeli-Arab sector. Her writers take on divisive issues like conversion and the rabbinate with long and intense essays.

A few years ago, her magazine was credited with what the Forward newspaper called "one of the most important but barely publicized rulings in the history of the Jewish state." It was a Supreme Court decision to cancel the privatization of the country's prison system, and it was influenced by an Eretz Acheret cover story: "Can the State Abdicate Its Role as Responsible for the Correctional System?"

In short, she's Israel's earnest answer to Jon Stewart.

What they have in common is a deep aversion to extremism of any kind. Stewart expresses his disdain for extremism by making fun of it. Sheleg expresses her disdain by creating an alternative.

Stewart will get up at a rally in front of thousands of followers and rail against "the country's 24-hour politico-pundit-perpetual-panic-conflicti-nator." Sheleg will talk to a small group and quietly say things like, "In the media, radicals get all the attention ... my goal is to build bridges between people rather than focus on what divides us."

They have similar goals, but they play different instruments. As I reflected on those two instruments after Sheleg's visit, a thought occurred to me: Maybe these two personalities need each other.

Stewart is the perfect opening act for Sheleg. He's the guy who can work the crowd and get them pumped up for the heavy stuff that's about to follow. He's no policy wonk, but he's wicked smart, and he knows a dumb debate when he sees one.

Sheleg is the ideal follow-up to Stewart. She does the heavy lifting of transforming the "dumb debates" into civilized dialogues that promote smart and humane solutions.

Israel needs a Jon Stewart to make Sheleg's moderation more noticeable, and America needs a Bambi Sheleg to make Stewart's brilliant rants more than just brilliant rants.

It's unfair to beat up Stewart because he doesn't offer solutions, just like it's unfair to beat up Sheleg because she hasn't made her centrist movement more entertaining. Still, it'd be nice to see what would happen if their movements joined forces.

I can just see it. After doing a bit on politicians who can't speak the truth, Stewart would hold up a magazine called A Different Place and say to his audience of millions: "Now go to this magazine's Web site and try to sit still for 30 minutes as my partner Bambi Sheleg leads a roundtable on the meaning of truth in politics. And then tell her what you think, because this woman's a really good listener."

In Israel, where ridicule and satire are common fare, I'm sure they can find an Israeli version of Stewart to break the ice for Sheleg's earnest offerings and add millions to her readership. This would be bridge-building at its highest level.

Maybe that's why Sheleg was so enthused at our Shabbat table about someone who is so different from herself. She has a weakness for bridges.

"I know that, for many people, spirituality and meditation will always be a tough sell. The experience seems too mushy. It doesn't feel as concrete as history, as artsy as poetry or as intellectually challenging as Talmud."

SEEING THE INVISIBLE

October 27, 2010

What is it about the word "spiritual" that throws so many people off? Why is it that when I invite people to a Torah salon, I get a great reaction, but when I invite the same people to a "spiritual" salon that includes meditation, I get a rolling of the eyes? Is it just that the notion of spirituality is too nebulous to be taken seriously?

I've had a chance to reflect on these questions over the past week as I've hosted Rabbi Yoel Glick, a spiritual teacher with an unusual background. Glick, who lives in France and Jerusalem, trained in the classic Modern Orthodox world of Yeshiva University but also spent years studying with the Chasidic mystic Rabbi Shlomo Carlebach and dabbling in the Eastern arts of yoga and meditation.

His blend of Torah intellect and spiritual intensity was on full display the other night as he led a session in my home on "Building the Temple of the Heart: The Three Pillars of the Spiritual Life."

It didn't take long for the 20 or so attendees to realize this would not be an ordinary class. As soon as we sat down, Glick asked us for something I don't recall ever experiencing in my house, especially when the kids are home: five minutes of total silence.

The idea was to put us in the mood to receive and experience the message itself.

For the next hour or so, Glick took us on a little expedition where the three pillars of the spiritual life became progressively deeper and more personal. He started in the classic tradition, quoting Pirke Avot (Ethics of the Fathers), which teaches that "the world stands on three things: Torah, avodah (worship) and gemilut chasadim (acts of loving kindness)." The combined practice of these three principles, the rabbi told us, brought "balance, harmony and firmness" to the world of our sages.

He connected the three pillars to the three paths in yoga: jnana (wisdom), bhakti (devotion) and karma (action). Torah is the equivalent of jnana, the path of the mind; avodah is the equivalent of bhakti, the path of the heart; and gemilut hasadim is the equivalent of karma, the path of the hands and feet, or action.

Glick went on to explain that each of us has one path that seems to come more naturally, that "resonates more fully with our soul."

At this point, he could easily have finished an excellent class. He would have tied classic Torah with Eastern philosophy and encouraged people to follow the spiritual path that speaks directly to them.

But it's what followed that took the session to a more intensely spiritual level. Glick took the three pillars and connected them to the ideas of "expansion of consciousness," the "remembrance of God" and "self-transformation."

He quoted from Bible stories, Chassidut and many other sources to further develop the three pillars. He spoke about the importance of "expanding the boundaries of both our inner and outer reality," of "bringing the awareness of God into every moment of our life" and of "transforming ourselves from animal creatures into Divine instruments — from what we are to what God wants us to be."

As he spoke, almost in a meditative trance, I couldn't help but think back to earlier that day, when Glick and I were having lunch with my marketing colleague Gary Wexler, and we were discussing how on earth one would market something as nebulous and intangible as "spirituality." There were no simple answers, we concluded, because while the idea of marketing is to make noise and be visible, the magic of spirituality is that it is quiet and invisible.

Selling spirituality with the usual tricks of branding and benefits would just cheapen it, Glick told us. And he was right. Maybe this is why spirituality is still on the fringes of mainstream Judaism.

Ironically, I realized a few days later that the secret to marketing spirituality was walking right beside me on Pico Boulevard. It was Glick himself. The way he concentrated on every moment; the care he took to prepare his drash at the Happy Minyan; his ability to explode in joy when the feeling overtook him; how slowly and little he ate at our Shabbat table while he told stories and encouraged everyone to sing; how he paid so much attention to the kids; the sweetness of his words.

I know that, for many people, spirituality and meditation will always be a tough sell. The experience seems too mushy. It doesn't feel as concrete as history, as artsy as poetry or as intellectually challenging as Talmud.

While there may be some truth in that, there's also something simple and powerful at work for the serious practitioner of the spiritual arts: It's what it does to you as a person.

I saw it with Rabbi Glick.

The rabbi explained that real spiritual work ends up permeating all of one's thoughts and actions — not just helping us handle crises but also influencing how we go about our daily lives. Inevitably, it permeates how we practice our professions and influences the quality of all our relationships.

The work might be silent, Rabbi Glick seemed to be saying, but the effects are loud and clear.

"As a Sephardic Jew, I can tell you that Jews who lived for centuries as good citizens of Arab countries would have loved nothing more than to pledge loyalty to a 'Muslim and democratic state' in return for the same freedoms, rights and protections that Arabs enjoy today in Israel."

WHY THE LOYALTY OATH IS A GOOD DEAL
October 20, 2010

M aybe it's because I was a Jew in an Arab country that I have a slightly different take on the loyalty oath controversy. Imagine, for a minute, that your name is Ahmed and you are a gay Palestinian living in Ramallah. You live in fear of being outed, ostracized, even jailed and tortured. A few miles away is a Jewish and democratic nation called Israel. Your partner, who is Arab and lives there, has been telling you for years that he suffers no discrimination from being gay. In fact, a few months ago, he danced in the Gay Pride Parade in Jerusalem with full protection from the Israeli authorities.

Lately, you've been doing research on Google to find out more about how Israel treats its minorities. You're doing this because since you were a child, you have been taught that Jews are the "sons of dogs" who have no connection to this land and are deserving only of hatred. How could such "sons of dogs" be so respectful of Arab homosexuals?

You learn in your research that Arabs living in Israel enjoy free health care and welfare benefits; democratic rights, like freedom of speech, freedom of religion and freedom to vote; full women's rights; and opportunities to learn at great universities.

You also discover the following items about Israeli Arabs: the existence of Arab political parties in the Israeli government like Hadash,

Balad and Ra'amTa'al, which have the right to promote even incendiary things like the Palestinian "right of return" and the dismantling of Israel's nuclear arsenal; NGOs like Adalah: The Legal Center for Arab Minority Rights in Israel, which helps minorities seek legal redress; Ali Yahya, Israel's Arab ambassador to Greece; Salim Joubran, Supreme Court justice; and Oscar Abu-Razek, director general of the Ministry of Interior.

You also learn about Raleb Majadele, the first Arab Cabinet minister in Israel; Jamal Hakrush, assistant commander in Israel's National Police; Rana Raslan, the first Arab to win a Miss Israel contest; Bnei Sakhnin, the first Arab soccer team to win Israel's State Cup; Asala Shahada, an Arab who won a gold medal at the Maccabiah games; and Majd el-Haj, an Arab sociology professor at Haifa University who was promoted to dean of research at the university.

You ask yourself: How could all these Arabs be so successful in a Jewish state that is supposed to favor Jews and discriminate against Arabs?

As you research the answer, you come across this finding from a report of the U.S. State Department: "Most of the Arab states are ruled by oppressive, dictatorial regimes, which deny their citizens basic freedoms of political expression, speech, press and due process." Ah hah, you say, maybe that explains why Arabs in Israel are not clamoring to leave the Jewish state and join their brethren in other Arab countries.

You then find Israel's Declaration of Independence, which affirms the full legal and human rights of all its citizens, Jew and non-Jew alike. Because you have been taught to believe that the birth of Israel is a "catastrophe" and that Jews have no connection to the land, you are surprised to discover the 3,000-year connection of the Jewish people to Israel. This helps you understand Israel's Law of Return, which states that Jews become automatic citizens when they "return home" to Israel.

Finally, you read about a recent and controversial amendment to Israel's citizen loyalty oath. The proposed amendment would require non-Jewish foreigners wishing to become Israeli citizens to declare loyalty not just to the State of Israel, but to the "Jewish and democratic" State of Israel.

So you think: I would be able to live as a proud and free homosexual and enjoy all the other civil rights and benefits in return for taking a loyalty oath to a "Jewish and democratic" state? Hey, that sounds like a pretty good deal to me. What's all the fuss about?

The fuss, Ahmed, is that a lot of people think this initiative is offensive and racist — that it is OK for a non-Jew to pledge loyalty to the State of Israel, but not to the "Jewish and democratic" State of Israel.

So what do I think?

First, I don't get all the hysterics. I might see the problem if the oath were only to a "Jewish" state, but to a "Jewish and democratic" state? Doesn't that addition make all the difference in the world? Isn't it democracy that enables Arab citizens to become Supreme Court justices, university professors or the second in command of the National Police?

A non-Jew gains a lot more by the word "democratic" than he loses by the word "Jewish." If an Arab man like Ahmed, for example, ever marries his partner in Tel Aviv and has to make his oath of loyalty to a "Jewish and democratic" state, he won't be thinking of how Jewish Israel is, but how democratic it is and respectful of his human right to enter into a gay marriage.

As a Sephardic Jew, I can tell you that Jews who lived for centuries as good citizens of Arab countries would have loved nothing more than to pledge loyalty to a "Muslim and democratic state" in return for the same freedoms, rights and protections that Arabs enjoy today in Israel.

But what about the fact that Jews become automatic citizens and don't have to take this oath? Isn't that a racist idea? Not according to my friend Yossi Klein Halevi, who writes in an e-mail from Jerusalem:

"There is a difference between an oleh [one who makes aliyah] who is repatriating home and a foreigner being naturalized. Many democracies require loyalty oaths of naturalizing citizens. The point of a Jewish state is that Jews aren't like naturalizing citizens — they are olim returning home. That distinction is crucial for affirming who we are. This is not about racism — it is about a reaffirmation of our right to define ourselves as a people returning home.

"If and when the Palestinians create a state, the first law they are likely to pass will be their version of our law of return, granting automatic citizenship to returning Palestinians. If an outsider wants to become a Palestinian citizen, he/she would no doubt have to go through a longer process."

Personally, whether it's part of a citizenship process or not, I'd love to see a national pledge of allegiance to a "Jewish and democratic" Israel. In fact, it ought to become a subject of study in Israeli schools and universities and part of a national conversation where every group gets to contribute its thoughts to this work in progress.

Both words — "Jewish" and "democratic" — are complicated and multilayered. Their marriage represents one of the great Jewish ideals — the collective project that Jews have come home to after almost 2,000 years.

Featuring this ideal in the loyalty oath reminds Israel of its obligations to all of its citizens, not just to its Jewish ones. As much as the applicant makes a formal gesture of loyalty, Israel makes a formal commitment of its democratic promise. The issue of who is required to take the oath is a fair one, but it shouldn't cloud the central fact that the oath itself is an especially good deal for minorities looking for official protection of their democratic rights.

That's why I can't understand the hysterical reaction of many Jews who have recoiled in shame and horror at this initiative, as if Israel had just decided to shut down every Arab newspaper or board up every mosque.

Yes, Israel could have done a better job of presenting the initiative, which suffered from awkward timing and its association with Yisrael Beitenu. But Israel's political clumsiness is even more reason for Israel supporters to reaffirm and defend the country's moral standing.

Despite all its faults, and despite being in a permanent state of war with enemies at its doorstep, Israel is still, by far, the most open and civil society in the Middle East. Think about that. The best place for an Arab to be free and successful in the Middle East is in a Jewish state under siege by Arabs. Incredible, no?

If Israel were smart, it would initiate a massive PR effort promoting the freedoms, rights and opportunities that Arabs get in Israel that they can never get in other Arab countries. It would show the world that its loyalty oath is a shining light in the Middle East cesspool.

A good place to start would be with Arabs like Ahmed from Ramallah, who dreams of signing an oath that would free him to be gay and dance in public with his Arab-Israeli partner next year in Jerusalem.

"Christians love to love. We love to kvetch."

LOVE WITHOUT BORDERS

October 13, 2010

What is it about Evangelical Christians and their support for Israel that really gets to me? I understand what makes some Jews — especially liberal Jews — nervous about this group: their conservative values (on issues such as abortion and separation of church and state); an uncompromising stance on the Middle East peace process; the theological slant to their support for Israel; and a propensity among some of them to proselytize to Jews.

Still, I couldn't help but be moved last Saturday night as I listened to Pat Boone talk about his deep and emotional connection to Israel. Boone was speaking at the home of Howard and Elayne Levkowitz with Rabbi Yechiel Eckstein, founder of the International Fellowship of Christians and Jews and guest scholar-in-residence at Young Israel of Century City.

At his talk earlier that morning in synagogue, Eckstein was passionate but walking on eggshells. This is a highly "unorthodox" Orthodox rabbi who for the past 35 years has spent most of his time with Evangelical Christians, drumming up support for Israel and raising tens of millions of dollars for the Zionist cause. He might be a graduate of Yeshiva University who can easily quote Soloveitchik, but he's equally at ease quoting Paul and the Gospels. (He was so sensitive to his surroundings that he said "J" instead of Jesus.)

Eckstein's message was twofold: One, Israel supporters must value the support of millions of Evangelical "ambassadors" for Israel throughout the world; and two, Jews need to strengthen their faith in God. We must remember, Eckstein said, that our first covenant with God was through Abraham, and it was based on faith. To strengthen our identity as Jews, we must incorporate this covenant with the subsequent covenant at Sinai, thereby enriching and deepening our Torah observance and connection with Israel.

Faith certainly permeated the discussion Saturday night between Boone and Eckstein. In front of a packed house, Eckstein talked about his epiphany almost 40 years ago, when he roomed with an 86-year-old black Baptist pastor on an organized trip to Israel. As a newly ordained 26-year-old rabbi from New York, Eckstein couldn't understand the pastor's passion for the Holy Land. That is, until the pastor told him: "Moses got to see the Promised Land; I get to walk on it."

Boone talked about one of his first encounters with rabbis, one of whom was highly skeptical and said to him: "If you really love us, then just leave us alone," to which Boone replied: "But I can't — you're God's people."

This is how the evening went: love for Israel on top of love for Israel and love for Jews on top of love for Jews. There was something almost non-Jewish about it. Jews don't talk a lot about love. It's not something that turns us on. We're more into debate, argument, challenge and outrage.

Christians love to love. We love to kvetch.

It's this unconditional love for Israel that unsettles me. Why do we find so little expression of it among Jews? Is it because we confuse love with support for policy? That is, if we disagree with Israel's policies, do we find it difficult — even impossible — to express unconditional love for Israel? And how many Israel supporters who disagree with Israel's policies can honestly say that their love for Israel is, in fact, unconditional?

Can you imagine, for example, a group that calls itself pro-Israel, like

J Street, ever doing a "Love for Israel" event where they just celebrate Israel? Can you even imagine them leading their followers in "Hatikvah" at the beginning of their next convention?

A lot of this made more sense to me when I reflected on a conversation I had last week with my friend Gary Judis and some of his Zionist friends. The subject was the worldwide movement to delegitimize the State of Israel, and the consensus among this group of businessmen was the following: Enemies of Israel are not looking for a debate. Their aim is not to engage but to undermine. Their opposition is not open to reason.

In short, their hatred is unconditional.

So, as I left the discussion last Saturday night, I started to put two and two together. Why am I so moved by the Evangelicals' unconditional love toward Israel? Well, maybe simply because it is unconditional.

How better to fight unconditional hatred than with unconditional love? What better weapon against the forces working to delegitimize Israel than a force that unequivocally loves Israel? Of course, we should never stop doing what we do best: argue, debate, challenge and rebuke.

But we can't love the process more than we love Israel itself. For Israel supporters, unconditional love is the emotion that ought to trump all others; the emotion that fuels and gives meaning to our actions. I can challenge my child and rebuke him, but I can never forget to show him unconditional love.

Our debates over Israel have become coarse and divisive. One reason is that in our zeal to express tough love, we have forgotten about pure love.

We don't have to agree with the theology or politics of an Evangelical like Pat Boone, but by expressing his unconditional love for Israel last Saturday night, he gave a group of Jews his version of tough love.

"Instead of new ways of thinking, we've been offered extremes. The Tea Partyers are extreme minimalists, the Latte Democrats are extreme spenders, and the Beer Republicans are extreme naysayers."

AMERICA NEEDS A COFFEE PARTY

September 21, 2010

The political world is all atwitter over the Tea Party movement that is sweeping America. Everywhere you turn, from Alaska to Delaware, it seems another Tea Party candidate is on the rise. What does this mean? So far, most of the analyses have been political: Will the uncompromising Tea Partyers help or hinder the GOP's chances to retake Congress in the fall? Are they revitalizing or fatally dividing the Republican Party? Can their radicalism end up rescuing the faltering Democrats? And so on.

While those questions are important, there's one question that's even more fundamental: What's good for America? And the answer, it seems to me, is neither the Tea Party nor the Democratic Party nor the Republican Party, but a brand-new kind of party.

Call it the Coffee Party.

Drinking coffee is not the same thing as sipping tea. Tea is for relaxation and laying back. It suggests an attitude of laissez-faire, not active engagement. Tea Partyers may yell a lot, but in fact, their policy prescriptions are very laissez-faire. No matter the problem, they want minimal government. Cut spending. Cut taxes. Cut regulations. Protect us from our enemies, but stay out of our way.

Meanwhile, what have the Democrats been drinking? Extra-large foamy lattes with whipped cream — the kind that make you feel really bloated. Under their watch, America has been on a borrow-and-spend binge that is weighing down our economy with enormous debt while doing little to reverse near-record unemployment. This has created a perfect storm for an "Enough already!" backlash — hence the Tea Party phenomenon, which has tapped into the growing anger at the spending addicts in power.

And what are the Republicans drinking in response to all this? Beer. So much beer, in fact, that they have become drunk, obnoxious and forgetful. They have forgotten, for instance, that they were the original bloated folks who started this whole mess of spending trillions above our means. Now that they see the Democrats making things worse, they're hoping they can transfer some of that amnesia to the voters and get back in power. They've gotten so drunk on this possibility that they're incapable of cooperating or offering any real solutions.

All of this has gotten me to fantasize about an alternative political party, one named after America's favorite wake-up drink: coffee.

A few years ago, a study from the University of Queensland in Australia suggested that drinking coffee makes people more open to different points of view. Apparently, coffee makes you more engaged, more alert and thus more open to new ways of thinking. It's an ideal metaphor, I think, for what our country needs and hasn't been getting.

Instead of new ways of thinking, we've been offered extremes. The Tea Partyers are extreme minimalists, the Latte Democrats are extreme spenders, and the Beer Republicans are extreme naysayers.

A Coffee Party would shun the extremes. Its ideology would be, "Let's do what works." It would steal from everyone to find optimal solutions. Branded by the hard-working, no-nonsense symbol of black coffee, the party would roll up its sleeves and work in a nonpartisan way to get the country out of its mess. It would bring passion to reason.

More important, it would treat us like grown-ups. If taxes need to be raised to reduce horrendous deficits, it would tell us. If entitlements need to be reformed to avoid bankrupting future generations, it would tell us that, too. If we could save the country $100 billion a year in health-care costs by reducing cigarette smoking and leading healthier lifestyles, it would call on us to do so. If bloated institutions have to be trimmed and reinvented to make America competitive again and create new jobs, it would make those hard decisions. If we each had to sacrifice a little to make our country more energy independent, it would ask us to step up.

In other words, it wouldn't be afraid to look America in the eye and tell it like it is. It would tell us not what we want to hear, but what we need to hear.

Maybe I'm dreaming, but I think in today's climate, a "coalition of candid candidates" could catch on. There's so much revulsion out there with our pandering and failing political class that brutal honesty might be the perfect tonic for our times. When things are falling apart, voters — especially centrist and independent voters — look for competence and real solutions, not empty promises or ideological grandstanding.

Unfortunately, our leaders today are great at haggling over ideology and party politics but terrible at crafting real solutions. Maybe that's why trust in Congress is at an all-time low. The Tea Party movement may be one big primal scream without serious solutions, but its phenomenal success is a sign that America is desperate for something different.

The Coffee Party — the party of reason, urgency and tough love — can be that something different. It would be as if a bloated and sluggish America hired a personal trainer to whip it into shape. "Hope and change" was a sleeping pill compared to this triple espresso.

I can already see the campaign slogan: "America's wake-up call."

"As I go through the Days of Judgment, the Days of Awe, the Days of Harvest and the Days of Too Many Stuffed Zucchinis, I will try to keep my eye on the spiritual ball."

AIMING HIGHER

September 8, 2010

Here in Pico-Robertson, many of us approach the month of Tishrei with a certain amount of ambivalence, if not culinary dread. Especially this year, when the holiday meals are back to back with Shabbat, we are bracing ourselves for 30 days with — I'm not kidding — at least 20 Thanksgiving-level meals, if you include the High Holy Days, the first and second holidays of Sukkot (eight meals right there) and the weekly Shabbat feasts.

That's a lot of guest coordination, shmoozing and baba ganoush.

Meanwhile, the rabbis will be imploring us to embark on a deep and personal spiritual trek that would lead to things like personal transformation, clinging closer to God and returning to our better selves. The bigger question they might ask is: How will the ingestion of 50,000 calories a week amid a freight train of festive meals contribute to this spiritual journey?

I don't have an answer, but I have an idea: maybe we ought to find a two- or three-word mantra that summarizes what these High Holy Days mean to us and use this mantra as a handy guide to help us navigate the many distractions we are sure to encounter.

I wrote my own mantra after hearing from three rabbis over the past week: Rabbi Donniel Hartman of the Shalom Hartman Institute in Jerusalem; Rabbi Chaim Seidler-Feller of UCLA Hillel; and Rabbi Kalman Topp of Beth Jacob Congregation.

So what's my mantra for this holiday season? Aim higher.

"Rosh Hashanah and Yom Kippur are not primarily about atonement, about being forgiven for our sins and indiscretions," Rabbi Hartman wrote. "While originally in the Bible this was the primary intent, the revolution of the rabbinic tradition was to shift the focus from attaining atonement from God to the human responsibility to repent and change our behavior. It is not about God's love and acceptance of the sinner, but rather God's expectation that humankind overcome sin and live up to our tradition's expectation."

Hartman goes on: "To assume one's righteousness and concentrate one's efforts on pointing out the failures of others is again to ignore the principle of teshuvah and its spirit on which our tradition is founded."

In other words, it's easy to be humble and ask God for forgiveness, or to focus on criticizing others, but it's a lot harder to ask yourself how you will change your behavior and become a better person. You have to handle the blows to your ego of admitting how often you messed up during the past year, and then you have to commit to the hard work of actually becoming a better person.

But what kind of better person?

"Avoiding transgressions is not enough," Rabbi Seidler-Feller said in his holiday message. Quoting Maimonides, he spoke about the importance of going beyond "simply avoiding sins like sexual transgressions and stealing."

It's all about character, the rabbi says. Controlling one's anger. Never humiliating others. Avoiding the pursuit of honor. Not coveting the success of others. Those are all issues of character, and they're much tougher to work on than the avoidance of basic sins. Rosh Hashanah is a holiday that reminds us that the act of refining one's character is never complete, that it represents "the very act of living."

And where do we find the strength to aim so high, to do such difficult work?

According to Rabbi Topp, Rosh Hashanah also reminds us that because we are created in the image of God, we already have this strength inside of us — we just have to tap into it. That was his message last Sunday morning at a pre-Rosh Hashanah breakfast at Beth Jacob.

The rabbi took us through the four key insertions to the Amidah prayer during the High Holy Days and showed us how with each insertion, we keep asking God for more. It's not a coincidence that at each level our identity gets stronger and stronger: We start by being anonymous, then we are "God's creatures," then we are "members of the covenant at Sinai," and, finally, we are the "Nation of Israel," with all the privileges and duties that go with it.

It's at that final level that Rabbi Topp spoke about our "built-in specialness," the idea that whatever personal improvement we are seeking, God has already given us the strength to "return" to it — to return to our better selves.

(On that note, one of the most effective ways I have found to rebuke my kids when they do something wrong is simply to say to them, "You're better than that," even when I'm not sure I mean it.)

So that will be my mantra during these High Holy Days — aim higher. As I go through the Days of Judgment, the Days of Awe, the Days of Harvest and the Days of Too Many Stuffed Zucchinis, I will try to keep my eye on the spiritual ball: Don't focus on just seeking forgiveness or not criticizing others; don't settle for just avoiding sins; do the hard work of refining my character and remember that God is there to give me strength on my journey.

And if I fail to reach that high, and the baba ganoush and single malts get the better of me, well, there's always next year.

"Every time I saw something that drove me nuts, my Zionist bias made me look for positive signs, for a redeeming feature, for a ray of hope."

A MESS IN PROGRESS

August 31, 2010

I s Israel going in the right or the wrong direction? If the glass of Zionism is half full, is it in the process of being filled or depleted? And how do we even define the "right" direction? These are the kind of questions that have been going through my mind as I've been reflecting on my 30-day journey to the Holy Land.

In one respect, my trip was a failure. Before leaving, I swore to myself that I would be totally objective, that I would look at Israel's negative side with a cold eye, that I wouldn't let my Zionist emotions get in the way. I wanted to view Israel through the skeptical lens of a journalist, rather than the warm lens of familial love.

I failed royally. How could I not? How could I be unbiased about a country that touches me so deeply? A country Abraham Joshua Heschel calls "An Echo of Eternity"?

Every time I saw something that drove me nuts, my Zionist bias made me look for positive signs, for a redeeming feature, for a ray of hope.

If I saw a Charedi establishment that made it extremely difficult for non-Jews to convert to Judaism, I would find a courageous Charedi rabbi in the Knesset who is fighting for a more flexible interpretation of Jewish law.

If I saw signs of discrimination toward minorities, I would meet with people like Gerald Steinberg of NGO Monitor, who would remind me about the numerous human rights organizations in Israel that use the Israeli legal system to defend the rights of Israeli Arabs and other minorities. Or I would see a demonstration to protest the deportation of illegal immigrants. Or I would see police officers lining the streets of Jerusalem to protect the rights of gays to parade in front of ultra-Orthodox Jews.

If I saw signs of tension between the many ethnic groups in the country, I would meet someone who would inform me that there are over 100 different nationalities in the Israel Defense Forces.

If I despaired about the ability of Jewish settlers to ever get along with Palestinians, I would meet settlers in the West Bank who are collaborating with their Palestinian neighbors over things like water conservation and getting more fire trucks.

If a Jewish university professor would drive me nuts by spewing anti-Zionist venom and supporting the international boycott of his own country, I would remind myself that it is to the credit of Israel that he has the freedom to spew that very venom.

It's true that viewed from the outside, Israel's image is heading south. Books like "Start-Up Nation" are nice, and so are signs of a recent thaw in the relationship between Israel and the Obama administration with the opening this week of direct peace talks with the Palestinian Authority.

But those are minor causes for optimism in the face of the global movement to delegitimize the Jewish state, documented in excruciating detail by the Reut Institute. No matter how positively I viewed my Israeli experience, it was impossible to forget that the view from the outside is quite different. We could moan all day long that Israel is subjected to a nasty and unfair double standard, but that is still the reality.

This assault on Israel's legitimacy has created an almost hysterical polarization among the Jews of the Diaspora, and I understand both sides. One side feels the need to defend and push back against the assault; the other feels the need to reaffirm the Jewish ideals of self-criticism and self-correction. And both sides seem to be digging in their heels. As a result, two things are being lost — complexity on one side, and expressions of love on the other.

This is why I loved being in Israel. I saw both love and complexity. A perfect example was Micah Goodman, the head of the Israeli Academy of Leadership, Ein Prat, who is relentless in his critique of Israeli policies and the need to "renew Zionism," but who also overflows with love for Zionism and had this to say to keep things in perspective:

"The mark of a good idea is whether it works in extreme circumstances," he told me one morning in Jerusalem. "Liberals of the world should love Israel, because it proves that democracy works. Israel is a country under siege, in a state of permanent war, and, still, it manages to grant freedom of speech, freedom of religion and more human rights than most democracies."

So yes, Israel is a mess, a noisy, resilient, frustrating, vibrant, complicated mess. But it's also a mess in progress, not least because the most vicious critics of the state are free to be the most vicious critics of the state.

Will the rest of the world ever catch up to the balance and complexity of Micah Goodman's thinking, and to his deep and poignant love for Zionism? I doubt it.

But it'd be nice if the Jewish world could — and that includes emotional Zionists like yours truly.

"As the voices of the verbal slugfest echoed outside, I wondered what it'd be like to live with demonstrators camped out in front of my house virtually around the clock."

SHOWDOWN AT SHEIK JARRAH

August 24, 2010

In this land of a million arguments, it's easy to get so exhausted by the back-and-forth that you just want to tune out and say, "Well, there are two sides to every argument, so you're probably both right — or you're both wrong."

I was tempted to feel that way recently when I visited a notorious flashpoint of the Palestinian-Israeli conflict, the East Jerusalem neighborhood of Sheik Jarrah. This is the place where leftist demonstrators from around the world gather regularly in front of an eager press corps to protest the eviction of a Palestinian family, who are now camped out in an ongoing vigil across the street from their former home.

Accompanied by Chaim Silberstein, who runs Keep Jerusalem, an organization that promotes keeping Jerusalem united under Israeli sovereignty, I went to check out the scene. I had no idea I'd end up witnessing a verbal slugfest.

It started harmlessly enough, when we approached a small group of demonstrators milling around a tent where a few Palestinians were sitting on an old sofa. I greeted one of the Palestinians, an elderly man, in Arabic, to show him we didn't have any hostile intentions.

A young man then approached us, as a few cameras started rolling. He said he was a freelance reporter from San Francisco.

"So, what have you learned so far?" Silberstein asked him.

"Well, it seems there has been somewhat of a contention over the land since '54 or '56. The UN-RWA set up all these houses with the Jordanian authorities, but then the people have been having a legal battle over it. They [the Israelis] kicked out the family and literally moved in another [Jewish] family."

"Do you know the history, what happened 100 years ago?" Silberstein asked the journalist.

"Well, I know in 1948, the people from here, from Sheik Jarrah, were refugees that came from Haifa, Jaffa and other places and built homes on the land that was empty land with the Jordanian authorities," he said.

"It was empty land; it didn't belong to anybody?" Silberstein asked.

"No," the reporter replied.

"OK, so I know a little about the background, and that's not correct," Silberstein told him. "This whole area was purchased by Jews in 1875. They still have the documents — it was ratified by the Supreme Court."

"But Nasser [the Palestinian whose family got evicted] also has a document from the Ottoman Empire that was before that," the reporter said.

"Actually, I've seen that document," Silberstein said. "It is dated back to 1897, and the Israeli court did a forensic test, and it came back [that it was] completely forged."

For the next 15 minutes or so, including several interruptions, Silberstein gave what amounted to a mini-history lesson: How Jordan took control of East Jerusalem during the War of Independence in 1948; how they evicted the Jews and brought in Arab families; and how Jordan's "illegal annexation" of East Jerusalem was recognized by no country except Pakistan.

At one point, a Palestinian man got up, moved toward Silberstein and said, "Can I answer? My name is Mohammed."

Mohammed explained that he has a document showing that Jews didn't own, but rented, the Sheik Jarrah property for 140 years. When Silberstein said the document was forged, Mohammed answered that it only appeared to be forged, because some words were not clear and had to be filled in by hand. Silberstein shot back that a forensic lab had done a chemical test on the paper and that "it was shown to be 5 or 7 years old, not 140 years old. The Israeli Supreme Court even ratified the results. That's why Israel won the case."

It got ugly after that.

Other people jumped in. Voices were raised. The subject shifted to the Israeli occupation of the West Bank. A Palestinian kid yelled, "Go f——g back to Brooklyn." An olive-skinned man approached Silberstein and said, "You are a fascist." The reporter from San Francisco made a few sarcastic remarks.

By now, Silberstein had also lost his cool: "The Palestinian nation is an invention!" he told the hostile crowd. "Tell me one place before 1964 where there is one mention of a Palestinian Arab nation, and I'll give you a thousand dollars!"

The insults were flying. I absorbed the scene, thinking about something Silberstein had said in the car on the way to Sheik Jarrah: There are about 220,000 Jews living in "Arab" East Jerusalem, he told me. How on earth do they think they can ever divide this city?

I walked across the street to visit two of those Jews. A young man with a beard greeted me, and, when he saw my kippah, opened the security gate. His pregnant wife, who didn't look a day over 18, was preparing for Shabbat. I saw a flute on a coffee table and asked who played it. His wife did, the man said.

As the voices of the verbal slugfest echoed outside, I wondered what it'd be like to live with demonstrators camped out in front of my house virtually around the clock.

In this crazy and holy part of the world, when you "win" a battle you just never know what the victory will look like.

"'I'm Charedi,' he told me, 'but I'm also Sephardic. The Sephardic way is a paradox: to keep tradition but to stay open. The Torah is not there to put handcuffs on you.'"

CHAREDI REBEL

August 17, 2010

Few issues have generated as much heat in the Jewish world this year as the Rotem bill, which is now on hold pending further review. Presumably, a key goal of the bill was to make it easier for the hundreds of thousands of Russians in Israel, who are not halachically Jewish, to convert to Judaism. There is sharp disagreement among critics of the bill over whether it would, in fact, accomplish that goal.

The bill would formalize control of the conversion process with the Charedi-controlled Chief Rabbinate. This is of great concern to the non-Orthodox streams, who are afraid this might impact the Law of Return, which currently honors non-Orthodox conversions performed outside of Israel. In addition, the bill would make it difficult, if not impossible, to challenge the Chief Rabbinate in the Israeli Supreme Court, something that has been done successfully in the past.

The emotions have run high. Machers across the Diaspora have expressed their outrage. In response, Rotem and others in Israel have accused Reform and Conservative leaders of "purposefully misleading their constituents."

As Gary Rosenblatt, editor and publisher of New York's The Jewish Week, who himself has gone back and forth on his views about the bill, wrote this week: "Bottom line, the conversion conflict underscores the fissures and frustrations within and between the Diaspora and Israel. Front and center is the rigidity, if not corruption, of the Chief Rabbinate itself, which is a tragedy."

One Orthodox rabbi who feels this rigidity especially hard is Rabbi Seth Farber, an Orthodox activist whose Jerusalem-based organization, ITIM: The Jewish Life Information Center, handles between 150 and 200 conversion-related calls each month.

"There needs to be serious reform of the existing conversion authority, which will lead to greater transparency and a more user-friendly system," he told me the other day. "The Rotem bill does not represent a meaningful response to the demographic crisis in Israel, and it is certainly not worth it if it alienates the broader Jewish community."

Farber is now suing the Chief Rabbinate in an attempt to stop the annulment of a conversion of a woman who was told she could not get married because she converted in the IDF. "The couple was Jewish enough to fight in the Lebanon war for Ashdod, but not Jewish enough to be married in Ashdod," Farber said.

If you're not part of the Charedim, it's easy to be outraged by their rigidity. But what if you're a Charedi scholar who is highly respected in the Charedi world? Can you also be outraged?

Yes, if your name is Rabbi Chaim Amsellem.

Amsellem is an MK from the Charedi Shas party, and he has been making waves. One reason is that he has written a serious book of halachah that supports a more lenient view of conversions.

The book is based on the concept of Zera Yisrael, or progeny — someone who, while not halachically Jewish, is very close to Jews and has even risked his or her life to defend the Jewish nation.

There are hundreds of thousands of such potential Jews in Israel. If Rabbi Amsellem were ever put in charge of the Conversion Authority, there would be a revolution in the Jewish state, if not the Jewish world.

How does a Charedi scholar and politician come to display such extraordinary flexibility in a world that is hardly known for it? I wanted to see for myself, so I managed to corral him last week at a Jerusalem hotel, and I spent three hours listening to a Jewish rebel express outrage at his own community. Sound familiar?

"I'm Charedi," he told me, "but I'm also Sephardic. The Sephardic way is a paradox: to keep tradition but to stay open. The Torah is not there to put handcuffs on you. We try to find solutions. We put unity first."

As he spoke, I was experiencing my own paradox. Amsellem sounded almost exactly like my late father, a Torah-observant Sephardic French teacher who was anything but Charedi and who was incredibly tolerant. How could someone who had the tolerance of my father be part of such a rigid world?

"I studied only in Sephardic yeshivas," Amsellem told me. "I was taught that Torah and tolerance go hand in hand. Most of the Shas voters are also Sephardic and tolerant, but many of them are just being manipulated by the system."

Normally, such a dissenting and rebellious voice would be easily neutralized by a monolithic and all-powerful Charedi establishment. The problem is that Amsellem is not easily neutralized. It's not just because of his halachic reputation. It's also his character— he's a scholar and a fighter.

There have already been a few attempts to undermine him and cut him out of the Charedi mainstream, but so far they have failed. You can bet that he will continue to face internal opposition in the coming months and years. Let's face it: His halachically based tolerance is a threat to the Charedi way. But Amsellem is undaunted.

"A man who has nothing to lose is most dangerous," he told me. "I don't fear losing, because I know I will get up and keep fighting."

Somewhere, my father must surely be smiling.

"It's not that Eid isn't loyal to the Palestinian cause. He is. It's just that he's a fine practitioner of that popular Jewish sport we call tough love. He puts a large part of the blame for the plight of the Palestinians on the Palestinians."

HUMMUS AND WHIPLASH IN RAMALLAH
August 10, 2010

I t was the best hummus I've ever tasted. It came in a bowl, drenched in olive oil, with a few small garbanzos and shreds of parsley and hot green peppers sprinkled on top, and just the right amount of lemon juice. The elderly Palestinian man had made the hummus from scratch and served it to us with a salad plate, a bowl of falafels and a tall stack of hot pitas for just under 8 shekels.

I was eating in a refugee camp in Ramallah with Bassem Eid, the founder and director of an NGO called Palestinian Human Rights Monitoring Group. We ate at this hole in the wall off a skinny alleyway nestled in a labyrinth of ramshackle houses, tiny grocery stores and one little mosque, with a U.N. mini-truck riding around the alleyways picking up random garbage.

Outside the camp was a different story. Ramallah is a happening city with construction everywhere and a sea of people lining the sidewalks of boulevards teeming with commerce. Eid, it seems, knew every street.

I met him the way I've met a lot of people in Jerusalem — one meeting leading to another. In this case, I was having dinner in Jerusalem with my friend Hillel Neuer and professor Irwin Cotler, a Canadian Member of Parliament and a well-known human rights activist. We were talking about the many human rights NGOs in Israel, and I mentioned that we rarely hear about NGOs that monitor Palestinian society.

At which point the professor exclaimed: "Oh, you must meet my friend Bassem Eid!"

The next day, I was at the American Colony Hotel in East Jerusalem surrounded by foreign correspondents wearing crumpled linen — it could have been a movie set right out of "Lawrence of Arabia" — having one coffee after another with my new best friend, the chain-smoking Eid.

For Israel-lovers tired of seeing Israel get beaten up by the world press, Eid is your dream come true. I sat listening to him for hours in scorching heat, and I didn't want to leave.

It's not that Eid isn't loyal to the Palestinian cause. He is. It's just that he's a fine practitioner of that popular Jewish sport we call tough love. He puts a large part of the blame for the plight of the Palestinians on the Palestinians.

As much as he loves peace, he hates violence even more.

In fact, had he been running the Palestinian Authority 10 years ago, when Ariel Sharon made his provocative visit to the Temple Mount — allegedly triggering the Second Intifada — there probably never would have been a Second Intifada.

"I would have received him at the Temple Mount with honor," Eid told me. "I would have had 10 prominent Palestinian personalities receive him and explain to him how holy the Temple Mount is to us and give him a sightseeing tour."

In other words, he would have provoked Sharon right back, but not with violence; never with violence.

He thinks the extraordinary violence of the Second Intifada killed more than people. It killed the Palestinian cause, which has become, he says, a "profitable enterprise for the people on top." Because Arafat chose violence even in the face of Ehud Barak's peace offer at Camp David, Eid doesn't see trust being rebuilt or peace breaking out for at least a generation.

So he immerses himself in the only arena he knows: human rights. He worked with the Israeli NGO Betselem for many years before starting his own NGO about 15 years ago, because, he says, "I didn't see too many NGOs criticizing my people and holding them to account."

He started to document cases of financial corruption and torture inside the Palestinian Authority and, along the way, was arrested once and has been routinely defamed and slandered as an "Israeli collaborator." About seven years ago, to get away from the pressure he was feeling in his hometown of East Jerusalem, he moved his family to Jericho.

As we drove through Ramallah the other day, it was hard to make sense of it all. For every sign of hope I saw — like busy people on busy streets looking like they love life — there were the forlorn looks on some of the faces in the refugee camp.

For every building with a sign of hope — like the one for the Sartawi Center for the Advancement of Peace and Democracy — there was a large poster promoting "One Indivisible Struggle for Palestinian Return" by a committee to commemorate the Nakba.

When we sat down for our homemade hummus, the whiplash continued. Eid reminisced about the good old days before the two intifadas, when thousands of Israelis would visit Ramallah on weekends to taste the hummus and contribute to the local economy. The sound of those words tasted too good.

On a whim, I asked Eid to ask the old man making the hummus if he'd like to see Jews from Israel visit his restaurant and give him more business.

"Jews are forbidden here," the old man replied in Arabic, and, for the first time all day, it occurred to me that I was glad I wasn't wearing my kippah.

"Given the possibility that Jewish settlers may stay on one day as part of a Palestinian entity, it's not a bad idea to begin planting the seeds of co-existence."

SETTLER, WARRIOR, HEALER

August 4, 2010

In many ways, Ron Jager is your typical religious settler who made aliyah from America to live out the Zionist dream. With a short beard, laser-sharp eyes and a sturdy frame, he looks the part of the diehard Zionist from the Bronx, where, in fact, he grew up. So how did this tough guy turn out to be a "kumbaya" promoter of Jewish-Palestinian cooperation in, of all places, the West Bank?

When Jager arrived in Israel in 1980, at the age of 22, he already had two college degrees: a bachelor's in psychology from Baruch College and a master's in clinical social work from Yeshiva University.

He put those skills to work when he joined the Israel Defense Forces (IDF) and fought in the Lebanon War of 1982. His fight was to treat soldiers in the heat of battle who were experiencing trauma, like from seeing the bodies of their best friends mutilated by shrapnel.

"If you don't get to them right away and send them back to the war zone, the psychic damage can be permanent," he told me the other day as we were riding through the hills of Samaria.

Jager treated hundreds of soldiers through three wars over 25 years. He had a proven technique. First, he took care of the soldier's physical needs: a hug; then a shower, coffee and a meal; and then a little sleep.

Only after that would he begin treatment. He would start by helping soldiers remember why they were there in the first place — about their responsibility toward their children, their family members, their fellow Jews. This would take the focus away from their immediate pain by putting the trauma in a larger and meaningful context.

Once that larger context was established, he would convey the soldiers' accomplishment to boost their sense of self. "Not every soldier sees frontline combat," he would tell them. "You have to earn it. You're here because you can be here."

The final step was the traditional debriefing or retracing of the events leading to the trauma to help them "take control" of the events.

Usually within a day or two, the soldier would return to the combat zone.

After 25 years in the IDF, Jager retired in 2005 with no idea what to do next. On a whim, he followed up on an ad from Haifa University recruiting for an MBA in "Jewish-Arab Cooperation."

He ended up holed up for two years with 18 Israeli Arabs, six Palestinians and 10 Jewish leftists.

"I was used to shooting at Arabs, not studying with them," he said.

During their travels for overseas conferences, his roommate was an Arab. They had endless late-night conversations. They didn't change each other's views, but one thing did change in Jager.

"I think the whole experience made me more pragmatic," he said, "more conscious that we need to come up with solutions."

So what did he do next? After graduation, he jumped into one of the toughest places on earth to find solutions: the West Bank, where he's been a longtime resident. He became strategic adviser to the Shomron Liaison Office, an independent NGO whose mission is to put a human face on the settler movement.

I know what you're thinking — good luck. But listen to this: They're making some progress. Jager and David Ha'ivri, the office director, have managed to develop a good rapport with the global press, including even The New York Times, whose reporters they've taken on several tours of the region. Their secret, he says, is to focus on humanitarian issues, not politics.

"We tell them that no matter what happens politically in the future, there are human needs that will always be here, like water conservation and sewage," he said. "So we show them what we are doing to help our Palestinian neighbors in those areas, thanks in large part to the scientists at Ariel University [Center of Samaria]."

Lately, they've been petitioning officials from the U.S. Consulate office in East Jerusalem to help fund joint cooperation projects with the Palestinians in areas such as firefighting and emergency response. Jager says he has surprised more than a few U.S. officials and reporters when he tells them how Jewish settlers who are paramedics will rush to the scene of an accident to rescue Palestinian victims.

"When the police call us after an accident, they don't tell us whether the victims are Jewish or Palestinians."

Of course, it's not all rosy. Palestinians, for example, have refused Israeli offers to treat their sewage because they think their water will be stolen. So the scientists at Ariel are developing new, simplified techniques for sewage treatment that the Palestinians can handle and maintain themselves.

The list of projects for joint cooperation is endless, he says. But he knows it will be an uphill battle to convince the world that Jewish settlers are not just impersonal "obstacles to peace"; that there is more to gain by talking about warming relations than freezing construction; and that given the possibility that Jewish settlers may stay on one day as part of a Palestinian entity, it's not a bad idea to begin planting the seeds of coexistence.

Uphill battle or not, who better than an expert at dealing with trauma to lead the way?

"The idea is not to change people's minds, but to open them; not to push for compromise but to push for authentic expressions of peace."

RADICAL PEACE

July 27, 2010

It's a sign of how the peace movement has fizzled out in Israel that even the peace process itself rarely cites peace as the goal — it's now the "two-state solution" that is the mantra. It's as if everyone realizes that after decades of mutual hostility and mistrust, real peace between the Jews and Palestinians is simply too much to ask for without being laughed at.

Being in the city of messianic dreams — i.e., Jerusalem — it didn't surprise me yesterday to meet a man who dreams of changing all that. His dream is to revitalize the peace movement in Israel by making it deeper, richer and more inclusive. He wants peace to be a hot topic not just among liberal peaceniks but also radical settlers; not just among poets and artists but also hard-nosed and cynical right-wingers.

Alick Isaacs is a teacher and philosopher who, for the past 12 months, has been matchmaker-in-chief for ideological opposites. With the help of expert staff, like Sharon Leshem-Zinger and Avinoam Rosenak, he has brought together 14 influential Israeli personalities from all walks of life and, about once a month, gathered them in the same room to talk about peace.

Not peace platitudes, but intimate, personal, even raw expressions of what peace means to each of them.

The program's core idea is to validate — and value — these individual visions of peace. But getting everyone to the table wasn't easy. Settler rabbis, for example, dismissed the project at first. Isaacs appealed to them by talking their language. In one marathon session, he recruited a leading settler rabbi by studying the texts of his hero, Rav Kook, and pulling peace quotes such as these:

"The Lord will bless his people with peace. And the blessing of peace, which comes with the [blessing of] strength, is the peace that unites all opposites. But we must have opposites so that ... something might be united, and the blessing is evident in the power of these, and these are words of the living God."

Isaacs and his group are trying to inject vitality and freshness into an idea that has been beaten to death by the corrupting world of politics. Politics' virtue is that it creates systems and structure to try to effect change. Isaacs'challenge has been to take a theoretical idea and give it structure.

So he has made his Talking Peace initiative a pilot program for a much bigger venture called the Center for the Advancement of Peace in Israel, which will be hosted by Mishkenot Sha'ananim, an international cultural and conference center located in Yemin Moshe in Jerusalem.

All group meetings have taken place at Mishkenot Sha'ananim, which also houses an art gallery, a restaurant and guesthouses (where I am staying, and where I met Isaacs). A major player in the venture is Uri Dromi, who is director of Mishkenot Sha'ananim and is helping put the whole project together. (Dromi, incidentally, is also a blogger for The Journal.)

Isaacs, who wears a kippah and has a doctorate in Jewish history and anthropology from Hebrew University, was careful not to put down the Israeli government's failed efforts to make peace with the Palestinians. But it was hard for me not to draw a contrast between the emptiness of the political peace process and the seriousness of Isaacs' initiative.

This seriousness was evident in the wrenching moments that have occurred among the 14 participants during their many encounter sessions. Animosities flared. Mistrust was common. They were strangers stuck in a room with people with completely different worldviews. It helped to have a professional group facilitator who ensured that meetings wouldn't unravel into nasty political arguments. As the months went by, and more and more participants got to "speak their peace," raw emotions gave way to empathy for differing viewpoints.

The real value of the program will come when Talking Peace goes on the road. As one example, Isaacs plans to team up a well-known leftist columnist from Haaretz, Akiva Eldar, with a prominent settler leader, Rabbi Eliezer Melamed. As a result, followers of Melamed will learn about Eldar's vision of peace, and Eldar's readers will learn about Melamed's.

The idea is not to change people's minds, but to open them; not to push for compromise but to push for authentic expressions of peace. Compromise is more likely to occur when these expressions of peace are ingrained in people across the ideological spectrum.

Isaacs hopes to leverage the success of Talking Peace to raise the funds that will make the Center for the Advancement of Peace in Israel a full-time reality.

Ultimately, Isaacs knows that a similar process will need to happen on the Palestinian side for real peace to catch on. At least he's not starting with illusions. He knows that it's useless to charge full speed ahead with a peace train that is empty. For peace with the Palestinians to have any chance, it will need a multitude of peace riders from both sides to hop aboard, even if that takes a generation or two.

Until then, the Center for the Advancement of Peace in Israel will be advancing an idea that also deserves its share of attention: the peace process among the Jews.

"Maybe his nomadic background has been a blessing. Nomads get attached to values, not to land or ideologies. They don't build permanent structures; they don't get bogged down if the land doesn't produce."

SHEPHERD ON A MISSION

July 9, 2010

I f ever there were an Israeli who could lead Israel to peace with its Arab neighbors, it might be the Israeli diplomat I met the other day in the lobby of the Century Plaza Hotel. This is your classic Zionist. He stands tall and proud of his country, doesn't ignore its faults, has a deep understanding of the issues from all sides and craves peace.

Of course, it helps that he's a Muslim. Not just a Muslim, but a Bedouin Muslim.

Ishmael Khaldi's official position is policy advisor to the Israeli foreign minister, but he's a lot more than that. He has become a one-man hasbara machine for the Jewish state, traveling around the world to make the case for the country he loves. When he encounters anti-Israel hecklers who spout slanderous words like "apartheid state," he has an easy answer:

"If Israel was a racist state, a Muslim like me would never have made it this far."

This notion of going far came early for Khaldi. Until he was 8, he walked four miles to school from his tiny Bedouin village of Khawalid in the western Galilee, then the same distance to get home again. He has fond memories of the family tent, where he lived with his parents and 10 siblings. He calls the tent an "extraordinary thing," because it was made of goat hair, which he says keeps you "warm and dry in the winters, and cool in the hot summers."

It wasn't just the memories of the goat-hair tents that marked him. It was also the ancient Bedouin lifestyle and the stories he heard from his grandmother, Jidda, who passed away in 2005 at the age of 96.

Khaldi recalls an early life that revolved around caring for animals, usually goats, sheep and cows. Because the condition of the land changed with the seasons, Bedouins were always on the move, looking for somewhere to nourish their flock. Their nomadic lifestyle lasted for thousands of years. Today, Khaldi says, many Bedouins have settled in more permanent dwellings in villages.

The turning point in Khaldi's life came when he decided, at 17, to visit America. He spent three months in New York City getting by on "one miracle after another," including one episode when he jumped onto subway tracks to get to the other side. "Bedouins always look for the shortest route," he says.

He met religious Jews in Brooklyn and Queens who gave him room and board. He learned what it was to be a "Shabbos goy," but he also remembers the joys of Shabbat and listening to the Torah portion of the week.

When he returned to Israel, higher education beckoned. Bedouins today do everything in their power to send their children to university, "even if I need to sell my clothes," his father once told him. So he enrolled at the University of Haifa, where he got a degree in political science and arranged cultural tours for overseas students, mostly Americans, to his Bedouin village.

After completing his college degree, he followed his brothers' footsteps in the national service and rose to second sergeant in the Israeli police force. He recalls his emotion when, after completing basic training, he was handed a Quran on which to swear his oath to his country, Israel.

He says that throughout history, Bedouins lived a life of tension with governing regimes, whether Ottoman, British or Arab. His own tribe developed a good relationship with the early Jewish pioneers in the 1920s, '30s and '40s. Bedouins and kibbutzniks always had a deep affinity for one another. His grandmother even learned a little Yiddish. So it was natural, he says, to want to enlist in the Israel Defense Forces and develop a loyalty to the Jewish state.

What I found fascinating about Khaldi is that at 38, with a graduate degree from Tel Aviv University and an important position in the Foreign Ministry, he's still a nomad at heart. He's always on the move, going from one country and city to another, telling Israel's side of the story. He's even found time to write a book about his story (A Shepherd's Journey).

Israel's story is his own, he says. No one stopped him from moving up. It was his choice to wake up at 3:30 in the morning to work to make enough money to buy a plane ticket to America. It was his choice to get an education and apply to work in public service. Israel is far from perfect, he says, but it gave him the freedom and opportunity to get where he is today.

Maybe his nomadic background has been a blessing. Nomads get attached to values, not to land or ideologies. They don't build permanent structures; they don't get bogged down if the land doesn't produce. They're used to being fluid, to moving on and looking for more fertile areas. And they never abandon their flock, or each other.

What better values for a diplomat? Loyal, practical, resourceful and travels light. Oh, and one more -- respectful of his elders. This one, though, has landed him in hot water.

"My father keeps asking me when I will settle down, get married and start a family," he says.

The only good excuse I can think of is that he'll first need to take care of another matter -- making peace between Muslims and Jews.

"While there were a few times during the evening when I felt like throwing sharp objects, I managed to escape with my love for Israel and the Jewish people intact."

CRASHING THE PARTY

June 29, 2010

I fully expected last week to be kicked out of an activist meeting for a leftist group at a private home in Mar Vista. I wasn't invited, but after hearing about the meeting from a friend, my curiosity got the better of me and I decided to take my chances and go.

I had promised myself that I wouldn't lie if they asked me who I was and where I stood politically. It turns out that was a moot point, because someone quickly said, "Aren't you that guy who writes in The Jewish Journal?" "Yes, I am," I said.

At that moment, with about a dozen peaceniks in their 30s, 40s and 50s looking straight at me in a living room, probably wondering what I was doing there, I said the only thing I could think of that would be honest but still keep them from calling the cops and charging me with trespassing.

"I live in Pico-Robertson," I told them. "Everyone's pretty much right-wing over there. And that's a lot of what I hear, right-wing views. I came tonight because I was curious to hear other views."

Well, wouldn't you know it — I got smiles all around. It felt like one of those Alcoholics Anonymous meetings where people feel your pain and can't wait to help you.

Maybe they thought I was ready to "convert" to their side? Who knows

— all I know is that they accepted me, and if I could control my Sephardic hothead impulses for a couple of hours, I would be there for the duration.

There were a few things in the invitation that had especially aroused my curiosity, like the word "Jew" in the group's name — LA Jews for Peace — and the first item on their agenda, what they called the Freedom Flotilla. A representative of the Free Gaza movement came to brief us on several items related to the flotilla, such as: the origin of the movement, the press bias in favor of Israel, upcoming flotillas, the status of legal action against Israel, planned protests in Los Angeles and so on.

Overall, while there were a few times during the evening when I felt like throwing sharp objects, I managed to escape with my love for Israel and the Jewish people intact. I think two things helped. One, I came in expecting some heavy-duty beating up of Israel (and I got it), and two, most of the people were really nice.

In fact, one of them even came to my defense. There was a moment when one of the presenters was going on and on about Israel's brutal treatment of Palestinians in Gaza. Hoping to inject a little "context," I asked about the thousands of rockets that Hamas had dropped on Israeli civilians for so many years before Israel took military action.

"What do I tell the people in Pico-Robertson when they ask me about the rockets?" I asked.

The presenter had a pat answer. Most of the rockets were cheap and homemade, she said, and, in any event, only three people were killed.

As if feeling my agony, one of the leaders of the group quickly jumped in and said, "That's not a good answer. Dropping rockets on civilians is never right." Of course, he did pull out some graphs to try to make the point that many of the rockets were in response to Israeli aggression. At least his tone was friendly.

That might be the one optimistic thing I took away from the evening — the tone. No matter how painful the subject and how sure people were, there was no anger or bitterness.

For example, one of the items on the agenda was "Continue Our

Study of the Goldstone Report." They do this at every meeting. It's like Bible class. That night, the person in charge took us through chapters 12 and 13. It was gruesome. He handed out pictures of the effects of phosphorous on the human body and described in talmudic detail the types of weapons used by Israel. He said it all with a matter-of-fact tone. There were sad faces all around, but no anger.

I almost jumped in to ask if anyone had read the many critiques of the Goldstone report, but I didn't want to wear out my welcome.

By the time the evening wound down and people started milling around, I could have been at any Jewish event in any Jewish home. I hugged and thanked the hostess (a Sephardic Iraqi) and took plenty of e-mail addresses. Feeling somewhat relieved that the serious part was over, I shmoozed with a writer from the Huffington Post, a self-described anti-Zionist former Communist from Israel, a recent candidate for Congress (Marcy Winograd), a well-known local poet and the woman from the Free Gaza movement.

I was happy and encouraged that the tone of the evening was so respectful. But I couldn't help feeling a little sadness that everyone was so sure of themselves.

As I walked back to my car, I wondered if we were all guilty of the same thing — meeting only with like-minded people and becoming more and more sure of ourselves.

Add up all those meetings, I thought — whether in Mar Vista or Pico-Robertson — and the distance between us only grows. Maybe we ought to crash more of each other's parties — even if it's only to see each other's faces.

"He was talking to Jews who pride themselves on following all of God's mitzvot, and yet, acting happy to make others happy hardly seemed like an obvious mitzvah."

SERIOUS ABOUT HAPPINESS

June 22, 2010

It's not every day that Orthodox Jews gather in a synagogue to learn about happiness. But on a recent Sunday morning at Young Israel of Century City, a standing-room-only crowd came for precisely that. The event was the seventh annual Ariel Avrech Memorial Lecture, and the speaker was author, radio host and happiness guru Dennis Prager.

The very idea of a serious lecture on happiness felt weird, and Prager sensed it. After all, synagogue sermons usually deal with sober topics like ethics, compassion, truth and justice. Personal happiness? That feels more like a selfish fetish of the secular world. The Torah world is supposed to operate on a more noble and altruistic plane.

Well, that is the misconception Prager came to correct.

Prager's thesis — which he expounds on in a book ("Happiness Is a Serious Problem") and a weekly "Happiness Hour" on his radio show — is that happiness isn't a selfish act at all, but might be, in fact, the ultimate mitzvah.

To dramatize his point, Prager used the religious language of altruism. If the Torah commands us to look beyond ourselves and consider the welfare of others, what better way than to act happy around others and elevate their own happiness? It's a worthy sacrifice, Prager explained, not to allow one's negative feelings to bring others down.

His subject touched a sensitive nerve. He was talking to Jews who pride themselves on following all of God's mitzvot, and yet, acting happy to make others happy hardly seemed like an obvious mitzvah; certainly not as natural or obvious as lighting the Shabbat candles or donating to charity.

Prager's thesis came to life when he talked about his "war on the moody" — people who put their feelings first, even at the expense of bringing others down. Judaism isn't about putting feelings first, he said. It's about actions, and actions that bring happiness to the world are supremely moral.

Prager explained how he stumbled onto his happiness philosophy. Many years ago, Rabbi Shlomo Schwartz invited him to speak to students at UCLA and suggested "something light, like happiness." When Prager responded that "happiness is a serious problem," Schwartz said he loved that title, and Prager crafted a talk that became one of his most popular.

He's been on a happiness mission ever since.

His mission isn't to promote the suppression of negative feelings — that's not realistic — but to make people aware of the power of a happy disposition to change the world around us and make it a better place.

His lecture hit home with me, since one of my pet peeves is moody or disengaged people who think they're being "authentic" when they inflict their moody vibes on those around them, especially in a festive setting. Of course, at the other extreme, I also don't enjoy people who try too hard to act happy. Faux happiness makes me feel guilty that they're faking it on my behalf. Maybe, then, Prager's lecture should come with this caveat: If you have to act happy when you're not feeling it, make sure only the happiness shows, not the acting. Eventually, Prager says, the more you act happy, the less you'll have to fake it.

This whole notion of happiness was on my mind last week when I went to an event at the Backdoor Art Gallery, a little space located off an alleyway behind Robertson Boulevard in Beverly Hills.

The gallery is run by my friend Bob Oré, a French-Moroccan Jew who is one of the premier producers of French cultural events in town. Last year, when he brought the popular comedian Gad Elmaleh to Los Angeles, several hundred French-speaking Jews packed a local theater. Oré is the kind of guy who can get a hundred fashionable people to show up at a party on an afternoon's notice.

At his event last week, you felt you were in a little nightclub in St. Germain, with a French poet singing love songs to a summer night crowd seeking a little moonlight bliss.

The singer was Pol-Serge Kakon, a painter and troubadour in his late 50s with long silver hair and a thin mustache who looked like he could have been married to Edith Piaf. I couldn't believe I was in Los Angeles.

As Kakon was singing to his adoring crowd, I thought about Prager's lecture on happiness. For all I knew, Pol-Serge could have had a real crummy day or been consumed by the sadness of a failed romance. But if that was the case, we saw none of it. All we saw was a singer exhaling happiness onto the people around him. It wasn't a showy kind of happiness, but an intimate sort that comes from being lost in the pleasure of the moment.

Kakon had the power to make us happy, and he used it.

Maybe Prager wants us to be a little like that French troubadour — to elevate those around us by simply exhaling happiness.

To Prager, this simple act is so important that he calls it a moral obligation. If that's still not enough to motivate you, well, just remember that happy people get invited to the best parties.

"Instead of spending so much time bickering among ourselves about how to help Israel, we ought to just get out
there and do it, each in our own way."

IN PRAISE OF DISUNITY

June 15, 2010

I t's painful to watch liberal lovers of Israel feel so isolated. I'm thinking especially of people like my friend Rabbi Sharon Brous, who wrote
about her disappointment with many in the pro-Israel community after last week's rally in front of the Israeli Consulate.

In her piece, she noted the animosity that Israel was up against in the
first days of the flotilla crisis. She mentioned the "tens of thousands crying
'Death to Israel' and burning flags in rallies around the world," but then
bemoaned the fact that "fairly quickly, the 'tragedy' of the incident was
superseded by the need, once again, to stand and defend Israel against
vociferous attacks on the very legitimacy of the Jewish state."

She then let the defenders of Israel have it:

"And thus a rally was born. Let's fight fire with fire, it is decided. We'll
bring thousands of Jews to the streets and show the world that we will not
stand by as Israel is delegitimized. 'You're either with us or against us!' a
speaker shouts. 'YES!' the crowd hungrily replies. And in a heartbeat, a
tragic episode, filled with complexity and nuance, becomes a Lakers' rally,
complete with flag waving, chanting and sloganeering."

Brous lamented the boos and jeers that greeted an official from Americans for Peace Now, and said that she was "devastated by what I can only
understand to be a tragic narrowing of the American Jewish heart and

mind." She closed with a heartfelt appeal:

"Wouldn't it have been heartening if the Jewish community's message to the world after the flotilla had been: 'What a painful and tragic event. We know that we will never have peace until we can mourn one another's losses. We affirm Israel's right to defend itself, but we also realize that the status quo is untenable and pray that the world, rather than delegitimize us, will join hands with us and work to achieve a lasting peace.' "

My first reaction after reading the piece was: Brous really feels strongly about this, and I'm sure she'd love to have me and others get behind her approach. But then I thought: If we're all on the same team, why do we all have to play the same position?

Brous called on the whole Jewish community, not just her community, to follow her approach and make her statement to the world. But why does she assume that this approach is good for all of us?

In any event, how realistic is it to expect that we should all choose the same way of helping Israel? Jews are as diverse as they come. I'm a hard-nosed Sephardic Zionist from Casablanca; Brous is a spiritual Ashkenazic liberal Zionist from America. I don't mind a nuance-free demonstration once in a while; she's more into self-reflection and understanding the other side.

I see the hypocrisy of a world that's demonizing Israel and trying to turn it into a pariah state, and I feel a need to fight and expose this hypocrisy. Brous sees the same mess that I do, but her inclination is to offer a more hopeful message. Brous sees the status quo as untenable and calls for conciliation; I see a Hamas takeover of the West Bank as even more untenable, and I call for extreme caution. I call my way Jewish; so does she.

What's wrong with two Jews seeing things differently?

Jews have this obsession with rebuking each other in the hope that they'll change one another — always chasing that elusive dream of a "united approach." But if that hasn't succeeded in 5,000 years, why should it succeed now?

The way I see it, we're better off trying to turn our disunity into a virtue.

How can we do that? By focusing less on each other and more on the world — where Israel's real troubles are. If Brous and her camp want to help Israel by showing a conciliatory and self-reflective side to the world — rather than a rah-rah side — they should just do it.

For example, they can have a community "pray-in" that would include an interfaith shiva to "mourn each other's losses" and a "Hands Across Los Angeles" event where peace lovers from all walks of life would hold hands for peace.

If other groups would rather promote Israel's contributions to the world, or fight the lies and hypocrisy against Israel with conferences and activist literature, they should just do it, too. In other words, everyone should feel free to do their own thing for Israel, even if that "thing" means holding a loud public rally to make a statement to the world of solidarity and support for Israel.

Now, if that kind of partisan atmosphere doesn't lend itself to groups like Peace Now, the organizers shouldn't force it.

Peace Now can do their own thing to help Israel, like dramatizing to the world how much Israel wants peace. For example, why don't they organize an annual Peace Now concert at the Hollywood Bowl with Israeli and Palestinian musicians? (One call to Craig Taubman will make it happen.)

You get the idea: Instead of spending so much time bickering among ourselves about how to help Israel, we ought to just get out there and do it, each in our own way.

Just as there are all kinds of Jews, Israel needs all kinds of supporters — lovers, fighters, jokesters, artists, lawyers, rabble-rousers, social activists, producers, etc. In my mind, that's the only thing we should all agree on.

"The major factor in being alienated from Israel, it turns out, is intermarriage. The more distant you are from your Jewish heritage, the more distant you are from Israel."

BEINART'S FAILURE

June 8, 2010

I love Peter Beinart. The last time we had breakfast, in Washington, D.C., about a year and a half ago, our conversation got so lively that I think someone asked us to quiet down. We don't see eye to eye on everything, but I've been moved by his compelling logic and sense of fairness in the many opinion pieces he has written over the years.

Not so with his latest, much-discussed piece, titled "The Failure of the American Jewish Establishment," in The New York Review of Books. The essay is sprawling and cleverly written; you feel you are reading something important that is revealing a big truth.

My problem, though, is that once I got over the drama, I found myself asking questions like, "What exactly does he want the Jewish establishment to do?"

For example, one of Beinart's key points is that a major reason for the alienation of liberal Jews from Zionism is the fact that the Jewish establishment has failed to criticize Israel's behavior on liberal issues, like its treatment of Palestinians and Israeli Arabs.

Let's unpack that argument. Let's imagine a liberal Jew in his 20s who hasn't gone on Birthright, doesn't go to shul and knows little about Israel. During Israeli Apartheid Week on his college campus, he sees pictures of Israeli soldiers portrayed as "Nazi baby-killers."

Through the media, he sees Israel as the world's most brutal occupier and favorite piñata: U.N. condemnations, global calls to boycott, accusations of crimes against humanity, Goldstone reports, the works.

If he does a little homework, he might come across a recent report from the Reut Institute describing a global movement afoot to delegitimize the Jewish state.

Now, what does Beinart think we should do to bring this liberal Jew closer to Zionism? Have someone from the Jewish "establishment" come on campus and educate him about how Israel is mistreating its Arab citizens? Is he serious?

Tough love is one thing, but showing tough love for Israel to those who have no love for Israel in the first place isn't tough love. It's just pouring oil on the fire.

Beinart loses me not when he criticizes Israeli democracy, but when he tries to pull a fast one by telling me that this criticism will help make alienated liberal Jews more sympathetic to the Jewish state.

His argument ignores some inconvenient facts. One of these facts is pointed out by Shmuel Rosner on The Jerusalem Post's Web site. Beinart quotes Steven Cohen of Hebrew Union College and Ari Kelman of the University of California, Davis, as saying that "non-Orthodox younger Jews, on the whole, feel much less attached to Israel than their elders, with many professing a 'near-total absence of positive feelings.' "

However, as Rosner notes, the study itself contradicts a key component of Beinart's thesis:

"Political identity, for the general population, has little bearing upon feelings of warmth toward or alienation from Israel. Whatever conclusion one may draw from the actions of political elites, or the writing of intellectual figures, left-of-center political identity (seeing oneself as liberal and a Democrat) in the general population exerts seemingly little influence on the level of attachment to Israel."

The major factor in being alienated from Israel, it turns out, is intermarriage. The more distant you are from your Jewish heritage, the more distant you are from Israel.

Nevertheless, let's give Beinart the benefit of the doubt and continue with his argument on the liberal value of criticizing Israel. Beinart is incredibly good at criticizing Israel. He's like Muhammad Ali: Move like a butterfly, sting like a bee. He'll cherry-pick the best facts and sources, bob and weave away from inconvenient context, and, by the time he's done, Israel might as well be a banana republic.

Beinart ignores the crucial context that Israel is a country under permanent siege and in a state of virtual war, surrounded by terrorist entities sworn to its destruction, and that it still manages, however imperfectly, to maintain a civil society — a society that boasts, among other things, the freest Arab press in the Middle East. He complains about the treatment of Israeli Arabs and Arab members of Knesset (MK) who coddle with Israel's enemies, but like a Likud MK said recently: "Imagine a member of the Taliban being a member of Congress." It makes me wonder: How tolerant would Beinart be if 6,000 Hamas rockets had fallen on his quiet suburb?

I'm not talking here about whitewashing Israel's mistakes; I'm talking about context. Appreciating this context might have led Beinart to a different approach toward his own goal. After all, if you want to appeal to a liberal Jew who has heard mostly poison about Israel, wouldn't you want to start off with some positive "liberal context" to break the ice? Wouldn't you want to tell the story, for instance, of the Palestinian homosexual who had to flee to Israel to have his rights protected?

In Beinart's world, however, the magic tonic for the revival of liberal Zionists is not context but criticism. Get bigwigs like Abe Foxman and Malcolm Hoenlein to publicly criticize Israel's democracy and liberal Jews will be more likely to flock to the Zionist tent. Where's the evidence for this? He never says.

He does say that the Jewish establishment's failure to criticize Israel's democracy is a major reason why liberal Jews have "checked their Zionism at the door." But how does he know that the opposite isn't true — that piling on establishment criticism on top of the world's hyper-criticism would have chased even more liberal Jews away?

What's ironic is that at the beginning of his piece, Beinart cites evidence that contradicts his own theory. He discusses focus groups among American Jewish college students in 2003 that showed how alienated they were from Israel. He then mentions an ad they were shown that was "one of the most popular."

Did that ad criticize Israel? No, it gave information: "Proof that Israel wants peace," with "a list of offers by various Israeli governments to withdraw from conquered land." In other words, instead of piling on the criticism, the ad gave alienated Jews some important context about the peace process that presumably might lessen their shame about Israel.

The fact that the ad was so popular might actually be a sign that these Jewish students are craving more context that shows Israel's side of the story — and that Jews like Beinart are just not hearing that part of their message.

Because he so downplays context, it's not a shock that Beinart is relentless in calling for more criticism of Israel on the peace process. As Jonathan Tobin wrote recently on the Commentary blog, "it's only by pretending that 17 years of Israeli concessions never happened that [Beinart] can hold on to the falsehood that the lack of peace is due to Israeli intransigence aided and abetted by American supporters."

Which brings me to this question: Does Beinart really believe there's not enough criticism of Israel in Jewish America? What's he been reading? The voices of influence today aren't just old-school establishment machers like Foxman and Hoenlein, who I doubt are Facebook friends with alienated liberal Jews anyway. The new world of influence also includes the multitude of voices in the social networks, in the blogosphere and in the established Jewish media, like The Forward, The Jewish Week and this newspaper, as well as in progressive Web sites like Tablet and Juicy — all places where you'll find plenty of Jewish criticism of Israel.

Go to any event from J Street, the Progressive Jewish Alliance or the New Israel Fund, or hang out at any of the social activist spiritual communities that have sprouted over the last decade, and you'll see lots of friendly venues for liberal Jews who want to criticize Israel and oppose its policies.

Yes, it's true that many defenders of Israel — especially since the Second Intifada and the Hamas rocket attacks that followed the Gaza disengagement — don't do much Israel-bashing. They're too busy trying to push back against the onslaught of hypocritical and disproportionate global criticism that is poured almost daily onto the Jewish state. Maybe that's their way of fighting for the liberal values of fairness and balance. Anyhow, if they won't do that dirty work, who will? Beinart?

Like many Jews, these Israel defenders are reluctant to second-guess the democratic choices of their Israeli brethren, who have to live with the life-and-death consequences of their decisions. If Beinart himself is so keen on improving Israel's democracy, instead of beating up on pro-Israel groups like AIPAC, why doesn't he talk to those Israeli voters and try to convince them to vote for Meretz? Or better still, why doesn't he work through any of the numerous human-rights NGOs or any other groups whose missions coincide directly with his? Not every Zionist needs to play the same instrument.

Beinart's own instrument is to criticize Israeli democracy, criticize establishment types for not criticizing Israeli democracy, and then hope that in the end, that symphony of criticism will attract more liberal Jews to come under the Zionist tent. Good luck. Whatever power there is in criticizing Israel, it surely won't seduce a Jew tainted by anti-Zionist propaganda to take a second look at Zionism, let alone enter the tent.

To have any chance with those alienated Jews, Beinart needs to go back to that popular ad he mentioned from the college focus groups. That ad was neither criticism nor propaganda: it was context — context that provided information to balance out the anti-Israel venom the students are routinely exposed to, while recognizing that Israel is still a messy and wonderful work in progress.

As part of that work in progress, Beinart can also point, with pride, to the many liberal Jewish groups in Israel who are using the Israeli legal system to defend the rights of Arabs and other minorities.

If all of that "context" helps alienated Jews care more about Israel, he can then introduce them to the Israel activist community so they can pick their own instrument, whether it be joining J Street, AIPAC or a human-rights NGO.

Of course, if he believes in the research he quoted, Beinart must also try to rekindle in those liberal Jews some kind of connection to their Jewish heritage.

In any event, all of these issues are multilayered and complex, and Beinart shouldn't pretend otherwise. Issues like Jewish alienation from Israel, the evolving role and nature of the Jewish establishment, the character of Israel's democracy and the revival of liberal Zionism in America are infinitely more textured and complicated than what Beinart reduces them to. But complexity doesn't make for hypnotic prose. Alarmism and finger-pointing do.

By largely abandoning nuance and context in favor of dramatic impact, Beinart has made a lot of noise and put a big part of the Jewish community on the defensive. But in the process, he has ignored less divisive approaches to our common problems and discouraged a deeper understanding of complex issues.

In my mind, I consider that a failure. And I say this with the same tough love that I know he has for Israel.

"Here are some of the most brilliant intellectual and spiritual Jewish minds in America, and all they can come up with is the same stuff we've been hearing ad nauseum for years."

EVA'S PEACE PROCESS

May 18, 2010

How could a frail, 83-year-old Holocaust survivor battling leukemia have a deeper understanding of the Israeli-Palestinian conflict than some of the great minds of the Jewish world? I asked myself that question last Friday night, while listening to my good friend Eva Brown, a Holocaust survivor who's a regular guest at our Shabbat table.

Earlier in the day, I had received an e-mail petition that invited me to "take a stand in support of peace for Israel and her neighbors" and lend my name to "an important new statement titled 'For the Sake of Zion.' " The statement was endorsed by a 34-member organizing committee of prominent American Jews, many of whom I know and admire.

The list includes Rabbis Elliot Dorff, Irwin Kula, Sharon Brous, Ed Feinstein and David Saperstein, along with Michael Walzer, Theodore Bikel, Judge Abner Mikva, Peter Edelman, Letty Cottin Pogrebin, Steven M. Cohen and Leonard Fein.

The statement is, essentially, a passionate appeal to advance the peace process that echoes the recent European "Call to Reason," initiated by French Jewish intellectuals. It declares: "We categorically condemn terrorism and we mourn the tragic loss of blood and treasure that has afflicted the region over the years. At the same time, we abhor the continuing occupation that has persisted for far too long; it cannot and should not be sustained."

The Americans quote the Europeans' text on the importance of ending the occupation — "Israel will soon be faced with two equally disastrous choices: either to become a state in which Jews are a minority in their own country, or to establish a regime that would be a disgrace to Israel and lead to civil unrest" — and adds that "recent and ongoing developments in Jerusalem, Ramallah and Washington give rise to a still extremely fragile hope that finally, both Israelis and Palestinians may be ready to revive the peace process and to engage in negotiations."

The statement declares that "advancing toward a two-state solution will require significant concessions and commitments by both sides," and it endorses "the American government's vigorous encouragement of the parties to make the concessions necessary for negotiations to advance."

The appeal didn't do much for me, not because I disagreed with it, but because it put me to sleep.

Such wasted genius, I thought. Here are some of the most brilliant intellectual and spiritual Jewish minds in America, and all they can come up with is the same stuff we've been hearing ad nauseam for years. Seriously, do the authors really expect that the zillionth repetition of the obvious will help longtime foes reconcile and revive the peace process? That all the peace process needs is more pushing?

I know; I'm a cynic. Or maybe I just yearn, after being burned by decades of peace process failures, to hear something really fresh that might make a difference.

All this ran through my mind as I listened to Eva Brown talk on Friday night about surviving a death march from the concentration camps in 1945, just hours before being rescued by American troops. Brown is a popular speaker at the Museum of Tolerance, where, when she's not fighting off the effects of her chemotherapy, she takes time to share her story of survival.

But here's the part of her story that I find so amazing: She talks about her enormous pain, yes, but she never sounds bitter. She believes in justice and in remembering, but not in revenge. As she reveals in her book, "If You Save One Life," the horror of the Holocaust taught her more about life than it did about death.

Her big thing is forgiveness. Without forgiving her captors, she says, she would never have found the inner peace that helped her savor the infinite pleasures of life. This is her simple message: If you feel you have been aggrieved, and peace and life are important to you, you must learn how to forgive those who have aggrieved you, no matter how difficult.

As she spoke, I had this vision of President Obama inviting Eva Brown to join him in Ramallah and Jerusalem to speak to Jews and Palestinians about forgiveness. If she can forgive those who murdered 59 members of her family, she would tell them, can't Jews and Palestinians find it in their hearts to forgive one another?

With President Obama standing by her side, and her message broadcast on Al Jazeera, CNN and throughout the world, she would hold up her tiny body with her cane and tell her message of peace to both sides of the conflict: Nothing good can happen until you make mutual forgiveness the first step in the peace process.

The very freshness of this message — not to mention the person delivering it — would get the world's attention.

In fact, if the 34-member organizing committee of prominent American Jews are serious about advancing the peace process, they ought to make mutual forgiveness their main message, and Eva Brown their spokesperson. That would certainly awaken and disarm everyone.

More important, it would also make sense. No proximity talks or construction freeze can cure a hundred years of accumulated bitterness. No passionate statement pushing for a two-state solution can make enemies reconcile.

Eva Brown, by her example, can teach us all a lesson: If you don't learn how to forgive, you'll have nothing to give.

"They are easily moved by little things. Ziman was moved by a little touch, Tessler by a little phrase."

TWO JEWISH MOTHERS

May 9, 2010

Sometimes all it takes is a few words or a little touch to ignite a motherly connection. In the case of Daphna Ziman, it was a little touch. A friend of hers needed to do community service in 1993, so Ziman took the friend to a charity that Ziman supported, the Sunlight Mission in Santa Monica. Ziman recalls seeing little cubicles with tiny cots along the walls.

Beneath the sheets, she could see kids, some sleeping with their drug-addicted or battered mothers, others alone.

As she passed through the kitchen, which prepared thousands of meals a day for the local homeless, she crossed a patio area, where she saw a young girl sleeping on a bench. She approached the girl, who Ziman says looked like a "ragamuffin" with dreadlocks and a caked face. Sensing a human presence, the girl opened her big green eyes and stared right at Ziman. After a short pause, with hardly any words spoken, the girl reached out to Ziman's hands, holding tight.

It was at that moment that Ziman realized it would be very hard to let this kid go.

So she didn't. After a long period of mentoring and legal wrangling, Michele became Ziman's adopted daughter. But Ziman also knew that thousands of other abandoned kids were still out there, longing to hold the hand of someone who would protect them. So she rallied all her Hollywood and political connections and started up, along with her friend and mentor Hillary Clinton, Children Uniting Nations, an organization that promotes the mentoring of disadvantaged kids.

The organization is now involved with everything from lobbying Washington for legislation to strengthen children's rights, to sponsoring neurological research to reduce dependence on drugs like Ritalin, to training mentors and monitoring the progress of the kids.

I checked out one of their signature events last November, Day of the Child, a large outdoor festival for several hundred mentors and mentees that takes place near the Santa Monica Airport. It turns out that the Sunlight Mission, where little Michele first reached out to hold Ziman's hand, is only a few minutes away. Now, 17 years later, thousands of disadvantaged and abandoned kids have been the beneficiaries of that little moment.

Six years after Ziman's 1993 visit to the Sunlight Mission, in the little Israeli town of Hadera, a girl in her late teens named Michal was at a bus station ordering a slice of pizza. She was waiting with her girlfriend for a bus to take them to Eilat for a little vacation.

But before she could get her change back from the pizza vendor, a terrorist bomb went off, killing Michal's friend and leaving Michal in critical condition, without her legs.

I heard of Michal's story last week from a woman named Aviva Tessler, who was in town to raise funds and awareness for her organization, Operation Embrace.

Tessler, who lives in Washington, D.C., first met Michal in the hospital a few months after the bombing. Tessler and her husband, a Modern Orthodox rabbi, were in Israel on a one-year sabbatical, and she went to the hospital that day to hand out mishloach manot (baskets of goodies), a ritual of Purim.

When she got to Michal, though, she couldn't go on. Michal said something that slowed her down. The bombing had been front-page news in Israel, as were the scores of terrorist attacks happening all over Israel in those years. Michal had received many visitors in the first days and weeks after the attack, including members of the press. Now, she felt mostly alone.

"Don't be a hi-bye friend," she told Tessler.

This was Michal's way of saying: "Don't come to show me your love and then leave, never to be seen again."

That little phrase got to Tessler. There was an old picture on the wall of Michal dancing in a disco with her boyfriend (who had already broken up with her), and Tessler saw an unspeakable sadness on Michal's face.

She told herself at that moment that she wouldn't become another "hi-bye" friend. So she kept in touch with Michal with regular visits and contributions to her rehabilitation, which she continues to this day.

And in Michal's honor, Tessler founded Operation Embrace.

Over the past 10 years, Tessler's organization has helped hundreds of terror victims in Israel, helping pay for medical care, post-traumatic counseling and rehabilitation therapy, as well as providing educational scholarships, adopt-a-family programs, free laptops and, of course, distributing hundreds of Purim baskets.

To keep all this going, Tessler goes to Israel about four times a year. She has become a ubiquitous presence in hospitals and shelters, especially in towns that have been the hardest hit, like Sderot.

I heard Ziman's and Tessler's stories about a week apart – Ziman's at my Shabbat table, Tessler's at a small theater in Beverly Hills. They are two Jewish mothers who don't know each other but who share at least one trait in common: they are easily moved by little things. Ziman was moved by a little touch, Tessler by a little phrase.

It's true that when you raise kids, you must learn when to let go. But sometimes, when the pain and trauma are so deep, what children need most is simply a mother like Daphna Ziman or Aviva Tessler to hold their hands ... and never let go or say "hi-bye."

Happy Mother's Day.

> "Halevi didn't buy the 'tough love' argument. He sees Obama's actions more as a combination of bullying and naive incompetence."

PRESIDENT OF HUMANITY

April 27, 2010

After listening to Yossi Klein Halevi speak at Nessah last week on the deteriorating relationship between President Obama and Israel, the question on many people's minds was: Why?

Why has Obama acted the way he has toward Israel?

Halevi laid out a sober recap of the relationship, from Obama's visit to Sderot as a candidate in 2008 — when he beguiled many Israelis with his comment that he'd do anything to defend his house if bombs fell on his children — to the personal humiliation of Prime Minister Netanyahu last month, when, as Jackson Diehl wrote in The Washington Post, the Israeli prime minister was treated like a "third-rate dictator."

Halevi didn't buy the "tough love" argument. He sees Obama's actions more as a combination of bullying and naive incompetence. A couple of years ago the Israelis and Palestinians were negotiating directly about all the important issues. Since Obama began his active engagement, the Palestinians haven't even agreed to enter indirect "proximity" talks.

Obama's key blunder, Halevi said, was his reaction to the historic agreement by a Likud leader to endorse a two-state solution and a settlement freeze in the major settlement blocks. Instead of crediting Israel and turning to the Palestinians and saying, "OK, now what will you do?" Obama pressured Israel for even more concessions, including unprecedented ones, like stopping Jews from building in Jewish neighborhoods of Jerusalem.

For about an hour, Halevi had us riveted with his anatomy of a deteriorating relationship. At the end, the big question lingered: Why would Obama act this way toward a great ally? If it's not anti-Semitism or tough love, is there a larger narrative that speaks to the soul of the man — a narrative that might explain why he bows to America's foes and mistreats America's friends?

Here's one possibility: Maybe Obama sees his calling as bigger than America, and he wants to be President of Humanity.

"His speeches and remarks are filled with references to himself in a ratio that surpasses anything yet seen in the history of the American presidency," writes professor James Ceaser in a recent piece in The Weekly Standard titled "The Roots of Obama Worship."

"He awakened at some point in the campaign to the realization that he was no longer running merely for president of the United States. He was being selected to the much grander 'office' of leader of a new world community."

Ceaser finds evidence for this grand narrative in many areas, like Obama's distaste for America's exceptionalism and his dogmatic stubbornness in foreign affairs: "Americans who thought that it is one thing to offer an initial hand to the likes of a Chavez or an Ahmadinejad think it something quite different to offer it after the hand has been flagrantly rejected. To persist is to invite dishonor, both for the office of the president and for the nation. Realism dictates an adjustment. The fact that such a change has been so slow in coming suggests that it is not realism that is Obama's guiding light, but a commitment to the dogmas of the Religion of Humanity."

He finds similar evidence in stubborn Bush bashing: "Persistence bespeaks something more than political miscalculation. For the Religion of Humanity, the attack on Bush, both the man and the 'substance,' is a matter of dogma. If Obama were to desist, he would relinquish his higher office."

Most seriously, Ceaser worries that "the conflicting demands of the Religion of Humanity and the presidency of the United States have become most apparent in the administration's approach to dealing with the threat of Islamic terrorism.

"Supporters of the Religion of Humanity [therefore] believe they have good reasons to deny or minimize the danger of terrorism in order to save the world from the even greater danger of the triumph of the retrograde forces. This is the dogmatic basis of political correctness and Obama and his team have gone to considerable lengths by their policies and by their use of language to hide reality. But reality has a way of asserting itself, and it is becoming clearer by the day that being the leader of Humanity is incompatible with being the president of the United States."

It's hard to say how much truth there is in Ceaser's analysis, but it does add to the debate of understanding Obama's behavior toward Israel. At least it gives us something more noble than the hysterical "Obama's an anti-Semite" accusations that I see in my inbox every day.

And let's face it, there is something noble about having a heart for all of humanity.

The problem for Israel, of course, is that most of humanity already hates Israel, and if you're Obama and you want to woo all of humanity, well, I can see how tiny Israel would be a major irritant.

Maybe that's why Halevi was so sober when he spoke last week — he knows a conflict of interest when he sees one.

"If there's a message to their stories, it's that we need the courage to fight for our cause, but also the wisdom to remember why we're fighting."

NAMING NAMES

It struck me during the Passover seders this year how impersonal the Jewish master story can be. We seem to jump so quickly to the grand themes. Slavery, freedom, responsibility. The characters are mythical, the drama is epic, the story laden with symbols. It all feels so overwhelming. It's as if God gave us a blockbuster movie that we must turn into an indie.

In this blockbuster, one thing that is clearly impersonal is evil. We're never told which Egyptian pharaoh we're dealing with. It's just a generic Pharaoh. One explanation for this (which I saw on the Seraphic Secret blog) is that, had his name been provided, "Historians and psychologists and novelists would have speculated about him, especially his childhood, suggesting probable reasons for his atrocious behavior." This would "open the door to excuses and thence to the erosion of personal responsibility."

That may be true for evil, but what about the victims of evil? Shall they also remain mythical and nameless?

This year, I found my own answer to that question. While I was going through the haggadah with my family in Montreal, as we were reflecting on a Passover story that overflows with nameless victims, I couldn't stop thinking about victims with real names.

I was haunted by two names in particular: Josh Friedberg and Gail

Rubin.

I came across Friedberg's name in the lobby of my niece Rebecca's Jewish day school in Montreal, Herzliah High School. His picture was framed behind a glass case, surrounded by diplomas, trophies, newspaper articles and other mementos. Friedberg was a star student, captain of the basketball team and an ardent Zionist. His dream was always to make aliyah.

He moved to Israel right after graduating from high school in 1991, during the first Gulf War. After learning in a Jerusalem yeshiva, he enlisted in the Israel Defense Forces' Golani Brigade. While on patrol in March 1993, he was kidnapped and murdered by terrorists. It took several days to find his body.

Thousands attended his funeral on Mount Herzl, among them Yaffa Ganz, who wrote on aish.com: "Like our father Abraham, Josh had left the familiar to follow his God and to join his people in the Promised Land. ... In ancient Egypt, Pharaoh had buried Jewish infants in the walls and monuments memorializing Egypt's dead. Now, Jewish soldiers stood shoulder to shoulder, forming a living wall to protect Jewish children and keep them alive. Josh stood with them.

"He was kidnapped, tortured and killed because of a khaki uniform, a blue and white flag, a Star of David."

Twenty-three years earlier, Gail Rubin, in her early 30s, was an editor at a major publishing house in New York, and she was restless. Zionism and politics had nothing to do with her move to Israel after a visit in 1969. As her cousin, journalist Elinor Brecher, wrote: "She fell in love with the irrepressible people who, with ceaseless labor, were turning a scrap of desert into fertile farmland."

It was in Israel that Rubin began her love affair with photography: "She captured the merry grins of sun-browned kids on the cobbled streets of Israel's ancient cities. Her color close-ups of tree barks rival the most spectacular abstract paintings. She made tender portraits of relaxed young Israeli soldiers. And she found them also as they lay wounded and dying in the Yom Kippur War."

During one spring in the mid-1970s, her photographs of Israeli wild-life went on exhibit in the Jewish Museum in New York.

A year later, on a Saturday in March 1978, Rubin was walking on a beach near Tel Aviv, on her way to photograph wild birds at a nearby kib-butz. She was alone when a group of terrorists landed on the beach.

As Brecher wrote: "One report said the terrorists asked her for direc-tions. She gave them the directions and they shot her. Another report said they asked her nothing. They just killed her."

Rubin was one of 38 victims murdered in that terror rampage, which was in the news recently because Palestinian Authority President Mah-moud Abbas dedicated a memorial to its mastermind.

The mastermind's name is now well known. I'm sure if I do a little research, I can find the names of other terrorists who became local heroes after murdering people like Josh Friedberg.

I doubt very much that I will look. Maybe it's for the reason I men-tioned earlier — that we keep Pharaoh nameless in the haggadah so that we will resist the temptation to rationalize or "explain" evil.

But there's also a simpler reason. The terrorists get enough media fame and glory. We need to honor those who honor life. Josh Friedberg and Gail Rubin loved life. They gave their lives in the service of life. Fried-berg gave his to defend his people. Rubin gave hers because she yearned to reinvent herself.

If there's a message to their stories, it's that we need the courage to fight for our cause, but also the wisdom to remember why we're fighting — so that people like Gail Rubin can be free to walk on the beach and photograph wild birds.

To honor these lovers of life, we must absolutely turn our blockbuster into an indie and name names.

"Just like Soviet Jewry was about the Jews' 'right to leave,' this new cause is about the Jews' 'right to stay.'"

LET MY PEOPLE STAY

March 24, 2010

W hy does the Israeli-Palestinian conflict seem so intractable? Why do we hear the same ideas over and over again, even though they never work?

At her AIPAC speech this week, Secretary of State Hillary Clinton spoke of the need to find "a new path" to the two-state solution. But nowhere in her speech did she actually challenge a key tenet of the current path: We can never have Jews living in Palestine.

She's not alone. For decades now, the world's most brilliant political minds have worked with this same unimaginative and racist assumption: To have peace with the Palestinians, we must have ethnic cleansing of the Jews.

As a result, a peace vocabulary has developed that suggests anything but peace: words like "freezing" and "dismantling" rather than "warming" and "creating." The Jews themselves who live in the areas of a future Palestinian state have been globally demonized as the biggest obstacle to peace.

Sure, there may be terrorist entities like Hamas and Hezbollah that are sworn enemies of any peace agreement, but as far as the world is concerned, the soccer moms in Ariel and Efrat are bigger obstacles to peace.

Never mind that when Israel tried to cleanse Gaza of all Jews a few years ago, it got rewarded not with peace and quiet but with a few thousand rockets.

It's gotten so absurd, that the headlines around the world two weeks ago weren't about the terrorist rockets flying into Israel, but about interim zoning permits for apartments in East Jerusalem. Had those apartments been for Buddhists or Hindus or Hare Krishnas, no one would have flinched. But they were for Jews, which makes them obstacles to peace.

The Obama administration's obsession with freezing Jewish settlements — including Jewish neighborhoods of East Jerusalem — has further demonized the settlements, made the Palestinians even more intransigent and pretty much frozen the peace process.

But what if the peace processors took a different view of these settlements and saw them not as obstacles to peace but as potential contributors to Palestinian society? What if, instead of forcing Jewish settlers to leave as part of a peace agreement, they were invited to stay?

In all these failed peace meetings over the years, has anyone considered that a Jewish minority in a future Palestine may actually be a good thing? That it would encourage mutual dependency and co-existence and democracy — and help the Palestinian economy? And that for Israel, it'd be good to have Jewish representatives in a Palestinian parliament — just like we have supporters in Diaspora communities throughout the world?

I know what you're thinking: How naïve of you, Suissa! How many Jews would want to be part of a Palestinian state? Who would protect them? It'll never work!

To which I reply: Maybe you're right! But nothing else has worked, so why not shake things up and try something new? Let's poll the Jews of the West Bank who'd be most likely to be evacuated and see how many would be interested in staying in a future Palestine, and under what conditions. Dual citizenship? Security guarantees? Equal voting rights? These are great questions for peace talks.

Even if you're a cynic who believes peace with the Palestinians is impossible in our lifetime, pushing for the right of settlers to stay in a future

Palestine is a game changer. It disarms critics who claim that settlements are the main obstacle to peace and shines a light on fundamental issues, like whether the Palestinians are willing or even able to deliver peace, and how they would protect a Jewish minority in their midst.

Just like Soviet Jewry was about the Jews' "right to leave," this new cause is about the Jews' "right to stay." And if the world ends up opposing the idea, well, we'll finally have our PR homerun: An international movement fighting for "Human Rights for Palestinian Jews!" Our mantra: The Jews of Palestine deserve the same rights as the Muslims of Israel.

If you're not a cynic but a hopeless romantic who believes in the power of co-existence, you should have been with me the other night at the Levantine Cultural Center, a storefront salon on Pico Boulevard co-founded four years ago by local activist Jordan Elgrably to foster harmony between all peoples of the Middle East and North Africa. The guest speaker was author and journalist Rachel Shabi, who was talking about her new book, "We Look Like the Enemy: the Hidden Story of Israel's Jews From Arab Lands."

Shabi, a Jew of Iraqi descent who grew up in London and now lives in Tel Aviv, has had a lifelong fascination with the story of Jews who come from Arab lands like Morocco, Egypt, Lebanon, Syria, Iraq, Algeria and Tunisia.

As she spoke about the long and complicated journey of these Jews of Arabia, she didn't sugarcoat their struggles, but you could feel her passion for the golden moments and possibilities of cultural co-existence.

Stuck between my cynical and romantic sides, and perhaps caught up in the moment, I couldn't help wondering whether there might be, one day, a Palestinian chapter to this Jewish-Arab odyssey — a chapter that wouldn't be about Jews being kicked out, but about Jews being asked to stay.

"Israelis understand that, compared to the threat of a nuclear Iran, an issue like building permits in Ramat Shlomo is a farce."

TORMENTING ISRAEL

March 16, 2010

I've never understood why the world goes absolutely bonkers when Jews try to build homes in Jewish neighborhoods of Jerusalem. Take the latest brouhaha about the announcement by Israel's Interior Ministry that it had approved a planning stage — the fourth out of seven required — for the eventual construction of 1,600 units in the Jerusalem neighborhood of Ramat Shlomo.

Mahmoud Abbas, leader of the Palestinian Authority, is not known for being too accommodating during negotiations. And yet, when negotiating a two-state solution two years ago with Ehud Olmert, Abbas agreed that several neighborhoods in Jerusalem would stay in Israeli hands in any final settlement. And guess which neighborhood was on that list?

That's right — Ramat Shlomo, a neighborhood made up mostly of religious Jews with big families and a shortage of housing. Abbas was surely aware that, as analyst Evelyn Gordon wrote March 14 in a Commentary blog post, "Its location in no way precludes the division of Jerusalem, which is what both Washington and Europe claim to want: Situated in the corner formed by two other huge neighborhoods to its west and south, it [Ramat Shlomo] does not block a single Arab neighborhood from contiguity with a future Palestinian state."

Nevertheless, Israel was crucified when its Interior Ministry made the Ramat Shlomo announcement last week during Vice President Joe Biden's visit to Israel — presumably because the timing was highly embarrassing. But really, what timing would have been more appropriate? An announcement two weeks later, when Israel would have been accused of being sneaky and deceitful during Biden's visit?

After all, Israel had nothing to hide: It was in strict compliance with the 10-month settlement freeze, which specifically excluded East Jerusalem and which the Obama administration fully supported and even characterized as "unprecedented."

In any case, Vice President Biden made a rare public condemnation of Israel's announcement, and Prime Minister Benjamin Netanyahu responded with an explanation and a rare public apology that Biden accepted. Normally, that is more than enough contrition to resolve misunderstandings.

But not in this case. The following day, Secretary of State Hillary Clinton berated Netanyahu on the phone for close to 45 minutes and followed that with public condemnation and demands for more Israeli concessions.

Ambassador Michael Oren has reportedly called this the biggest crisis between the United States and Israel since 1975. And why all this madness? Because Israel had this crazy idea to allow a zoning permit for housing units in a Jewish neighborhood of its capital city.

One wonders: What would have happened if Israel had done something really bad while Biden was in Israel? Like, say, announce a zoning permit for construction of a national memorial to a terrorist?

Well, it turns out that while the Obama administration was heaping abuse on Israel, the Palestinians were in fact dedicating a memorial to the mastermind of the worse terrorist attack in Israeli history. Now tell me, which act does more to undermine trust and the atmosphere for peace: a zoning permit for apartments or a memorial to terrorism?

The funny thing is, no administration official ever mentioned the terrorist memorial. As Barry Rubin, professor at the Interdisciplinary Center in Herzliya, reminds us: "Even though the Palestinian Authority has refused to negotiate for 14 months; made President Obama look very foolish after destroying his publicly announced September plan to have negotiations in two months; broke its promise not to sponsor the Goldstone report in the U.N.; and rejected direct negotiations after months of pleading by the Obama White House, not a single word of criticism has ever been offered by any administration official regarding the P.A.'s continuous and very public sabotage of peace- process efforts."

Obama's single-minded condemnations of Israel have done more than push Israel away; they've also emboldened the Palestinians to dig in their heels and pushed them even further away from peace talks of any kind.

My friend Yossi Klein Halevi, an author and political analyst who lives in Jerusalem, has a "strong sense that Obama was looking for a pretext. He's turned an incident into a crisis."

He adds: "If Obama thinks he's going to win friends in the Israeli public by treating Israel more harshly than any other country aside from Iran, he's going to have an even tougher learning curve than he's had in this last year of failed Middle East diplomacy."

According to Noah Pollak of Commentary, Obama's priority is to stop Israel from attacking Iran: "Obama's only option for restraining an Israeli attack is the one that we're seeing unfold before our eyes: a U.S. effort to methodically weaken the relationship; provoke crises; consume the Netanyahu government with managing this deterioration; and most important, create an ambience of unpredictability by making the Israelis fear that an attack on Iran would not just be met with American disapproval but also a veto and perhaps active resistance."

If Pollak is correct, then, the Ramat Shlomo crisis has clarified the stakes: The issue of Iran trumps everything.

Israelis understand that, compared to the threat of a nuclear Iran, an issue like building permits in Ramat Shlomo is a farce. By tormenting the Jews over such an issue, Obama is not just emboldening Israel's enemies, he's setting back the very peace process he so cherishes.

"This widespread Jewish illiteracy across America has made it easier for Jews and philanthropists to gravitate toward what they know best and what they feel most comfortable with: that is, the idea of tikkun olam."

BIRTHRIGHT JUDAISM

March 9, 2010

Why is it so expensive to live a Jewish life? Since Jewish continuity and vitality are such communal priorities, and since the great majority of Jewish students today are not getting a Jewish education, why has the Jewish community not done more to help in this area? And what could it do to change that?

These are some of the questions explored in "The High Cost of Jewish Living," a lengthy, brilliant and depressing article this month in Commentary magazine. The article's author, Jack Wertheimer, a history professor at the Jewish Theological Seminary and one of the leading lights of the Conservative movement, dissects the problem and comes to some pretty downbeat conclusions.

First, there's the numbers game. It's just really expensive to lead a Jewish life. Add it all up, Wertheimer says, and "an actively engaged Jewish family that keeps kosher and sends its three school-age children to the most intensive Jewish educations can expect to spend somewhere between $50,000 and $110,000 a year at minimum just to live a Jewish life."

This problem might be more acute today, but it's hardly new. Wertheimer quotes from an address to the General Assembly of Jewish federations almost two decades ago, when Jacob Ukeles spoke about the idea that "living Jewishly shouldn't force people into poverty." But, as

Wertheimer says, "The message fell on deaf ears ... and there is little evidence that the problem is drawing more attention today."

There are many reasons for this, he explains, not least the fact that the financial resources of Jewish organizations are "severely limited." But more important than money is the question of attitude: "The prevailing attitude of too many in positions of authority is that affordability is a private matter. If families want to live an observant life, they alone should bear the costs. Why privilege day-school families? Most Jewish children attend far less costly part-time Jewish schools or receive tutoring. Let those who want more pay for it themselves."

What this cold calculus misses, Wertheimer says, is "any recognition that Jews well-versed in their religious culture are adding to American Jewish society. A disproportionate number of leaders and activists have been shaped by the most immersive forms of Jewish education. As for the rank and file, we would expect a community that places a great value on general education for all to ensure a comparably high level of literacy in Judaica."

He bemoans the lack of "a principled appreciation for the responsibility Jews must assume for building Jewish social capital so that there will be a vital Jewish community in the future. A proud and self-confident community would do all in its power, or so one would think, to prepare its youth for active participation in Jewish life."

This widespread Jewish illiteracy across America has made it easier for Jews and philanthropists to gravitate toward what they know best and what they feel most comfortable with: that is, the idea of tikkun olam, about which Wertheimer quotes Cynthia Ozick's "dead-on" observation that "universalism is the parochialism of the Jews."

He writes: "The measure of Tikkun Olam's authenticity, it would seem, is that it be solely a Jewish mission to the Gentiles," and then wonders why "this effort to repair the world cannot also extend to aiding fellow Jews." He notes that this shift of attention away from our own community has had severe fiscal consequences, to the point that "insufficient resources are available to meet the basic needs of the American Jewish community."

Wertheimer has the courage to take on a sacred cow — tikkun olam — but he does so in the service of something just as vital: building Jewish literacy and connecting Jews to their tradition and their people. He lays out several ideas to advance this cause, from getting funding from government agencies to creating volunteer-based programs like a Jewish Teach for America.

Above all, he makes a passionate case that the advancement of Jewish literacy ought to be a communal enterprise.

So, what can the Jewish community do to help? Well, I think one way to approach this — and attract more philanthropic interest — is to make the advancement of Jewish literacy more of a mainstream project like Birthright Israel. If a journey to Israel is a Jewish birthright, shouldn't a journey to Judaism also be?

The idea would be to create a fun, free and adventurous "Birthright Judaism" program that would introduce thousands of unafilliated Jewish teens to the Jewish tradition.

The program would borrow from the classic camp experience, but would be more focused on advancing Jewish literacy. Birthright Judaism wouldn't really address the question "How can I afford to live a Jewish life?" but it might answer an even more important one: "Why should I want to?

"Maybe, just maybe, it is the Jewish comedians who are most responsible for the pro-Semitism in America."

THE COMEDIANS

February 23, 2010

A merica is different." Time and time again, when you hear experts discuss the state of the Jews in the world, you hear the same thing: America is different.

Sure, it's not as if there's absolutely no anti-Semitism here, but compared to the rest of the world there's little doubt that this country has been a haven for Jews.

How do we explain this? There are the obvious reasons, like the fact that this is a country governed by laws. It doesn't matter who you are, what God you believe in or what language you speak, the laws in America are designed to protect your rights. And if this country is obsessed with anything, it is obsessed with protecting individuals' rights. Since their arrival, and especially over the past half-century, Jews have taken full advantage of this protection to succeed in virtually every field of influence in American society.

This has earned Jews in America a degree of respect they have rarely enjoyed in other places in the Diaspora.

But respect is one thing — love is another. Respect doesn't begin to explain the long and ongoing love affair between America and the Jews — a love affair that has rendered the two cultures virtually interchangeable. How do we explain that love?

As it happens, I found one answer at a recent fundraiser for Maimonides Academy, my kids' Jewish day school. This year, maybe to provide some well-needed distraction from the economic crisis, Rabbi Baruch Kupfer, the head of the school, asked one of my favorite comedians, Mark Schiff, to produce a kosher comedy night at The Laugh Factory on Sunset Boulevard.

We've all been to comedy joints and seen Jewish stand-up comics, but what was different about this night is that everything screamed Jewish. The comics. The cause. The audience. The evening even began with the ultimate Jewish experience: a rabbi's sermon.

On the same stage where raunchy comics bring down the house every night with material that would make a free-speech activist blush, here was an Orthodox rabbi talking about the importance of Jewish education.

Needless to say, this sermon — and its length— was the brunt of jokes throughout the rest of the evening. But in a strange way, it also set a tone for the night. Yes, we can crack up and laugh until it hurts — and believe me, we did — but the rabbi's sermon reminded us that we should never forget the serious stuff like, for example, the future of the Jewish nation.

This mix of the serious and the comical hit home when Maimonides parent and kippah-wearing comic Elon Gold got up to do his shtick. At one point, he took on perhaps the most serious topic of all for Jews: anti-Semitism. Of course, he did it his way, by introducing a rarely used term — pro-Semitism. He spoofed a series of ads, one of which used a hick accent: "I was told that I had six months left to live, and then some Jew-doctor took my disease away — but left me with a case of pro-Semitism."

At that moment, while the crowd was in hysterics, I couldn't help but have a serious thought: maybe, just maybe, it is the Jewish comedians who are most responsible for the pro-Semitism in America — that is, for the mutual love affair between America and the Jews. While doctors, lawyers, academics, Hollywood moguls and other machers may have earned us the respect, it is the comedians who have brought us the love.

Think about it. Who was the most popular kid in class? Who's the most endearing guest at a dinner table? Is it the person who knows the most, or the one who can poke fun at himself and make you laugh?

Seriously, is there an ethnic group in America that has given this country more laughs than the Jews? From Jack Benny, Shelley Berman, Milton Berle and Sid Caesar to Mel Brooks, Billy Crystal, Jerry Seinfeld and Larry David, is there a group that better practices the art of poking fun at itself?

We can applaud all day long the work of Jewish groups that counteract anti-Semitism, like the Anti-Defamation League, the Holocaust memorials and the multitude of pro-Jewish and social activist groups — and I do applaud them — but for my money, the most underrated and underappreciated Jewish warriors against anti-Semitism have been our comedians.

No Jews have done more to endear us to America. And the fact that they don't take themselves too seriously hardly means that we shouldn't take them — or their contributions to our community — more seriously.

In fact, the upcoming holiday of Purim — that wild and crazy time of year when many Jews get drunk and a little rowdy — is an ideal time to take a more serious look at our comedians. While I was schmoozing about this subject the other day with Schiff, he shared a sober thought with me about comedy: If you laugh hard enough, it's like being drunk.

What a holy idea: This Purim, instead of getting drunk on Johnny Walker, we can get drunk on laughter.

It wouldn't be a bad way to honor the modern-day Jewish heroes who conquered the hearts of a great nation by telling a few good jokes.

"Yes, I know, this is called tough love, and God knows we all need tough love. But tough love is better received when it's balanced by pure love, the kind you feel when you get a hug."

WHEN TO BE AN EXTREMIST

February 10, 2010

What is it about criticism of Israel that is so hard to take for so many Jews? That question was on my mind this week as I was reading about the brouhaha with the New Israel Fund (NIF). In case you missed it, the NIF has been accused of funding human rights groups in Israel that provided much of the ammunition against Israel in the Goldstone report.

These human rights groups — like B'Tselem, Yesh Din, Machsom Watch and Breaking the Silence — are, in the words of Anshel Pfeffer in Haaretz, "nudniks" and "one-sided." As he says, "they pick up any story floating around, often giving exaggerated credence to hearsay testimony and they have a tendency for overkill, conflating every report into a phenomenon."

Yet, he asserts, we couldn't do without them: "With their resources and their zeal they are serving as eyes and ears, not just for the Israeli media, but for the Israeli public as a whole. Despite all the media's efforts, much of what goes on across the Green Line remains unreported, and without the researchers of these organizations and their local informants, we would know even less.... They draw attention to what many of us would prefer not to know about — but have to."

These groups are kindred spirits with the NIF, which since its inception in the United States in 1979 has provided, according to its Web site, "more than $200 million to more than 800 cutting-edge organizations."

Now, if you read the NIF's mission, it's hard to argue with what they're trying to do. They are "committed to democratic change within Israel" and they "fight inequality, injustice and extremism because [they] understand that justice is the precondition for a successful democracy — and the only lasting road to peace."

Regarding the latest fracas, the NIF didn't take a position on the Goldstone report, and, according to spokeswoman Naomi Paiss, "is very proud of the groups we have supported.... Their reports were carefully documented and in some instances were the only available information out of Gaza because the international press and the Israeli press were kept out."

So why, then, if its goals are so noble, has so much of the Jewish world not come to the NIF's defense regarding the charge that it contributed indirectly to the Goldstone report?

I see a specific reason, and a more general one.

The specific reason is the Goldstone report itself, which has garnered almost unanimous disapproval in the Jewish world, and which Elie Wiesel has called "a crime against the Jewish people." Really, no matter where you sit ideologically, which Jewish group would want to be associated with this piece of plutonium?

But I think there's also a general, more emotional reason: Many of us are simply tired of beating ourselves up and seeing our situation grow worse and worse.

It's not that we're blind followers who don't understand the importance of self-criticism. We do. Self-criticism is part of who we are. We must constantly challenge ourselves to be better. That's the Jewish way.

But there's something else that's also the Jewish way: not being stupid. When most of the world is already doing such an amazing job of pointing out our faults and turning us into criminals against humanity, what should be the appropriate Jewish response: To pile it on or to balance things out?

This is the word that seems to be missing with Jewish groups critical of Israel: balance.

For example, the NIF says they love Israel and are passionate about human rights, but on their Web site, there's hardly any positive mention of Israel's record on human rights — just one Israeli injustice after another.

Yes, I know, this is called tough love, and God knows we all need tough love. But tough love is better received when it's balanced by pure love, the kind you feel when you get a hug. What would a hug from the NIF look like? Well, for starters, a little recognition that Israel's record on human rights — whether with gays, women, Muslims and other minorities — is far superior to that of any of its neighbors. You'd never know that from seeing their Web site and fundraising pitch.

Relentless criticism that goes only in one direction might in fact be good for fundraising, but it's a form of extremism and it's divisive. So here's an idea for all Israel lovers, left or right: let's be more extreme with our love and more moderate with our criticism — of Israel and of each other.

But let's not be moderate at all when confronting this poison: the double standard that the world imposes on the Jews and Israel and the global assault on the legitimacy of Zionism and the Jewish state. This is an injustice on an epic scale.

As groups like the NIF fight to make Israel a more just and noble nation, they must remember our other fight — the one against enemies who don't give a hoot about how just and noble we are. This is also a fight we can't afford to lose.

"Maybe we're stupid and naive," he told me. "We just want to help."

STEP-UP NATION

January 27, 2010

Yonatan Yagodovsky, director of the international desk at Magen David Adom (MDA) in Israel, remembers exactly where he was when he first heard about the earthquake in Haiti. It was 6 a.m., and he was in the bathroom of his home in Jerusalem, shaving. He immediately called Ohad Shaked, the MDA's specialist in earthquake preparedness, who rushed to the Situation Room in the Ministry of Foreign Affairs, where, by 8 a.m., a group of experts from the humanitarian group ZAKA, El Al airlines, the MDA, the Israel Defense Forces, the Foreign Ministry and the Health Ministry were meeting to plan Israel's response to the disaster.

When Yagodovsky talks about the first 24 hours of the Israeli response, it's with the quick cadence of machine-gun fire.

"It's all about coordination and speed," he told me over a lunch in Beverly Hills with representatives of MDA and the Israeli Consulate.

This coordination took place internally, within Israel, and externally, with groups like the United Nations and Red Cross. Most importantly, the Israeli mission needed an OK to land in Haiti from the U.S. Army, which was already working to secure the Haitian airport.

Within 24 hours, Yagodovsky told me, two El Al cargo planes were on their way to Haiti — one carrying a field hospital and another carrying staff and supplies (including kosher food for those who required it).

Meanwhile, the Israeli Ambassador to the Dominican Republic, Amos Radian, had commandeered a caravan of Jeeps and trucks, which drove 16 hours straight to the Haitian airport to help unload and deliver supplies.

By Friday, the Israeli field hospital was being set up near the Port-au-Prince airport and included the following: 40 doctors, 25 nurses, a team of paramedics, a pharmacy, a children's ward, a radiology department, an intensive-care unit, an emergency room, two operating rooms, a surgical department, an internal medicine department and a maternity ward.

One of the first people rescued on Saturday was a top income-tax official who had been trapped for four days under the rubble of the collapsed government building.

Within a few days, 13 Israeli rescue missions had been sent out, 172 surgeries performed and more than 500 patients treated at the field hospital. And eight babies were born.

Yagodovsky didn't go to Haiti for the rescue — but he was in constant contact with his people. MDA provided staff and assistance to the Israeli mission as well to the international efforts that would follow. I asked him what made the Israelis respond so quickly.

"It's very difficult to transition from a state of routine to one of emergency," he told me. "So you have to incorporate the idea of emergency from the very beginning, in everything you do and everything you teach."

As he spoke, Shahar Azani, who works with the Israeli Consulate here in Los Angeles, did something perfectly Israeli: he jumped into the conversation in a wild burst of excitement to tell a story of his own.

Five years ago, while Azani was stationed in Kenya, he and a colleague were visiting a school in one of the slums when they saw a pregnant woman being carried in a wheelbarrow. They realized that this was because there were no ambulances. So they quickly contacted Yossi Baratz from MASHAV, the division of the Foreign Ministry that specializes in humanitarian assistance, and they all got to work.

Baratz called a friend at MDA, which just happened to have two old ambulances they had stripped and were about to sell as regular vans. Instead, they re-equipped them as ambulances and offered them to MASHAV. Meanwhile, Azani called a friend at ZIM, the Israeli shipping company, which offered to ship the ambulances at no cost.

The first ambulance made its way to the city of Kwale, southwest of Mombasa in Kenya. The ambulance was the first ever to serve nearly 500,000 people living in the district.

As Azani was telling the story, Yagodovsky jumped in with an interruption of his own. Guess who was Baratz's friend at MDA who had arranged for the two ambulances? That's right: Yonatan Yagodovsky.

Small world, indeed.

While Azani and Yagodovsky did their few minutes of high-octane Jewish geography, I just sat back and absorbed the scene that had just unfolded. Here were a couple of Israeli Jews whose greatest source of satisfaction seemed to be helping people in desperate need.

At no point did the idea of "good PR for Israel" come up.

When I mentioned to Yagodovsky that Israel's heroic efforts in Haiti were spreading a lot of much-needed positive vibes about Israel, he gave me an awkward look, as if to say: "That's nice, but that's not why we do it."

In fact, there may be many reasons why Israel "does it"— an empathy for human suffering, lots of practice at emergency rescue, a belief in tikkun olam, a desire to be accepted by the world — but Yagodovsky didn't mention any of those.

"Maybe we're stupid and naïve," he told me. "We just want to help."

"The ensuing 40 years saw both dreams unravel. Land couldn't buy the Zionism of Peace, and love couldn't buy the Zionism of Land."

ON A RAINY NIGHT, A NEW ZIONISM

January 20, 2010

If I ever decide to make aliyah and move to Israel, I can blame it on Micah Goodman. On a chilly and wet Sunday night last week at The Mark — a reception hall on Pico Boulevard that used to house Mamash restaurant — Goodman spoke on "The Crash of Old Paradigms: Why the Left and the Right No Longer Exist in Israel." Professor Goodman, who was hosted by the Israeli Consulate as part of their new speaker series for young professionals, is part of a new generation of young and bright Israelis who are seeking nothing less than a renewal of the Zionist idea.

Goodman, who's only 33, studied in a variety of yeshivas over the years and got a doctorate of philosophy from Hebrew University. He teaches, among other places, at the Shalom Hartman Institute in Jerusalem, has his own weekly television show and runs a "leadership academy" called Ein Prat, which he founded. On the invitation for his Sunday night talk, Ein Prat was described as follows: "Seeking to lead a sea change in behavior and culture, we hope to awaken Israeli society from its slumber."

I can tell you that he woke about a hundred young professionals in Los Angeles from their slumber, yours truly included.

He did it by laying out a dramatic and depressing problem — what he calls a "crisis of ideas" for Zionism — and then fearlessly taking it on with an equally dramatic and positive vision.

He began by discussing the two original strands of Zionism: the Zionism of Peace and the Zionism of Land, explaining why both are failing and need an injection of new thinking.

The Zionism of Peace is the classic view of Israel as a safe haven for Jews. Its champion, Theodore Herzl, had seen the failure of emancipation to ward off anti-Semitism, epitomized by the anti-Semitic rage exposed in the Dreyfus affair. By enabling Jews to join the brotherhood of nations, this view went, Zionism would not only protect Jews from persecution but might even help vanquish anti-Semitism.

The Zionism of Land, as championed by Rav Kook, was not about fighting a negative, but about celebrating a positive: the return to the mystical land of our forefathers.

From 1948 to 1967, neither Zionism won the day. The state was too close to hostile neighbors to be a Zionism of Peace, and too distant from biblical Israel to be a Zionism of Land.

The Six-Day War of 1967 changed all that. Followers of both Zionisms saw an opening to fulfill their own dreams. The Peace camp finally had something (land) it could trade for peace and acceptance, and the Land camp, after 2,000 years, could finally return to the land of their patriarchs.

The ensuing 40 years saw both dreams unravel. Land couldn't buy the Zionism of Peace, and love couldn't buy the Zionism of Land. Today, when Goodman looks at the physical threats to Israel and the success of Jewish emancipation in America, he laments: "Jews are haunted in their haven, and accepted in the Diaspora. This is an earthquake to the Zionist idea."

The original justifications for Zionism — both pragmatic and ideological — are under such attack that the crisis of ideas has become a crisis of legitimacy, where Jews must now answer this vexing question: Why Zionism? This crisis is compounded by the fact that, as Goodman says, Israelis are the "Olympic champions of not loving themselves."

Yet it was Goodman's deep love for Zionism and his people, as much as his scholarly analysis, that woke us from our slumber. Here was a man who quoted the great philosophers, but who just as easily quoted the soldiers who were under his command during the recent wars in Lebanon and Gaza.

When he critiqued his homeland, he did it with a heavy heart. But when he talked about the outbursts of solidarity in Israeli society — thousands of homes opening up to refugees of bomb attacks, 100 percent of Army reservists responding to the call of duty, scores of volunteers helping out in bomb shelters, etc. — it was with a sense of genuine wonder.

It is this sense of wonder at the possibilities of the Zionist experiment that Goodman and his ilk are hoping to rekindle in Israeli society. He calls it a Zionism of Solidarity — creating an exemplary and decent society that worries less about what the world thinks of us and more about what we think of ourselves.

It is the renewal of Zionism from the inside out. It calls for, among other things, better treatment of all citizens (including migrant workers) and a greater separation of synagogue and state, where Judaism and its values are part of education rather than legislation.

On the relationship with the Diaspora, Goodman called for a "reverse Birthright," where Israelis would visit Diaspora communities to experience the breadth of Judaism and the depth of Jewish solidarity.

Zionism is in need of constant renewal, but it is the product of a deep past. Will these new and old forces destroy each other or empower each other? That is the challenge for Micah Goodman and the New Zionists.

Seriously, with this kind of drama, who wouldn't want a front-row seat?

"Judaism has plenty to offer – it's one long buffet full of wonderful delights: morality, prayer, and Torah, yes, but also centuries of history, philosophy, poetry, music, literature, theater, mysticism and humor, among other things."

YEAR-END BUFFET

December 23, 2009

W hat's wrong with Judaism?" "Why do so many Jews discon- nect from their faith?" "Why is it so hard to get them to go to shul?" "If Judaism is now a choice, why do so few Jews choose it?"

I thought I would end the year by ruminating on some of these ques- tions, which I hear time and time again from concerned Jews. But instead of just ruminating, I thought I would also try to put an answer on the table — or at least an idea that can guide efforts to make Judaism more relevant to all Jews.

What got me thinking about all this is the recent emphasis in the Jew- ish community on the issue of ethics. I can't tell you how many articles I've read or sermons I've heard that have touched on this. Ethics is now the subject of many conferences and debates. It's the Jewish topic du jour.

Now, at first glance, it's impossible to criticize a message of morality. I mean, how can anyone argue with Thou Shalt Not Steal? How can you be against a sermon or conference that reminds us of the importance of fol- lowing the laws of the land and being impeccably honest?

I guess, though, that that's precisely my problem: this stuff is too easy. It doesn't really challenge us. It admonishes the guilty and reminds the innocent, but it doesn't seduce us into exploring our Judaism.

In fact, I think if there's anything stopping Judaism from thriving today, it's the fact that it's being hijacked by the moralists. Do good. Be good. Speak good. The message is so obvious and true and important that rarely does anyone look at it and say, "Is that all there is?"

Imagine yourself as a bright Jewish college student who doesn't see or feel a need to connect to Judaism. Zionism is not your thing. So what will entice you to connect to your faith? A pitch on the goodness of Jewish values, or the goodness of peoplehood, or the goodness of tradition or tikkun olam or doing mitzvot?

What if goodness is not really a hot button for you — either because you already see yourself as a good person who does good deeds, or because you feel you can get this goodness message from other places?

Well, then, Judaism won't have much to offer you, which is sadly true for millions of Jews today.

Of course, Judaism has plenty to offer — it's one long buffet full of wonderful delights: morality, prayer and Torah, yes, but also centuries of history, philosophy, poetry, music, literature, theater, mysticism and humor, among other things.

The problem is that individual groups or movements have attached themselves to one section of the buffet, ignored the others, and said, "Here! This is Judaism!" Torah-observant Jews might ignore history and literature. Cultural Jews might ignore Torah and prayer. Spiritual Jews and tikkun olam Jews might ignore both, and so on. Yet each one will claim, "This is Judaism!"

Rarely will any group present the whole buffet or cross outside of their comfort zones (Limmud being a notable exception). I've spent twenty years in Orthodox shuls, for example, and I think I can count on one hand the classes or sermons that have dealt with Jewish poetry or literature.

By the same token, many of my friends who are "cultural Jews" have written off Torah study as being outdated and irrelevant.

My point is this: Jews would be a lot more interested in exploring their Judaism if they saw it as a buffet full of different delights, rather than a restaurant with one or two items on the menu — especially if those items are predictable servings of morality.

We focus so much on the obvious virtues — honesty, faith, compassion, integrity, humility, generosity, etc. — that we seem to forget the one virtue that makes us feel the most alive: curiosity.

Yet curiosity is the virtue that not only can entice disconnected Jews to explore their Judaism, it's also the virtue that can bring Jews closer together. What is real love if not the desire or curiosity to get to know — rather than judge — the Other?

Unfortunately, there's no money in curiosity. It's not easy to control your flock when you encourage them to spread their wings and sample the many delights of their faith. Who knows where they might end up? Falling for Jewish literature or history? Becoming more Torah-observant? Joining another Jewish community?

Ironically, for Judaism to thrive in the next century, we will need to violate the first rule of marketing: finding your niche and promoting the hell out of it. We're niching ourselves to death. Whichever niche you're in, whichever section of the buffet you're promoting, it would behoove all movements of Judaism to mix it up and add a few more items to their menus.

Think about it. If you see a beautiful spread with an array of choices, you might criticize one of the choices, but chances are you won't criticize the whole buffet. Judaism deserves nothing less.

Happy New Year.

"Just like we can draw strength from the master story of the Jewish people, we each have our own stories that we can nurture and shape and draw strength from."

THANKFUL FOR WHAT?

November 25, 2009

I t's one thing to know what to do; it's another thing to be able to do it. We know we are supposed to be grateful for all of life's blessings. We know that when hardship or tragedy strikes, we're supposed to keep our chins up and try to transform tragedy into action — turn negatives into positives, move forward no matter what, and so on.

But over the past few weeks, as we approached this period of Thanksgiving, it dawned on me that gratitude is a lot easier said than done. We can talk about this virtue and easily buy into it, but when reality strikes, it's another story.

This hit home the other night at a memorial service for a 3-year-old girl who was run over by a school bus in Jerusalem. The girl's extended family in Los Angeles, close friends of mine, asked me to say a few words. I had no idea what to say. I got up in front of 300 people and told them exactly that: I have no clue what to say.

I was in no mood to "spin" the situation and hand over the clichés of transformation and gratitude. Sure, there are always blessings to be thankful for, but how can anything alleviate such a singular and unspeakable loss?

A few nights later, I attended a fundraiser at A Cow Jumped Over the Moon, a kosher restaurant and music club on Rodeo Drive, for the manager, Sacha Chalom Louza, who recently underwent surgery to remove a brain tumor. Louza is a Sephardic Jew who prays at the Chabad of South La Cienega (known as SOLA), and his friends in the community are raising money to help cover his living expenses while he undergoes treatment.

At the fundraiser, the SOLA rabbi got up and spoke powerfully about the Jewish way of reacting to tragedy and hardships. He mentioned the worldwide efforts to commemorate the murders a year ago of the Chabad emissaries in Mumbai, Rabbi Gavriel and Rivka Holtzberg, and how Chabad was aiming to transform that atrocity into a positive force for the world. Yet as he spoke, I couldn't help thinking about the parents of the murdered couple and wondering what kind of "transformation" or "gratitude" could possibly alleviate their loss.

A third event also made me think about the difficulty of gratitude. A couple of weeks ago, our family hosted about 40 special needs kids, along with teenage volunteers and some parents, for a Friday night meal. They were all part of Etta Israel, a local organization that helps kids with Down syndrome, autism and other special needs.

At the end of the evening, as we were all saying our goodbyes, one of the more severely disabled kids kept making a "phone me" sign toward me. He wanted me to call him and stay in touch. As I looked at his forlorn face, again I thought: What does this kid have to be thankful for?

As things would have it, something did happen that night that helped me see things in a broader light. By some divine coincidence, the grandfather of the 3-year-old girl killed in Jerusalem was in my neighborhood that Shabbat, and he ended up joining us for the Friday night meal. Knowing that he was in deep mourning, I was uncomfortable at first. But then he told me the story of how the Lubavitcher Rebbe, while mourning his beloved wife, was able to "switch off" his grief during Shabbat because the mitzvah of joy transcended everything.

Well, my friend was able to emulate his Rebbe. Surrounded by the loud and happy Etta Israel kids, he switched from his state of mourning to a state of Shabbat joy. As I watched him sing and tell stories of the biblical patriarchs, I saw a transformation that came not from a self-help cliché, but from the story of a 5,000-year-old tradition.

It struck me that perhaps this idea of having our own story is itself transformational.

Just like we can draw strength from the master story of the Jewish people, we each have our own stories that we can nurture and shape and draw strength from. As Rabbi Naomi Levy told me a few days ago, while talking about a new book she is writing, some of these stories are more difficult or tragic than others, some are easier, but for better or for worse they are our stories — the stories that we are called upon to make our own.

As we live out these stories, we make choices. We can choose to rally a community and help a friend with a brain tumor; we can choose to give a few hours of joy to a group of kids with special needs; and we can learn to appreciate the gifts of our tradition, which include a day of the week that can transcend the deepest grief.

Maybe, then, this is the blessing that we have to be most thankful for: the very idea that we each have a story we can call our own, and that we have the power to shape and influence that story — even if we can never write its ending.

Happy Thanksgiving.

"Toameh sees no hope in the 'top down' approach to peace. The soil is too rotten, he says. The Arab moderates have been undermined."

PEACE IN ARABIC

November 17, 2009

I t's not that I get tired of listening to Jewish speakers. More often than not, they motivate and inspire me. Whether I agree with them or not, there's a familiarity, a connection. I learn from my people and I embrace their diversity.

But no matter how diverse, it's still the same Jewish tent.

That's why it was so fascinating the other night to listen to someone who describes himself as an Israeli-Arab-Muslim-Palestinian. His look, his dress, his accent and body language all felt different. His mother's "large clan," he said, lives in Ramallah, where he visits almost every day from his home in Jerusalem. I could easily imagine him drinking tea and eating hummus with them.

The man was Arab journalist Khaled Abu Toameh, and he spoke at the home of Steve and Rita Emerson in Westwood.

Toameh has been reporting on Arab affairs for close to 30 years, for both Jewish and Arabic media. There's a quiet nonchalance about him, an old-school Middle Eastern dignity. Even when he says something familiar, it sounds different coming from him.

Toameh is in the middle of a U.S. tour sponsored by StandWithUs and was in Los Angeles for their annual "Israel in Focus" weekend conference, which gathers student activists from around the world. Of course, he wouldn't have been chosen if his views toward the Jewish state weren't sympathetic.

But when Toameh spoke, what stood out was not that he is pro-Israel, but that he is pro-Palestine.

For example, he spoke about the virulent anti-Israel atmosphere he is seeing on U.S. college campuses, about which, he observed, "there is sometimes more sympathy for Hamas than I see in Ramallah."

When he asked these students, "What makes you pro-Palestinian?" the answers were usually the same: "Israel is an apartheid state, Israel is a violent occupier, etc."

"But that's anti-Israel," he challenged them. "That's not pro-Palestine. I'm pro-Palestine. What makes you pro-Palestine?

"If you're really pro-Palestine, come help us instead of just spewing poison about Israel. Come teach my people democracy. Instead of Israel Apartheid Week, why don't you have Palestine Democracy Week?"

There was something authentic and disarming about him. His words didn't smell like propaganda or activism. He spoke for moderate Palestinians like himself, and he spoke from his heart, not from talking points.

He brought up a private meeting he'd had with President Obama a couple of years ago, while Obama was still a U.S. senator. Toameh told Obama that the key obstacle to peace is the hatred and incitement to violence that prevails throughout Palestinian society — in schools, the media and mosques — and is endorsed by the Palestinian leadership.

Commenting on the charge of incitement, Obama asked: "Is it true?" and later asked: "What can we do about it?"

Toameh suggested that the United States and other donor countries should predicate aid to the Palestinians on their stopping the incitement, to which Obama responded, "Isn't this political extortion?"

Toameh clearly thinks not. He thinks it is in the interest of the Palestinians to stop incitement, and he shared an Arab perspective on the subject.

"Look at the language that is now flying back and forth between Hamas and Fatah," he said. "It's the same poison you hear about the Jews: sons of pigs, infidels, etc. Incitement has spread and backfired on the Palestinians."

This incitement has also hurt the Palestinians' ability to make peace: "How do you tell people to make peace with the people you've called monsters and sons of pigs?"

Toameh sees no hope in the "top down" approach to peace. The soil is too rotten, he says. The Arab moderates have been undermined. "If I go to Ramallah and talk about Palestinian concessions on the right of return, I'll get shot in five minutes."

He says the Palestinians "already got their two-state solution — Gaza and the West Bank," and if it weren't for the Israeli presence in the West Bank, "Hamas would take over and Mahmoud Abbas would be lynched."

But lest you think there was no ray of hope in this Arab gentleman, he closed by discussing the people who he believes hold the key to an eventual peace between Jews and Arabs.

The Arab citizens of Israel.

"They are the ones who can build a bridge between Jews and Arabs," Toameh said. "They know what democracy is. They know about a free press and about freedom of religion. They know both sides."

He acknowledged the many obstacles — mutual mistrust, dual loyalties, Muslim radicalization, etc. — but he says Israel has no choice. If it wants a peaceful future, it must do a better job of embracing its Arab citizens.

The fact that some of them are becoming more radical is an even bigger incentive to embrace the moderates and preempt further radicalization.

It's true, he said, that Arabs have it better in Israel than anywhere else in the Middle East. But that's not the point. Israel must see its Arab minority not as a threatening nuisance that must be tolerated and contained, but as potential allies who can eventually help bring peace to the Holy Land.

From your mouth to Allah's ears, Mr. Toameh.

"Gordis is both an idealist and a realist. He knows that nowadays, peoplehood is a tough sell. It smacks of tribalism, exclusivity, discrimination and dual loyalty."

FIGHTING FOR PEOPLEHOOD

November 11, 2009

I t's not fun to hear bad news on Shabbat. The whole idea of Shabbat is to take a spiritual break from the rest of the week, to reconnect with the essential stuff of life and to do it all in a spirit of joy. The last thing we need is to have our spirits brought down by depressing reminders.

And yet, there I was last Shabbat, at Young Israel of Century, listening to a riveting sermon by Daniel Gordis on the movement to delegitimize the State of Israel.

Gordis started with the Torah portion of the week, making the connection between "place" and "nation" in the biblical story of the Jews and establishing the importance of the modern-day revival of Jewish sovereignty.

But then he quickly brought us to the reality of the moment. As he explained it, there is a movement afoot to undo the 1947 decision by the United Nations to establish the state of Israel.

"If the establishment of Israel came up for a U.N. vote today," he said, "chances are it wouldn't pass."

The decision last week by the U.N. General Assembly to endorse the Goldstone report is just the latest sign of this movement, he said, because it undermines Israel's very ability to defend itself.

Gordis is no fire-and-brimstone rabbi trying to pump up a crowd through fear and alarmism. He's a passionate Zionist, yes, but he's also studious and reflective. His latest book, "Saving Israel" (Wiley), is full of nuanced discussion about Israel's complicated predicament.

He also has a big fan base in Los Angeles, where he lived for many years before immigrating to Israel with his family 11 years ago. He's now senior vice president and a senior fellow at the Shalem Center in Jerusalem, a Zionist think tank where he heads their efforts to establish Israel's first liberal arts college.

On Shabbat, this intellectual, who received his Ph.D. at the University of Southern California, was in no mood to play professor. His emotions were most evident when he let the second shoe of his sermon drop: his sadness that Jews are losing their sense of peoplehood, and this at a time when we really need it. We are more than a nation or a culture or a religion, he said. We are a clan, a tribe, a people.

And the best way to fight the forces that try to delegitimize Israel is to stand together as one people.

Gordis is both an idealist and a realist. He knows that nowadays, peoplehood is a tough sell. It smacks of tribalism, exclusivity, discrimination and dual loyalty. And, for many, it's not a very sophisticated idea — not too far from the cries at Staples Center to "cheer for the home team."

But that won't stop the idealist in Gordis. Our sense of peoplehood is a core element of the Jewish identity, he reminded us, and it has helped sustain us through the millennia. We must find a way to revive it. He spoke as if it was a winnable fight.

Is it?

It's hard to say. For the significant number of Jews who don't feel a need for Jewish peoplehood in their lives — and that includes Jews from across the denominational and ideological spectrum — it will take some very clever arguments to make them feel part of a "family" with whom they have little in common except for a shared ancestry.

Gordis delved further into the nuances of the problem when he spoke on Saturday night at a private home. He acknowledged that for the notion of peoplehood to catch on, it will need to be adapted for modern realities and be reconciled with opposing notions like individual identity and ideology.

For example, how can I be a "person of the world" and also be part of the exclusive Jewish family? And if I can't stand what you believe in, why should I be part of your family in the first place?

There are no obvious answers, but a good start, Gordis said, would be to make all Jews of good faith feel at home in the tent of Jewish peoplehood — even Jews who criticize Israeli policy.

But he also drew lines. We need to balance the ability to criticize Israel, he said, with the need to defend it. It's one thing to have debates within our community about difficult issues; it's another to take our critiques of Israel to Capitol Hill and turn them into a media circus.

Like he wrote last week in The Jerusalem Post, we shouldn't censor ourselves or squelch debate, but, at the same time, we need to remember that whatever we say can and will be used against us by forces who'd love nothing more than to see us commit national suicide.

Gordis is the ultimate struggler. He's got every side of a complicated problem dangling inside his nimble brain, yet he still aims for a message of clarity and passion.

He reached the height of clarity and passion when he spoke about the extraordinary transformation of the global Jewish community over the past 60 years and the power of Zionism to "manipulate history" and "rejuvenate the idea of hope." With that note of optimism, he bookended his stark morning sermon with one idea that has driven this little people forward since the days of Abraham: hope for a better future.

That's an idea that's always welcome on Shabbat.

"If the Jews can rally their own for peace, why can't the Arabs? Why should Jews have an exclusive on self-criticism and internal pressure?"

WE NEED "A STREET," NOT J STREET

November 5, 2009

I don't quite get the brouhaha that is going on in the Jewish world about J Street. Some Jews are convinced that this new organization poses a threat to Israel's interests, while others are equally passionate about the need for an organization that will counter AIPAC and critique Israeli policy for the sake of peace.

I've heard all the critiques of J Street, and I share many of them. But what I still don't get is why people are making such a fuss about an organization whose message is so outdated and unoriginal.

Listen to some of their pronouncements and tell me if they don't equal a triple shot of Valium. Hey, did you know, for instance, that J Street believes in diplomatic solutions over military ones? And in a negotiated end to the Israeli-Arab and Israeli-Palestinian conflicts?

And get a load of this: They believe in a two-state solution! Two states living side-by-side in peace and security! Because, they say, ending the Palestinian conflict is in the best interests of Israel, the United States, the Palestinians and the region as a whole.

Talk about going out on a limb. J Street believes it's really important that we resolve the Israeli-Palestinian conflict. No kidding. And what's their brilliant brainstorm for how to do that? "Consistent and concerted diplomatic engagement by the United States."

Wait a minute. Haven't we heard all this before? Like maybe 30 years ago — and at every failed peace meeting since?

Well, yes, but J Street has put a fresh coat of paint on this fixer-upper. They've mastered the art of preaching mind-numbing clichés and making it look like they've found the Holy Grail.

Let's look, for example, at the cliché that "consistent and concerted diplomatic engagement" — a euphemism for pressuring Israel — has a positive impact on the peace process. A good example of this engagement has been the demand on Israel to freeze all its settlement construction, a policy that J Street actively promotes. How has that engagement worked so far?

Let's just say that since the United States made this demand six months ago, the Palestinians have taken to it like a pit bull discovering a tasty dog bone.

Does anyone remember that in the past, the Palestinians would come to the negotiating table without ever asking for this construction freeze — and that just over year ago, Mahmoud Abbas was knee deep in negotiations with Israel?

J Street is so sure of itself that it is still pushing for this construction freeze, even after it's clear that it has pushed the parties further apart and even after the United States itself has softened its demand.

This shouldn't come as a surprise, because groups like J Street are still stuck in the old paradigm that the key to reaching peace is for Israel to make more concessions. History suggests otherwise. If the other side has been so poisoned that they want your destruction more than they want peace, making unilateral concessions only makes things worse, as we saw after the Gaza withdrawal.

But recognizing this sober reality would wreak havoc on J Street's marketing and fundraising. It's too messy and inconvenient. It would require too much original thinking. Better to stick with milquetoast themes like "pro-peace and pro-Israel" and the need for "broad public and policy debates."

This idea that what's missing right now in the Middle East is a "healthy debate" among American Jews is a narcissistic fantasy. Many "pro-peace, pro-Israel" American Jews, myself included, had plenty of debates when we supported the many concessions for peace Israel made over the years.

Now that Israeli society has decided to proceed more cautiously, the fact that we're not critiquing the Israeli government doesn't mean we follow them blindly; it means that we agree with them.

And the reason we don't scream so loudly for peace is not because we don't have a group like J Street to help us express ourselves, but because we'd love to see, for a change, more screaming for peace coming from the other side.

If you ask me, what the Middle East needs more than anything today is not a J Street but an A Street.

This would be an Arab organization that would do what no Jewish organization can do: rally peace-seeking Arab moderates to the cause of peaceful coexistence with a Jewish state. If the Jews can rally their own for peace, why can't the Arabs? Why should Jews have an exclusive on self-criticism and internal pressure?

Can you imagine how transformational it would be if a high profile, "pro-Arab, pro-peace" organization pressured Palestinian leaders to dismantle the teaching of Jew-hatred in Palestinian society — a hatred that has made a mockery of all moves toward peace?

Can you imagine the impact on the peace process if 1,500 Palestinian peace activists gathered in Washington, D.C., for a conference against hatred?

Sure, it all sounds like a pipe dream, but not any more so than the outdated delusions coming out of J Street.

"For 20 centuries, the ancestors of these Ethiopian Jews heard the same message: Moses didn't make it, but we will."

CHILD OF MOSES

October 28, 2009

A thousand Jews were gathered for the Passover seder. There were no tables or chairs or haggadot. The matzot were handmade. No one had gone shopping at the local markets, since they had grown all the food themselves. The plates were brand new; each family had broken their old ones in a wild ceremony and made new ones by hand, as they did every year.

The village had one rabbi, whose name was Kess Edene. Before the seder, he led all the Jews of the village, who were dressed in white for the occasion, up a small hill to make special prayers in their language of Amharic.

When everyone sat down for their seder meal, the rabbi got up and told the people the same story he told them every year, based on this idea: Our father Moses didn't make it all the way to Jerusalem, but one day, we will.

In fact, for 20 centuries, the ancestors of these Ethiopian Jews heard the same message: Moses didn't make it, but we will.

In the early 1980s, thousands of these Ethiopian Jews finally made their way to Jerusalem as part of Operation Moses. A girl from that village, Yarden Fanta, who was 11 at the time, remembers having to carry her 2-year-old sister on her back for a month as her extended family trekked toward the refugee camps of Sudan.

Late one night, Israeli Mossad agents, armed with a list of names of Jewish refugees, plucked Fanta and the other Jews out of their camp and led them by bus to a waiting airplane.

They were now huddled together on their very first flight, hundreds of them, on the way to the place they and their ancestors had been promised for 2,000 years.

Twenty-four years later, Fanta, who was introduced to me by Gil Artzyeli of the Israeli Consulate, is sitting at the Coffee Bean on Pico Boulevard telling me her story. I can't help noticing that she rarely stops smiling.

"It's like now you have a dream to touch the sky and you reach it," she tells me, trying to explain in her broken English the feeling of journeying to Israel. "One day you think you gonna die, one day you think God will help you.

"When something happen that you never believe will happen, you become like freeze, like shock."

Once she settled in Israel, though, it didn't take long for Fanta to feel other shocks. After getting bounced around several absorption centers during her first year and a half, she finally landed in a boarding school. But since she had no previous education, she had to start in first grade, even though she was almost 14.

"What, you just came down from the trees?" a teacher said to her, in a mocking tone.

But what shocked her even more was that the teacher wanted her to take only home economics classes, like sewing.

"Not this," Fanta would tell her in the little bit of Hebrew she had picked up. "I want something else."

Luckily, there was another teacher, a woman named Aliza Soen, who responded to Fanta and was able to give her that "something else": reading and writing classes and the beginning of a real education.

Fifteen years later, Fanta became the first Ethiopian woman in Israel to earn a doctorate, completing her Ph.D. at Tel Aviv University in, what else, education.

Today, she's married with children (her married name is Fanta-Vagenshtein), and she is a post-doctoral fellow at Harvard University's Graduate School of Education. Her field of research is on how illiterate immigrants adapt to modern societies.

She's also writing a book on her story. The book will cover, no doubt, what she says are "the three times she was born" — the first being when she was actually born, the second when she landed in the Holy Land, and the third when she visited, during a school field trip, a piece of the Holy Land she says changed her life: the Weizmann Institute.

She calls it her "wow moment." She recalls walking around the campus, visiting laboratories and conference halls and student lounges and thinking, "Wow, I can have the same air."

She eventually did have the "same air," but not before she struggled to climb, in her words, "the highest possible mountain."

She'd love to see more Ethiopian Jews in Israel climb that mountain. Although she says things have improved somewhat, it's been a rough ride for many of them, not least because the chief rabbinate often makes them go through impossible hoops just to prove they're Jewish.

But nothing seems to faze Fanta. She still has her smile on. She's learned that the promised land Rabbi Edene talked about at their seders in the village — the land Moses never entered and her ancestors dreamed of entering — well, that magical place was not the end of her yearnings, but the beginning of new ones.

She's learned, in other words, that to be Jewish means to always have something to yearn for.

Maybe that's why they call it the Promised Land — it's a land full of hardships, yes, but also full of promises.

"Why do polite people become impolite, cool people become agitated, witty people become humorless, loving people become hateful, holy people become ungodly and peaceful people become potentially violent when they're confronted with views that deeply offend them?"

CAN WE ARGUE WITHOUT FIGHTING?

October 15, 2009

If you want to ruin a Shabbat meal in my neighborhood of Pico-Robertson these days, just say one word: Obama. Within minutes, one of two things is likely to happen. If everyone around the table is anti-Obama, you'll get a grown-up version of a verbal piñata, with people taking turns bopping the man who is "selling America and Israel down the river."

But if some of the guests happen to be pro-Obama, and they're not afraid to speak up, you're likely to get a mini-bloodbath.

How do I know this? I've seen it happen — more than once.

In fact, it happened at my home, on a recent Friday night, when we had some wonderful out-of-town guests over for Shabbat dinner. The conversation at the table was joyful and friendly, and my daughter Mia's cooking was a hit. The Shabbat drug of choice — really good kosher wine — helped us all float in a state of Shabbat bliss.

Then someone said the word — "Obama."

For the next 30 minutes or so, the conversation progressively got more unpleasant. My out-of-town guests were rabid Obama supporters, while my other guests were anything but. I tried to steer the conversation back to the parasha of the week or to the Lakers, but it was too late. The forest fire had already been lit.

I made a blunder when the "fire" spread to the subject of Israel. I shared what I hoped would be seen as an unarguable fact (a Jerusalem Post poll this summer reported that 4 percent of Israeli Jews polled believe Obama is pro-Israel), but when the reaction from an Obama supporter was, "Are you crazy? There's no way!" I lost my cool. I got angry and raised my voice ("How can you just blab away like that? I study this stuff!"). My anger lasted only a few seconds, but the damage was done. I hated myself for it. I still do.

I should have resisted the urge to take things personally. I should have realized that at the precise moment when I lost my cool, there was something a lot more important in my life than showing that I was right. There was my role as the host of a Shabbat dinner.

And there was the example I was setting for my kids and for everyone else within earshot of my outburst.

Since that episode, I've been paying more attention to how we argue — to what we should do when we're in the company of people whose views make us want to toss an eggplant salad in their direction.

Why do we find it so hard to argue without fighting? Why do polite people become impolite, cool people become agitated, witty people become humorless, loving people become hateful, holy people become ungodly and peaceful people become potentially violent when they're confronted with views that deeply offend them?

I took my questions to someone who's well versed in contentious debates, Rabbi Yosef Kanefsky of B'nai David-Judea Congregation. Over the years, Kanefsky has weighed in on some of the more controversial issues in the Orthodox community, and despite the heat his debates have generated, he's always conducted them with the utmost dignity.

Why can't we all do the same?

"We live in challenging and dangerous times," Kanefsky told me. "Problems are extraordinarily complex. There are no easy answers. The only way some of us can find emotional security is to latch onto an idea about why things are the way they are and what is the solution. It gives us a sense of comfort.

"When someone challenges us," he went on, "we defend ourselves like we would defend our lives."

My friend Yossi Klein Halevi, a political analyst and author who lives in Jerusalem, elaborated on this view.

"One reason for our difficulty to manage civil discourse, especially in Israel, is because our issues really are life and death," he wrote in an e-mail. "The territorial issue is self-evident. But our other issues are also perceived as existential. Secular Israelis fear that a theocratic Israel would deepen our estrangement from the West and the Diaspora and leave us totally isolated, while Orthodox Israelis fear that an Israel totally divorced from Torah risks Divine retribution, another exile."

"So how can you maintain a live-and-let-live attitude when your ideological opponent threatens your existence?"

Halevi, who a few years ago wrote a spiritual book titled "At the Entrance to the Garden of Eden" (Harper Perennial, 2002), then went back a few thousand years to shed some more light on the subject.

"Maybe it's so hard for Jews to argue rationally because we were imprinted in our formation as a people with the experience of revelation, and ever since we're looking for that Sinai moment to clarify the world for us. We treat our partial insights — political and religious — as though they were revelations."

The problem, of course, is that when we give our individual insights the weight of revelation, we don't allow much room for different or conflicting insights, let alone the chance to have a debate about them.

This idea of looking at more than one "truth" is at the heart of the epic debate in the Talmud between the house of Shammai, which represents the strict, uncompromising voice of Jewish law, and the house of Hillel, which represents the more lenient voice.

Rabbi Moti Bar-Or, who runs Kolot, a bridge-building Torah-study institution in Israel, explained to me that "the uniqueness of Hillel is that he truly believes there is validity in the Shammai approach, although he totally disagrees with him."

In Shammai's world, there's "no room for pluralism" because it's the world of "true or false." It is Hillel's ability to see the other side, Bar-Or says, that makes Judaism follow his approach today — not the fact that he was "smarter or right."

As the Talmud explains in Tractate Eruvin 13b: "On what basis did the School of Hillel merit that the law should be determined in accordance with its positions? Because they were gentle and kind, and they studied their own rulings plus those of the School of Shammai. They were even so humble as to place the words of the School of Shammai before their own."

For many Jews, myself included, the overriding lesson in the Hillel-Shammai dispute is that despite their intense disagreements, they never split up.

Like the Talmud says in Tractate Yevamot 14b: "Beth Shammai did not abstain from marrying women of the families of Beth Hillel, nor did Beth Hillel refrain from marrying those of Beth Shammai, or eat with one another. This is to teach you that they showed love and friendship toward one another."

Perhaps this love and friendship was rooted in the fact that they argued, as it says in Pirkei Avot, "for the sake of heaven."

But this "sake of heaven" idea can be a double-edged sword. When one is arguing over the word of God, or anything else that feels supremely important, the stakes get pretty high, which makes us more emotional and more easily offended.

And as we know too well, when the stakes are high and the passions and disagreements run deep, it's a short road to anger and animosity.

An even worse result, in some ways, is that we simply tune each other out: I hate your views so much that I see no point in having any contact with you.

That's why so many of us prefer to hang out with like-minded people. It's a lot more comfortable and pleasant.

A few years ago, during the Second Intifada, I was invited to speak at a weekend conference organized by Tikkun, a leftist organization whose views are distinctly at odds with mine. My comrades on the right were shocked that I accepted the invitation. And to be honest, when it came time for me to speak, I really didn't know what to say.

Should I have fought back and represented the right-wing view in the middle of this liberal love-fest? The probability that I would change anyone's viewpoint was nil, so what would be the point of riling people up?

Luckily, on a whim, I found something to say. I asked the audience: "How many of you ever wake up in the morning and ask yourself: 'What if I'm wrong?' Raise your hands if you do." Nobody did.

Now that I had their attention, I explained that, initially, I was against the Oslo agreement, because I didn't feel it dealt with the fundamental issue of Palestinian and Arab rejection of Israel. But for the sake of peace, I asked myself "What if I'm wrong?" and I became an Oslo supporter.

I suggested to the Tikkun community that maybe it was now their turn to ask themselves that question, and that, in fact, we should all constantly be asking ourselves that question — what if we're wrong? Compassion for the other is a Jewish virtue, I told them, but so is humility.

Being surrounded for two days by people with views opposed to mine was not comfortable, but it challenged me to refine and elevate my own thinking. For me, one of the benefits of having constant contact with the "opposition" is that it keeps me from becoming a one-note extremist.

My ongoing conversations with left-wing friends like Rabbi Chaim Seidler-Feller temper my passions. I get to hear another side of the story, one that I may not agree with but that is nevertheless highly knowledgeable and deeply loving of Israel.

Do we change each other's views? Not really, but so what? We're different people. We see things differently. How could it be any other way?

The truth is, if I'd had the same upbringing as my left-wing buddies, chances are I'd be just like them, and vice versa.

Once you see people that way, you stop seeing them as ideological opponents who must be bludgeoned into submission. You see yourself in the other and the other in you, and you hear better what the other has to say. You feel more secure inside, more curious, less threatened.

This moderation comes not from nullifying your own views, but from allowing space for other's views.

Unfortunately, in today's Jewish public space, the enormous pressure and competition to raise money seems to have suffocated the civil and pluralist voices of our community. Moderation is a boring brand. What sells is single-minded passion. Oversimplification. "Never again!" Another crisis!

Try raising money for an organization that promotes deep understanding of both sides of an issue.

In a recent piece in The New Yorker on the ideological battle between the Pentagon and the White House over what to do in Afghanistan, George Packer reports on the "battle of the books" — how each side is reading only what nourishes their own argument — and he concludes as follows:

"The rule for administration readers should be: no books that you already know will confirm the views you already hold. If that's asking too much, at least the advisers and officers should be required to exchange volumes and read what their policy opponents are reading, before the book group meets and decides the fate of the world."

I saw a good example of such a healthy exchange the other night at UCLA Hillel, when Rabbi David Wolpe and American Jewish University professor Michael Berenbaum sat on a panel with UCLA professor David N. Myers to discuss Myers' latest book, "Between Jew and Arab: The Lost Voice of Simon Rawidowicz" (Brandeis, 2008).

This was no literary love-in. The two panelists, especially Wolpe, challenged Myers with some tough and incisive questions. The debate even got a little heated.

But here's the thing. There was no name-calling or offensive language of any kind. Not even close. The focus was strictly on the issues. Sure, there was plenty of conviction and passion, but there was also, as Myers himself pointed out, a "shocking degree of civility."

So this, in the end, might be the most useful model for our community. Instead of allowing our ideologies to split us apart, we ought to emulate Hillel and recognize other views, emulate Shammai and "still eat together," focus on the issues when we debate each other, and aim, no matter what, for a "shocking degree of civility."

By engaging each other in this fashion, the pain of ideological tolerance will be more than offset by the gains of deeper understanding and the creation of new relationships.

And, worse case scenario, if things ever get too hairy at the Shabbat table, we should agree to change the subject by talking about the Lakers or, better yet, the parasha of the week.

"One-sided activism and one-sided self-criticism might be emotionally satisfying, but they're not enough. It's time to add something new."

ISRAEL PR 2.0

October 7, 2009

O ver the past few days, several people who read my column last week ("Dayenu Moments") have asked me what I think Israel should do to counteract its worsening image.

My thinking got jumpstarted by a piece I read in The Forward by noted historian Jonathan Sarna that discussed the "waning American Jewish love affair with Israel."

Sarna quotes Hebrew Union College-Jewish Institute of Religion sociologist Steven M. Cohen, who warns of "a growing distancing from Israel of American Jews ... most pronounced among younger Jews."

The new generation, Sarna explains, doesn't see Israel through the rose-colored glasses of the Zionist dream, which Louis D. Brandeis once characterized as "nothing less than heaven on earth."

"In place of the utopia that we had hoped Israel might become," Sarna writes, "young Jews today often view Israel through the eyes of contemporary media: They fixate upon its unloveliest warts."

A growing movement of pro-Israel activism — through organizations like The Israel Project, StandWithUs, ZOA and CAMERA — has counteracted this fixation on Israel's "warts" by aggressively promoting the Israeli position and exposing the hypocrisy of the world's condemnation of Israel.

I've always been a big supporter of these efforts. If our enemies attack us so viciously, and often so unfairly, shouldn't we defend ourselves? If they're looking for confrontation rather than a dignified debate, should we not respond in kind?

Lately, though, I've started to question myself. Maybe it's because I'm just coming off a month of self-appraisal, where I've been forced to look inward and challenge my own thinking.

Also, for way too long, I've been facing this sad fact: nothing seems to be working. Despite our heroic efforts to promote Israel among American Jews — whether through aggressive activism or projects like Birthright Israel — we're still left reading articles and surveys on the "waning American Jewish love affair with Israel."

Finally, I've resigned myself to the fact that the world's fixation with Israel's warts will probably never go away, and we must find new and fresher ways of dealing with this reality.

So, what can we do? How can we supplement our pro-Israel activism with something that will bring renewed sympathy for the Jewish state, especially among young American Jews?

Contrary to some current thinking, it's not as simple as doing PR that is "beyond the conflict" — that is, promoting Israel's many accomplishments in science and technology (something I myself have done through a Web site), as well as its vibrant culture.

These well-intended efforts, just like aggressive pro-Israel activism, serve a useful purpose, but they don't address the warts that get such enormous play in the media. They can even backfire if they're perceived as propaganda meant to distract attention from Israel's mistakes.

It's also not enough to simply fess up to our warts, as many leftist organizations are wont to do, especially when we know that our enemies will just use these admissions to put another PR nail in our coffin.

As it happens, I found the seed for a new PR direction in the unlikeliest place: a little news item about a Jewish settler from Hebron who is being tried in an Israeli court. The charge? Two Palestinian schoolgirls accused him of endangering them while he was parking his car. No one got hurt, but the girls filed a complaint and they are getting their day in court.

What's my point? Simply this: Sure, we make plenty of mistakes, but God knows we also try to correct them. Our ideals demand it.

We need to exploit this idea. Yes, we should continue our efforts to confront the media's bias against Israel; and we should continue to make the case for Israel and even express outrage when it is warranted.

But I'd love to see us add this new element to our PR and branding efforts: Let's fess up to our mistakes, but focus on what we do to correct them.

This is a key tenet of the Jewish faith, and it ought to become a key tenet of Israel's PR efforts. We're far from perfect, but just like all good and noble societies, we are a work in progress.

Treatment of gays, women and minorities? Yes, we've made mistakes, but look at what we've done and are doing to correct them.

Corruption in our political ranks? You bet. But look at how our legal system is working to fix it and instill accountability.

Whether it's the disproportionate influence of the Charedi community, a flawed electoral system, IDF actions, environmental pollution, child abuse, poverty, etc., the Israeli way is to work to correct its mistakes and make things better.

Even with the vexing subject of the "occupation," Israel's PR should aggressively promote what it did to try to "correct" the problem: the fair and generous offer Prime Minister Ehud Olmert made to the Palestinians as recently as a year ago.

One-sided activism and one-sided self-criticism might be emotionally satisfying, but they're not enough. It's time to add something new.

There's no guarantee this will work, but at least it'll make Israel look more human. And compared to the way we look now, that would be a major upgrade.

"It's bad enough that this global and hypocritical anti-Israel hit parade is so painful to watch. But there's another, more subtle price that Jews pay when confronted with such exaggerated maligning."

DAYENU MOMENTS

September 30, 2009

I don't know if anyone's noticed, but it seems like there's been an unusually high number of "dayenu moments" for the Jewish people over the past few months.

A dayenu moment is when the criticism or pressure against Israel gets so ridiculous that a large majority of Jews from across the ideological spectrum recoil and say, "OK, enough already!"

The latest hit parade started when professor Neve Gordon of Ben-Gurion University called for a global boycott of Israel in a Los Angeles Times op-ed — similar to the international boycott against the racist apartheid regime of South Africa in the 1980s.

Never mind that Israel provides more freedom and human rights for Arabs and Muslims than any country in the Middle East. No, according to professor Gordon, only a debilitating global boycott would "save Israel from itself" and force it to make peace — as if that would magically create a partner on the other side willing and capable of making peace.

And then there was that protest letter signed by some prominent Hollywood folks at the Toronto International Film Festival. They accused the festival of taking part in pro-Israel propaganda by featuring 10 Israeli films as part of Tel Aviv's 100th anniversary celebration.

Had these movie people done a little movie watching, they would have discovered that the last thing anyone can ever say about Israeli films is that they are "pro-Israel propaganda."

But that wasn't all. The Toronto hit squad also attacked the legitimacy of Tel Aviv itself, treating this vibrant and free city as if it were an illegal outpost in the West Bank.

That was a double dayenu, implying that all of Israel is occupied territory. Even progressive, anti-occupation Jewish liberals got up in arms over that one.

The list goes on. More recently, we've seen the Goldstone report on the Gaza war, which was so biased against Israel that people like Michael Oren and Alan Dershowitz called it a "victory for terror" and a "barrier to peace."

In Israel, where polls show that only 4 percent of respondents believe President Obama is pro-Israel, Israeli Jews have had their own dayenu moment.

Obama's loud and humiliating demand for Israel to freeze every ounce of construction in all Jewish areas of the West Bank and in East Jerusalem has not gone over well — especially since Palestinians have used the freeze request as a pretext to back away from peace talks.

My favorite dayenu moment was an interview in The Forward with Omar Barghouti, a rabid anti-Israel activist and founding member of the Palestinian Campaign for the Academic and Cultural Boycott of Israel. Well, guess where Barghouti is currently studying for a master's degree in philosophy? That's right, Tel Aviv University.

When The Forward asked him about his affiliation with an institution he wants boycotted, Barghouti "refused to discuss his personal life."

It's bad enough that this global and hypocritical anti-Israel hit parade is so painful to watch. But there's another, more subtle price that Jews pay when confronted with such exaggerated maligning.

It becomes harder for us to criticize ourselves.

David Landau, former editor of Haaretz, captured this phenomenon perfectly in a recent op-ed in The New York Times. Commenting on the incendiary and "fundamental premise" of the Goldstone report that "Israel intentionally went after civilians in Gaza," Landau lamented the unfortunate result — it "thwarted ... honest debate" and "shut down the argument before it began."

As Landau points out, there could have been a healthy internal debate in Israel on such questions as: Are widespread civilian casualties inevitable when a modern army pounds terrorist targets in a heavily populated area with purportedly smart ordinance? Are they acceptable? Does the enemy's deployment in the heart of the civilian area shift the line between right and wrong, in morality and in law?

Of course, it's hard to engage in such reasonable debate when an international council has just concluded that you have acted essentially like terrorists. In the face of such brazen accusations, who wouldn't get a little defensive?

Similarly, when building kindergartens and synagogues in established settlement blocks is portrayed as a bigger obstacle to peace than having terrorist entities next door breathing down your neck, it's hard to engage in any reasonable critique of the settlements that might reinforce this distorted perception.

In other words, when the pressure and the attacks on Israel are so widespread, single-minded and extreme, it doesn't leave much room for Israel's supporters to jump in with their own critique. It spooks us. It makes us feel like circling the wagons — like saying "dayenu."

Some might say this is a good thing, because in times of danger, the more unity the better.

Viscerally, I agree. But there's still a little voice inside of me that tells me we shouldn't go too far; that Israel should always keep the Jewish ideal of looking inward and reflecting humbly on its own mistakes — even if it sometimes means doing so out of earshot of our enemies.

In this period of facing up to our own sins and repairing ourselves, it's a good time to remember that our enemies might define how we fight, but they don't define who we are.

"Let's face it, for Israel, no price is too high to eliminate the threat that the Jewish nation might be obliterated in 'a few minutes.'"

STOPPING IRAN

August 18, 2009

There is no issue of greater concern to Israel supporters than the threat of a nuclear Iran that could destroy Israel "in a few minutes," as Ambassador Michael Oren recently put it.

So you can bet I wasn't going to miss a gathering of local Jewish leaders last week that aimed to "begin a conversation" on what the American Jewish community can do to help.

The gathering was off the record, which is not a problem here, because all I want to share with you is a lightning bolt that came to me after the meeting was over:

The issue of a nuclear Iran might be messy, nuanced and horribly complicated, but the next step for the Jewish community is remarkably clear.

We must convince America that a nuclear Iran is as great a threat for America as it is for Israel, and that stopping Iran from obtaining the bomb is as much in America's interest as it is in Israel's.

In other words, in this debate, America needs to catch up with Israel.

This didn't seem so true a year ago, when presidential candidate Barack Obama stood at the AIPAC convention and declared:

"The Iranian regime supports violent extremists and challenges us across the region. It pursues a nuclear capability that could spark a dangerous arms race and raise the prospect of a transfer of nuclear know-how to terrorists. Its president denies the Holocaust and threatens to wipe Israel off the map. The danger from Iran is grave, it is real, and my goal will be to eliminate this threat."

But today, the language seems to have shifted. There is an emerging school of thought that fears that America, despite all the huffing and puffing, is not ready to do whatever it takes to "eliminate" the threat of a nuclear Iran.

The Obama administration's current policy of "engagement and possible sanctions" is seen by many critics as soft and unlikely to succeed. While the nuclear clock is ticking, President Obama, in contrast to his former forcefulness, has stated that "deadlines are artificial" and has spoken only of having "a fairly good sense by the end of the year as to whether they are moving in the right direction."

I don't know whether Obama has anything up his sleeve, but if I were Ahmadinejad, this recent statement from Secretary of State Hillary Clinton would not make me shake in my boots: "In the absence of some positive response from the Iranian government, the international community will consult about next steps, and certainly next steps can include certain sanctions."

Of course, getting global players to support any kind of meaningful sanctions would itself be highly unlikely.

As professor Barry Rubin wrote in the Jerusalem Post: "Obama is neither wildly popular, nor has he made progress with the two biggest barriers to strong sanctions: Russia and China ... [and] Europeans have spent years at engaging Iran. Their motives are economic self-interest ... desire to avoid confrontations with Iran ... [and a] belief that a nuclear-armed Iran can be managed."

Recent statements by Clinton about a Middle East "defense umbrella" have further stoked Jewish fears about America going soft. Israeli Intelligence Affairs Minister Dan Meridor was quoted as saying: "I heard without enthusiasm the American declarations according to which the United

States will defend their allies in the event that Iran uses nuclear weapons, as if they were already resigned to such a possibility.... This is a mistake."

My point here is not to suggest that the Obama administration has decided to accept a nuclear Iran, but rather to ask this question: If the current policy turns out not to work, what if America decides that the price to "eliminate" the Iranian threat is simply too high?

Let's face it, for Israel, no price is too high to eliminate the threat that the Jewish nation might be obliterated in "a few minutes."

But this is not necessarily the case for America. The potential repercussions of a "last resort" military strike against Iran (whether by Israel or America) for American troops and citizens within Iraq, Afghanistan and elsewhere, not to mention possible global political and economic fallout, might make a policy of "management" more palatable to America than a policy of "elimination."

If that's the case, we might well be left with a sobering, fundamental conflict of interest between two great friends and allies, America and Israel.

Which brings me back to my lightning bolt: American supporters of Israel must convince their country, the White House and Congress that a nuclear Iran is as much an American problem as it is an Israeli one.

Is it? I'm honestly not sure, but if anyone is interested in starting a movement, I have registered the domain name HelpAmericaStopIran. com.

Here's a suggestion for whoever might design the site: Put a bold banner across the top that says, "The danger from Iran is grave, it is real, and my goal will be to eliminate this threat."

And just below, name the author of those words: the current leader of the free world.

"For several years, Rivka worked, studied and built friendships. Inside, though, she never stopped dreaming about one particular Jewish ritual: finding a soulmate."

RIVKA'S SPECIAL NEED

August 11, 2009

When I asked Michael Held what was "different" about Rivka Bracha Menkes, he had trouble answering. It wasn't as severe as Down syndrome or autism or cerebral palsy, he said. It was more in the general category of "developmental disabilities," or "special needs."

It's true that ever since she was a little girl, Rivka, who is now 27, has had a special need. She dreamed of getting married, and having a beautiful wedding.

Rivka was part of the first group of students in 1993 that joined Etta Israel Center, the nonprofit organization founded and run by Held. Every Sunday, Rivka would go to their Talmud Torah at Maimonides Academy, where she would learn about Judaism and play with other kids.

Over lunch at Pat's the other day, Held explained that the important thing was to give the kids a social network, an opportunity to build friendships. "We wanted them to have something to look forward to every Sunday," he said.

In Rivka's case, she had plenty of experience with "looking forward" to things. Growing up in a Chabad family, her life revolved around preparing for the many Jewish rituals that enrich the Torah-observant life.

Over the years, she became somewhat of an expert in these rituals.

She got to know all the popular Shabbat songs, the brachas, the holiday recipes and the prayers.

She also got to know wedding rituals.

She went to enough Chabad weddings that she learned, for example, the exact order of dancing partners for the bride: mother, mother-in-law, grandmothers, sisters, aunts and closest friends. She even knew that the bride had to change into fancy sneakers between the ceremony and the dancing.

Rivka's knowledge of Jewish rituals served her well when she moved into Etta Israel's first rooming house for girls in 2002, when she was 20. The idea, Held says, was to give the girls a taste of independence and prepare them for adult life.

For several years, Rivka worked, studied and built friendships. Inside, though, she never stopped dreaming about one particular Jewish ritual: finding a soulmate.

In the world of developmental disabilities, this is a big deal. It hadn't happened yet with an Etta Israel kid. So Rivka and her family weren't the only ones dreaming about her finding a soulmate — the dreamers also included Michael Held and the extended Etta Israel family.

Thankfully, it turns out that they have a really good matchmaker in New York for Jews with special needs. So last year, Rivka was introduced to a Chasidic single man from Brooklyn named Avraham Chaim Weiss.

How good was the matchmaker? Well, the first time I saw Rivka and Avraham was on a beautiful night in June at the Chabad in Tarzana — and they were both under a chuppah.

How do you describe a wedding that transcends the norms of weddings? It's not easy.

All weddings are filled with love and simcha; this one had a little something extra. It had soul. You could see the joy on Rivka and Avraham's faces, but you sensed they were also a little vulnerable. It was like they were being carried by the love that was all around them.

You felt something special in the air, and somehow you knew everyone else was feeling the same thing.

There was one moment in particular that stuck with me. Avraham comes from a Chasidic tradition different than Chabad — so unlike the classic black hat, he wore a shtreimel (fur hat).

At one point, while he was dancing furiously with a Chabadnik, he decided to exchange hats. So there he was, dancing with a Chabad hat, while the Chabadnik was dancing with a shtreimel. Call it his little contribution to Chasidic unity.

Avraham couldn't stop dancing (I brought him a glass of water — this is my personal wedding ritual). As I saw him jump for joy in the middle of a human mass of Chasidic dancing, I turned to my friend Rabbi Yossi Shusterman and said, "This is the power of Torah, isn't it?"

"This is Torah," he replied.

When the rabbis weren't looking (I hope), I took a quick peek in the women's section to see Rivka, in her fancy sneakers, also dancing and jumping for joy. I have no doubt she followed the exact order of dancing partners that she had learned over the years.

At our lunch the other day, Held went out of his way to give credit to other people for Rivka's success, especially to her family. You could see the satisfaction on his face. His organization's whole mission is to help bring quality of life to kids with developmental needs and help integrate them into the "natural flow" of life.

A marriage is a breakthrough milestone on that journey.

But there's also a lot of pain on this journey. Held is haunted by something he once heard from one of the kids: "Why did God make my life so painful?" He didn't have an answer.

Lately, he's been getting another question from some of the kids at Etta Israel that he hopes, one day, to have many answers to: "Dr. Held, when am I getting married?"

"We were now leaving that house and village for other ones nearby. Where would all the memories go — the memories that were engrained in the walls of the house we could no longer see?"

MOVING

August 5, 2009

After three years of living in the 'hood, and with a mixture of sadness and excitement, I'm moving to the 'wood — Beverlywood, a more residential and quieter section on the "Upper West Side" of Pico-Robertson.

On the surface, it feels like I'm going from downtown to the suburbs; from the jazzy to the leafy; from the playing field to the nosebleeds.

Another view, though, is that I'm actually moving to the "heart" of the 'hood. Beverlywood has a heavy concentration of Modern Orthodox families who can boast of having the ultimate Shabbat gathering place: a modern-day public square called Circle Park.

Circle Park is the beating heart of Beverlywood. On any Shabbat afternoon, the locals and their children will slowly trickle in and spend several hours just hanging out.

For families who don't drive, watch TV or use computers on Shabbat, a park where kids can play and parents can schmooze is an ideal time-killer, especially during the long summer days.

My kids love Circle Park. Our new house is half a block away, so I assume we'll be regular visitors, and I'll be more in tune with the local happenings.

As it turns out, on our first Friday night in our new place, I was invited to speak at one of the bigger shuls in Beverlywood, Congregation

Mogen David.

I couldn't help but speak about the move, but I found myself speaking more about the old house than the new one. My mood was somber and reflective, maybe because we had just finished the period of Tisha B'Av. In a fit of near-blasphemous exaggeration, I spoke about how leaving a home full of great memories was like seeing your own personal temple get taken down.

I spoke about the shock of seeing an empty dining room, where hundreds of holiday meals and classes had occurred. I spoke about seeing an empty kitchen, where my kids had gathered every morning and every night, and where my mother once served moufletas for a packed house at Mimouna, a North African post-Passover celebration.

I spoke about seeing emptiness everywhere. An empty living room where we had my daughter's sweet 16; where the Happy Minyan and JconnectLA came for Shabbatons; and where guests would learn all night long on Shavuot.

So while I was excited about moving to Beverlywood, for some reason I couldn't stop talking about the old house. The new house looked great, but it had no memories yet, just promises.

The old house had all the memories — and it had already delivered on its promises.

Just when I needed it three years ago, it had given my kids something they'd never had: a cozy Jewish neighborhood. Instead of the sushi bars and trendy boutiques of West Hollywood, we now had Pico Glatt, Jeff's Gourmet and 40 shuls to pick from.

We had a village.

We were now leaving that house and village for other ones nearby. Where would all the memories go — the memories that were engrained in the walls of the house we could no longer see?

Luckily for me, there was something in the parasha — Vaetchanan — that helped answer that question. It came from one of my favorite Jewish thinkers, Rabbi Jonathan Sacks, chief rabbi of the United Kingdom.

Rabbi Sacks took one word from the parasha — shema (hear) — and ran with it. He explained how there were two civilizations in antiquity that shaped the culture of the West: ancient Greece and ancient Israel. The Greeks were the supreme masters of the visual arts: art, sculpture, architecture and the theater.

The Jews were different. God, the sole object of worship, is invisible, and reveals Himself only through speech. Therefore, the supreme religious act in Judaism is to listen. Ancient Greece was a culture of the eye; ancient Israel a culture of the ear.

The Greeks worshipped what they saw; Israel worshipped what they heard.

So as I spoke Friday night, I realized that a lot of my sadness about the old house originated in my eyes — what I saw and could not see. I could no longer see the visual cues that held all those great memories. My heart saw only the emptiness of lost memories.

But Rabbi Sacks' meditation suggested that perhaps our deepest memories come not from what we see, but from what we hear.

And upon reflection, it's true that even in our colorful old house, my most meaningful moments came from what I heard — the singing at the Shabbat table, the stories of our guests, the words of the teachers, the jokes and laughter of my children.

No matter how cool the kids' rooms look, it is my ability to hear them — hear their needs, their ideas and their stories — that will create the deepest bonds and memories.

That will hold true whether we're walking on Pico Boulevard, or hanging out in a beautiful park in Beverlywood.

"It seduces you by its silence. It makes no claims or promises whatsoever – because it doesn't have to. It's the 'real thing.'"

THE WALL

There are few places on earth that move Jews like the Western Wall in Jerusalem. After my visit this summer, I think I've discovered why this ancient structure has such a magical hold on us.

First, there are the obvious reasons. It's a piece of our national and religious history — a remnant of the Second Temple destroyed more than 1900 years ago.

You touch the Wall and you feel your ancestors. You feel the Bible. You feel the Jewish story.

You also feel Jewish unity. Go on any Friday night and you will see unity in action. Everywhere you look, there's a different prayer service. Sephardic services coexisting with Ashkenazi and Chasidic services. Dancing bohemians dressed all in white right next to straight-laced daveners dressed in sharp suits.

Outside the Wall, Jews pray and hang out in their little bubbles. But when they come to the Wall, their bubbles connect. They might not pray together, but they pray right next to each other.

It might be the only place in the world where this happens: All the voices of Judaism singing simultaneously. Unity without uniformity. Diversity not as a theoretical construct, but as a real-life experience that you can see, hear and feel.

Because of my background in marketing, I've also been sensitive to something uniquely seductive about the Wall: It's anti-marketing. It doesn't try to sell you.

This is the ultimate coup. The biggest enemy of marketing today is marketing itself. Consumers are hip to our tricks. They're suspicious of any commercial agenda.

That's why marketers are desperate to create the illusion of authenticity.

Imagine for a moment if the Wall didn't exist. Some Jewish entrepreneur might raise $100 million to build a memorial to the Second Temple. Just like at other tourist sites, you'd see big banners on the walls promoting one thing or another, ticket offices, ushers, brochures, velvet ropes and so on. No matter how authentic the monument would try to look, it would still be a commercial enterprise.

It would scream marketing.

The Western Wall doesn't scream anything. It has no logo, no signs, no slogans. It's not designed by Frank Gehry. It's not a marketing brand.

It's a monument to authenticity.

It seduces you by its silence. It makes no claims or promises whatsoever — because it doesn't have to. It's the real "real thing."

Over the years, this authenticity and connection to our ancestors and feelings of unity are what have moved me the most. This year, however, I felt something new.

It was something in the idea of a wall itself.

The idea that a wall actually pushes you back. It tells you to go away.

It's not like a building with a door that invites you to come in and make yourself comfortable. The Wall says, "Touch me, feel me, ask for blessings, but then leave. Take these blessings to the world. Go spread the light and the lessons that I represent. Take the memory of your people and create your own memories and your own stories."

In a way, it's like the Torah that we unfold and read on Shabbat. We read it, we feel it, we learn it — and then we go away. In the Jewish tradition, we are expected to go back into the world and live out the Jewish message.

When I shared these musings with a rabbi friend the other day, his eyes lit up and he told me about this cryptic talmudic story.

It's a story of King David going against God's will and digging the foundations of the Temple. When he hits the spot for the Holy of Holies, the chaotic waters burst out and flood the world. It's only when David writes and sings the psalms of Shir HaMa'alot that the waters return to their original place.

As the rabbi explained, when King David stopped trying to build a monument, he accessed the feminine side of his personality — he wrote and sang the psalms that brought peace and balance to the chaotic waters.

Thus, the Jews don't need to touch the Holy of Holies. We are attracted to the mystery of Jerusalem — where the world was founded, where Abraham tried to sacrifice Isaac, where our collective story was shaped — but we cannot enter this mystery. We can only touch one of its remnants — the Wall.

Because it's "only" a wall, we can't stick around for too long and wallow in its greatness.

But we can do more: We can sing and dance and wallow in its holiness.

Instead of admiring it, we can absorb it. We can absorb the Jewish unity that we felt on Friday night; the yearning for blessings that we put in the cracks of the stones; the joy we felt when we sang and danced; and the tingling emotions that touched us when we recalled the story and hardships of our people.

It's as if the Wall, in its utter simplicity and humility, is saying to us: "I am so old now, I am so small, it's OK if you take me with you."

"By focusing on freezing Jewish bedrooms while a Persian madman is focusing on nuking 6 million Jews, Obama has frozen the hearts of Israelis."

CHAOS AND UNITY

July 14, 2009

I srael is not a great country for neat freaks. The place is all mixed up. The trivial mixes with the existential, the silliness with the deadly serious, the sacred with the irreverent.

Every impulse gets a hearing, and every hearing gets an argument.

This messiness was obvious to me during my two weeks in the Holy Land. And it was captured perfectly one morning on the front page of the Jerusalem Post. Study this page and you'll understand Israel.

On the top left was a controversy over an annual "water fight" event in Tel Aviv — yes, people frolicking with water guns — right next to a story on the looming geopolitical battle between the United States and Russia.

The Tel Aviv frolickers were battling their critics, who were outraged that anyone would think of holding a water fight in a drought-ridden country. The frolickers countered that they would use only water from a public fountain to "prove that you can have fun while conserving water."

Just below the water drama was a story about how Israel was preparing itself for a nuclear attack. "In Face of Iranian Threat, IAF to Train Overseas," the headline blared. The story reported that "Saudi Arabia green-lights IAF flyover" (which Israel denied), as well as Vice President Biden's statement that the United States "won't stop Israeli attacks on nuclear facilities" (which his boss later contradicted).

Israel has a large Russian population, so it wasn't surprising to see a story on "Decoding Russia: A Six-Step Plan, as Obama heads to Moscow."

Right next to the Russian story was one on Israeli and Palestinian teens collaborating on a "song of peace."

Below the fold were three stories on the Israel-Palestinian conflict. On the left was Prime Minister Netanyahu uttering to his cabinet, for the first time, the "two states for two peoples" formula, which Washington had urged him to do. But lest you get too encouraged by that news, another story on the far right reported that "new home buyers [are] still offered incentives to move to settlements."

And lest you get too discouraged by that news, the story in the middle reported that Israel had approved the transfer of 1,000 Kalashnikov rifles to the Palestinian security forces to help them fight terrorism.

In all those stories, there were vigorous internal debates and disagreements.

Open the paper and the mess continues: A story on a petition filed by Peace Now calling for the dismantling of the illegal outpost of Migron, right next to one on the Palestinian Prime Minister saying that "Jews would be welcome in a future Palestinian state," right next to a controversial decision not to send ambulances into Arab villages without a police escort.

By now you're probably thinking: "Hey, there's nothing new here. Israeli society has always been chaotic and full of contradictions and disagreements. Those are the hallmarks of a robust democracy."

Well, yes. That's why it was fascinating for me to see that, in Israel today, there is one thing that almost all Israelis agree on.

It has to do with President Obama.

Over my two weeks there, I talked to all kinds of people — cab drivers, peaceniks, right-wing hawks, religious and secular Jews, artists, academics, bellboys, rabbis and more — and asked them how they felt about Obama and the "conflict with the Palestinians."

Just about everyone I spoke with is wary of the American president. They think his obsession with a settlement freeze has overshadowed much bigger threats (like a nuclear Iran) and much bigger obstacles to peace (like a terror state in Gaza). They see him as naïve at best and abusive at worst — abusing a friendly ally to curry favor with the Arab and Muslim worlds.

What I found most fascinating was that in a country that argues about everything, I couldn't find anyone — not even opposition parties in the Knesset — who would argue that a radical settlement freeze should be the centerpiece of the peace process.

Many Israelis I spoke with aren't pleased that Obama has ignored previous understandings with the Sharon government that allowed for "natural growth" in the settlement blocks. Even those who are against the settlements have seen how the relentless U.S. pressure on Israel has given the Palestinians the perfect excuse to be even more intransigent, and pulled the two sides even further apart.

Above all, unlike many Jews in America who are still under the Obama spell, Israelis understand that a total settlement freeze is extreme and absurd. How do you tell a family in Efrat that they need to get special permission from the leader of the free world if they want to add a bedroom or bathroom to their house?

By focusing on freezing Jewish bedrooms while a Persian madman is focusing on nuking 6 million Jews, Obama has frozen the hearts of Israelis. A recent poll in the Jerusalem Post backed up what I saw: Only 6 percent of Israelis consider him pro-Israel.

I'm sure the president saw something "neat" in pressuring Israel for a perfect freeze. But in his zeal to bring neatness to a messy conflict, President Obama has pulled off a double miracle — he has united the Jews and made things even messier.

"In my white outfit, no matter where I was, I felt like the middle of an Oreo cookie."

WAR AND PEACE

July 8, 2009

For the first time in my life, I was surrounded by Jews and I felt fear. Not too much, mind you, but just enough to give me the chills.

It was late Shabbat afternoon in Jerusalem's Mea Shearim, and thousands of enraged Charedi Jews were demonstrating against the opening of a city parking lot adjacent to their neighborhood.

My friend Rabbi Chaim Seidler-Feller and I were walking through their neighborhood looking for the shul of the Slonomer Chasids, who are known for their beautiful and mystical davening.

But before we knew it, we were interrupted by riot squads, horses, police cars, media trucks and screaming demonstrators. We needed to get through the mob to get to the Slonomers. We got past two police guards and then found ourselves literally trapped by demonstrators who were yelling "Shabbos, Shabbos, Shabbos!"

I was dressed all in white (not a smart move), so I clearly stood out. My yarmulke didn't help. A group of Charedim looked at me with threatening eyes. It felt so weird to feel anxious in front of Jews. Their utter certainty in their beliefs spooked me. It's one thing to see these mini-riots in the news, but when you're in the middle of it — when you can smell the breath of a demonstrator — it gets personal.

I thought: "How on earth can a stupid parking lot create such rage?

Why should the 'sin' of other Jews be the source of such anger?"

So I let my instincts take over. As I heard the screams of "Shabbos!" I decided to scream the word "Shalom!"

As in "Shabbat shalom."

This did not go over too well. By now, Chaim had come to see what was going on, and if you know Chaim, you know he can exhibit the passion of three Sephardi men overdosing on Turkish coffee.

Chaim overheard one of the Charedi men saying something to the effect that Jews who desecrate Shabbat should be killed.

This was not good.

Instantly, Chaim got into a heated debate with the Charedi man, who was so skinny he looked like a bearded ghost. They went back and forth. Chaim was familiar with the Torah sources the man was quoting, and he shot right back with his own.

I'm guessing the Charedi man was not used to being challenged by a Jew who knows his Torah, because the more Chaim talked, the more upset the man got.

In a strange way, though, Chaim's passionate Torah talk protected us, because at least it showed them that we were not secular spies.

Still, the place was going crazy, and this was no time to engage in a Torah salon.

So we quickly took off in the direction of the Slonomers, hoping to get there in time for Mincha.

We snaked through the narrow alleys of the shtetl, where hundreds of posters plastered the walls — the same form of public communication used in European shtetls for centuries.

We found our way to the Slonomer shul. Chaim asked a man when they would daven Mincha, and we followed him. The man, like all the other Slonomers, looked just like the demonstrators — long black kapote (caftan), beard, payos and fur shtreimel.

We asked the man why the Slonomers were not demonstrating with the other Charedim. The man paused, slowed his walk, made a little smile and said he could not answer that question on one foot.

We followed him into the shul, which was surprisingly large and packed with Slonomer Chasids (how do they have enough apartments for all these people in this little shtetl?).

I wanted to get a closer look at the Slonomer Rebbe, so I wound my way to the front of the shul. In my white outfit, no matter where I was, I felt like the middle of an Oreo cookie.

After Mincha, everybody moved next door to what looked like a mini airplane hangar with metal bleachers and one little window. It was time for the third meal, which in many Chasidic traditions is the most important meal of Shabbat.

The Rebbe himself showed up about 30 minutes later. Even though we were the only ones not dressed like them, we were warmly received with offers of food and drink and a place to sit. In fact, after the Rebbe did the Hamotzi, someone brought us a tiny piece of bread directly from the Rebbe's portion, a big honor.

These Charedim were clearly men of peace.

After their beautiful and haunting nigunim, the place went deathly quiet. Chasids were standing on benches and hanging on rafters. I don't think you could have fit another person in the room. The place was appropriately dark and mystical. In a very soft voice, the Rebbe spoke.

I didn't hear or understand anything he said, but I didn't have to.

Earlier, in the shul, Chaim had shown me the book written by the Rebbe's father, which all the Slonomers study.

The title of the book was, "The Ways of Peace."

"Bouskila has no particular problem with these traditional approaches. It's just that for him, if you want the message to 'really stick,' there's nothing like the magic of an Agnon story."

MAN OF AGNON

June 24, 2009

C an sarcasm, irony, surrealism, irreverence and Joycean word-play with Talmudic references help bring us closer to Torah and to God? Can you turn the rabbinic tradition upside down and still honor it?

Is it possible to understand a religious message better when you play with it, challenge it and even mock it?

These are not questions that have often crossed my mind. Until, that is, I started hanging out with Rabbi Daniel Bouskila, spiritual leader of Sephardic Temple Tifereth Israel in Westwood.

Bouskila believes there's one Jew who can revolutionize the way Torah and Judaism are taught, and, in the process, bring a generation of Jews closer to their Judaism.

That one Jew is the late Israeli novelist and Nobel Prize-winner Shmuel Yosef Agnon.

Agnon (1888-1970) was a religious Jew and talmudic scholar who was raised in a shtetl in Ukraine and who, after moving to Israel in 1907, became a world-famous novelist and storyteller. He used traditional religious sources and folklore, played with sacred and secular texts, blended classic and rabbinic Hebrew and fused irony with religious storytelling to create a body of work unlike any other.

The problem, however, is that because Agnon was seen mostly as a literary figure, he was never embraced and given his due by the Torah and religious world. Bouskila, who fell in love with Agnon years ago while studying in Israel, would love to change that.

Over lunch at Shilo's the other day, the rabbi spent several hours giving me examples of Agnon's potential to revolutionize Torah study.

His argument came down to this: For people who get bored easily (most of us?), the best way to teach is to surprise, challenge and provoke.

For example, let's say you want to teach the importance of not speaking lashon harah. You can go through the laws of the Talmud and Shulchan Aruch, analyze and debate the commentaries of the Chofetz Chaim and other great thinkers, study the relevant biblical stories, meditate on the mystical dimension of the mitzvah or give a passionate sermon on the ethics of avoiding hurtful language.

Bouskila has no particular problem with these traditional approaches. It's just that for him, if you want the message to "really stick," there's nothing like the magic of an Agnon story.

To help make his point, he read me an Agnon story of a woman who sits at home knitting on Shabbat instead of gossiping with her neighbors. One day, the great Moses happens to walk by her house and notices that God's spirit hovers above the house. Moses is shocked that the woman is desecrating the Shabbat by violating one of the 39 prohibited Shabbat labors.

He instructs her to sit with her neighbors so that she should not violate the Shabbat, yet the following week, when he once again passes by her house, he notices that God's spirit no longer hovers above the house. Moses understands that her original practice was better, so he instructs her to return to it.

Agnon, a Torah-observant Jew his whole life, had the chutzpah to challenge the notion of "violating the Shabbat," and through the character of Moses — God's lawgiver, no less — he suggests that idle gossip is more of a legal violation than the other 39 prohibitions. He concludes his story by mocking rabbinic authorities who concocted a cover-up to protect Moses' reputation.

Amazingly, Bouskila says, even though the story challenges halachah, a reader can walk away with a deeper appreciation for both the holiness of Shabbat and the importance of avoiding lashon harah.

Because Agnon's stories are so fertile and real and often surreal, they can touch you in a way that a typical Torah class cannot. And because the stories are textured with hard-core talmudic elements, they have enough Torah credibility to be taken seriously. The resulting brew is like midrash on steroids: it plays with your mind, sneaks up on you, tantalizes you, enchants you, provokes you, and, finally, invites you to challenge away.

After all that, Bouskila says, the reader begins to own the message.

At a Torah salon at my house recently, Bouskila took us through Agnon's "Fable of the Goat," a short story that touched on the themes of intergenerational conflict and the yearning to return to Zion. The story was only three pages long, but we debated its meaning for hours. After a while, the story became ours.

Bouskila, who's written about Agnon in The Jewish Journal in the past, has hundreds of these rich Agnon stories in his repertoire. The stories are his ammunition to spark a greater interest in Judaism — both with his flock and the community at large. He'd love to publish an anthology one day that will connect specific Agnon stories to each week's Torah portion and make Agnon "an engaging and thought-provoking guest at every Shabbat table."

He's banking on the notion that a lot of Jews are not turned on by the traditional ways of the religious trade — the preachy classes and sermons, the easy stories, the mitzvah pitch, the talmudic micro-debates, etc. — and that it's time to try a new, provocative and literary approach to Torah studies that can open up and energize Jewish minds.

At the very least, he'll have a ball trying.

"For most of those leaders, power comes before peace. The Palestinian conflict is their suckling milk, their Al Jazeera-fueled drama that diverts attention from their own brutal and oppressive ways."

DEAR PRESIDENT OBAMA

June 3, 2009

Now that you have brought your can-do spirit and sense of optimism to that most intractable of conflicts between Israelis and Palestinians, I thought I'd share a few words of caution.

First, Mr. President, be prepared to fail and to cut your losses. Be open to the possibility that this conflict is bigger than you are and there is nothing you can do to "solve" it.

When I hear you wax eloquently about creating a Palestinian state, I see you holding a flower in your hands. This flower, which represents the Palestinian state you so yearn for, needs to be planted, watered and nourished.

For several decades now, whenever anyone wanted to plant that flower, no matter how hard they tried, they couldn't do it. The flower had no roots, and the ground was full of sand. Nobody cared enough to give the flower the key nourishment it needed — preparing the Palestinian people for peace with their Jewish neighbors.

Today, as I see you holding aloft this rootless flower, I see you falling into the same trap.

Which brings me to my second point: Don't be so sure everyone wants peace. When you hear Arab and Muslim leaders tell you that "if only you could solve the Palestinian problem," they would have better relations with America, help you fight terrorism, help you confront Iran, etc., be skeptical. They will do anything, including exploit your weaknesses and put you on the defensive, in order to stay in power.

For most of those leaders, power comes before peace. The Palestinian conflict is their suckling milk, their Al Jazeera-fueled drama that diverts attention from their own brutal and oppressive ways.

Listen to the words of one of the world's foremost experts on the subject, your special adviser on Iran, Dennis Ross:

"Of all the policy myths that have kept us from making real progress in the Middle East, one stands out for its impact and longevity: the idea that if only the Palestinian conflict were solved, all other Middle East conflicts would melt away. This is the argument of 'linkage.'"

Of course, as you have often reminded us, a peaceful Palestinian state would be in Israel's interest, as it would ensure that the country stays Jewish and democratic.

So here's my third point: Don't assume the Palestinians want a state as badly as you do.

Consider this fact. The last Israeli administration made unprecedented concessions to the Palestinians, offering 97 percent of the West Bank, the evacuation of tens of thousands of settlers and even offering what was previously unthinkable: accepting the principle of a "right of return" to Israel for Palestinian refugees and offering to resettle thousands of Palestinians in Israel.

The offer was rejected by Palestinian leader Mahmoud Abbas, who said that "the gaps were too wide" and who later added, "No to the Jewishness of the Israeli state."

These latest Palestinian "nos" from our "moderate partner" continue a pattern of rejection that started more than 60 years ago, way before the first Jewish settlement was ever built, and traces to a poison you recently noted — anti-Israel and anti-Jewish incitement.

There's a perverse logic at work here. If you constantly demonize Jews in your schools, media and mosques, glorify suicide bombers and teach your children that there was never a Jewish presence in the land where Israeli Jews now live, how can you then turn around and tell them you will now make peace with these evil "foreign invaders"?

This Jew-hatred is independent of Jewish settlements, and is the longest-running impediment to a peaceful resolution of the conflict. The fact is, the Palestinians have invested a lot more energy in hating the Jewish state than in trying to create their own.

With that as background, Mr. President, perhaps you can understand why many of us don't see how a showdown with Israel over "natural growth" in the settlements will improve the prospects for peace. Israel hasn't built a new settlement in years. How will your relentless pressure on existing settlements help deal with the Hamas charter calling for the destruction of Israel or the ongoing Palestinian refusal to accept a Jewish state?

A more even-handed approach would have been to put equal pressure on both sides to begin a "dismantle for dismantle" plan: Israel dismantles the buildup of illegal outposts while the Palestinians dismantle the teaching of Jewish hatred.

As it is, your single-minded pressure on Israel has backfired. Instead of encouraging the Palestinians to move forward and offer their own concessions, it has emboldened them and other Arab leaders to set new conditions for restarting peace talks, and given them a perfect excuse to do nothing.

"I will wait for Israel to freeze settlements," Abbas told The Washington Post. "Until then, in the West Bank we have a good reality.... The people are living a normal life."

Unfortunately, there are others who are not living a normal life, and those are Jews in places like Sderot and Ashkelon, who over the years have been at the mercy of thousands of Palestinian rockets from Gaza that have rained down on their homes, schools and synagogues.

Which brings me to my final word of caution: You might not like the status quo, but believe me there's worse, like the West Bank turning into a terrorist state with a thousand rocket-launchers pointed at Israel's major population centers.

If you can find a way, Mr. President, to convince a few million Israelis that the Palestinian state you have in mind will be free of the Jew-hatred that is behind all these rockets, you will find plenty of Jews ready to help you water that plant.

"UN Watch's actions at Durban II reflect the group's position that 'it is legitimate for UN bodies to criticize Israel, but not when they do so unfairly, selectively, massively, sometimes exclusively and always excessively.'"

EXPOSING HYPOCRISY

May 20, 2009

Hillel Neuer is not your classic Jewish macher with a Florida tan who walks into a room and commands instant respect. He doesn't speak with the savvy and calculated tone of the experienced operator whose main agenda is either fundraising or political survival.

No, Neuer looks more like your basic preppy with a small frame, boyish face and plain eyeglasses.

So you'd never figure he'd be the nemesis of dictatorships and human-rights abusers the world over. You see, Neuer, a trained international lawyer from Montreal, is the executive director of UN Watch in Geneva, an organization affiliated with the American Jewish Committee that monitors the work of the United Nations on the basis of its own charter.

In other words, Neuer exposes UN hypocrisy.

It's no secret that the UN's first human rights conference in Durban in 2001 became a hatefest against Israel. The UN's Human Rights Council in Geneva, which organized the just-completed conference in Geneva dubbed Durban II, has suffered from a similar obsession with Israel: In 2007, for example, out of 192 countries under its purview, Israel was the only country condemned — in nine separate resolutions.

It is this obsession with Israel and the simultaneous neglect of other countries' human rights violations that Neuer and his group expose. On

April 17, at the conclusion of the Durban II conference, Neuer spoke out on the floor of the main assembly hall:

"In a conference that promised to review country performance on racism, why did the conference, in fact, fail to review a single country that perpetrates racism, discrimination and intolerance?

"Why did the conference fail to review a single abuser?

"Why is it silent on women facing systematic discrimination in Saudi Arabia?

"Why is it silent on gays persecuted and even executed in Iran? On ethnic repression in Tibet?

"Why is this conference, which promised to help Africans, silent on black Africans now being raped, slaughtered by racist Sudan?"

Neuer could have gone on, but he was interrupted by the representative from Iran, who asked the conference chairperson to "kindly pronounce the speaker out of order and stop him from continuation of his statement."

At that point, Neuer replied: "I shall conclude merely with one question: Has this conference really helped millions of victims worldwide? If so, who are they?"

Neuer's group, UN Watch, didn't just expose the hypocrisy of the conference, it also set an example. A few days earlier, they organized, in coordination with 40 human rights groups from around the world, a counter conference, across the street from Durban II, called Geneva Summit for Human Rights, Tolerance and Democracy.

The conference provided a platform for more than 500 human rights victims, scholars and activists from countries like Rwanda, Bulgaria, Libya, Burma, Egypt, Cuba, Iran, Zimbabwe, Sudan and Belarus.

With the support of pro-Israel allies, including our own StandWithUs, UN Watch arranged other events during Durban II, which prompted anti-Zionist agitator Michel Warschawski to conclude:

"Though Israel boycotted the conference, it was nevertheless omnipresent: 1,500 young Jews organized by UN Watch ... were sent to Geneva, and literally conquered the place ... [their presence] created a climate of occupied territory, both in the UN venue and its close vicinity and in the city of Geneva, where several mass rallies were held, with the participation of prominent figures like Elie Wiesel, Nathan Sharansky and Alan Dershowitz....."

UN Watch's actions at Durban II reflect the group's position that "it is legitimate for UN bodies to criticize Israel, but not when they do so unfairly, selectively, massively, sometimes exclusively and always excessively."

So while Israel did take more than its share of hits at Durban II, it was still a huge improvement over the nightmare of Durban I — proof that when Jews get their act together and take the high road, good things can happen.

Neuer was in town recently to share some of those things. He was staying at my house for Shabbat, and he asked if I could set up a few speaking gigs. With a few days' notice, I got three takers: Rabbi David Wolpe of Sinai Temple, Rabbi Yosef Kanefsky of B'nai David-Judea Congregation and Rabbi Elie Spitz of Congregation B'nai Israel in Tustin.

Neuer's first talk was at Sinai Temple on Shabbat morning. We walked about 90 minutes from Pico-Robertson to Westwood in what felt like desert heat. When we arrived, several hundred people were in the main sanctuary.

After Wolpe's introduction, Neuer walked to the podium and told the story of the "Six-Day Durban War" that he and other activists had just fought in Geneva; what they did behind the scenes to prevent another Durban I fiasco for Israel, and how Durban II became "a little piece of good news" in the ongoing struggle to expose human rights abuses that are systematically ignored by the UN.

Neuer did not appear imposing at the podium, but his voice and his message pierced the hall. And then, as if on cue, it happened again: just like on that day in Geneva when he spoke out in the main assembly, a man from Iran interrupted him.

This time, however, it wasn't to rebuke him, but to applaud.

"It's this back and forth between reality-biz and showbiz that has defined her life. It seems that whenever one side starts to dominate, the other wakes up, as if to say: "Hey, don't forget about me.""

WOLMAN OF VALOR

May 6, 2009

Lesley Wolman was having trouble breathing. She was in a small room on a hot and muggy day in New York City in August 1993, singing and auditioning for the George Gershwin Broadway musical, "Someone to Watch Over Me." A little earlier, Wolman had been breastfeeding her 21-day-old son, Yale, who was now safely in the arms of her husband, Jeff, in the waiting area. The three of them had taken the bus from their apartment on the Upper East Side.

"I can't believe you can sing like this 21 days after delivering your first baby," one of the casting directors in the room said to her.

"Personally, I prefer dogs," said another.

Sixteen years later, sipping iced tea at Pat's Restaurant, Wolman laughs at the memory of that day and seems amused that I'm asking for so many details. But looking back now, it's clear to her that that was the day she decided she would never be a "killer."

"Killer" is the term Wolman uses for artists who are obsessed with success, who put getting a part in a Brad Pitt movie on the same level as a Lubavitcher Chasid seeing his Rebbe revealed as the Messiah.

But if she will never become a showbiz killer, she will also never stop being a showbiz lover.

It is this love for performing that the packed house at the Pico Playhouse saw the other night at Wolman's cabaret show, "Jewish Women in Song ... a Celebration."

I knew very little about Wolman when I went to see her show at the suggestion of a friend. So when she came out sparkling like a jewel in a silky outfit, singing soulful and timeless songs accompanied by a three-piece jazz band, I had no idea that this was a PTA mom involved with the Bureau of Jewish Education and Camp Ramah, who sat on the board of Sinai Academy and who was about to fly to Washington, D.C., for the AIPAC convention.

All this stuff came out when we had lunch a few days later. Our conversation took on a schizophrenic quality, because I couldn't decide what interested me more — her views on Jewish education or her performance on Broadway in "Shenandoah"; her thoughts on the Israeli-Palestinian conflict or who did the choreography for her latest show.

It's this back and forth between reality-biz and showbiz that has defined her life. It seems that whenever one side starts to dominate, the other wakes up, as if to say: "Hey, don't forget about me."

She recalls the many times she was stuck in an audition in West Hollywood, calling one of her friends to ask: "Can you please pick up the kids from school? There's no way I'll make it back in time."

Wolman grew up in Winnipeg, Canada, and has been singing and performing in one way or another since she was a kid. Her singing didn't stop her from getting a university degree in nursing. During her many years of struggle, auditions and performances on Broadway, she spent countless hours caring for celebrities in an exclusive rehab hospital in Manhattan.

She moved to Los Angeles in the mid-1990s with her husband and their young boy, and shortly thereafter had a baby girl. Not knowing too many people in their neighborhood on Melrose Boulevard, they hooked up with the Sinai community in Westwood, joined the temple, put their kids in the day school and she soon became your classic, devoted, enthusiastic member of the Los Angeles Jewish community.

But she could never stop singing.

Her new show is an attempt to blend her two lives — devoted showbiz performer and devoted wife, mother, Jew and community member. The show celebrates great Jewish women performers throughout the ages, and while it has completed its limited run, her dream now is to expand it into other cities and communities.

As circumstances would have it, the night after experiencing the pure joy of Wolman's show, I was at the Odyssey Theatre experiencing the trauma of the Holocaust, in a play by Bernard Weinraub called "The Accomplices."

The play is about the struggle of one man, Peter Bergson, who comes to America during the Holocaust to mobilize the Jewish community, the White House, Congress, Hollywood and the media to try to do something about the genocide of his people.

There's a scene where Bergson, pleading his case, explains how many Jews he'd love to save. He starts with huge numbers and then simply says, "even just one."

For some reason, when Bergson said those words — "even just one" — my mind went back to Wolman's show from the previous night.

I thought about how Bergson was fighting to save millions of Jews, but he knew that this meant millions of "even just one" — millions of singular Jews of valor like Lesley Wolman, Jews who just wanted a chance to breathe and live out their story.

"It was as if we all realized that tolerance is only the beginning, not an end, and that settling for just tolerance means settling for a community of discrete and disconnected bubbles."

BEYOND TOLERANCE

April 29, 2009

Over a 48-hour period last week, through a series of Jewish events, I discovered the limitations of tolerance. On Thursday night, Rabbi Dr. Benny Lau, representing Beit Morasha of Jerusalem, came for a "conversational dinner" at my house. Lau was in Los Angeles as part of a citywide celebration of religious Zionism, and he spoke to a group of us about his and his organization's efforts to build bridges in Israel between the Torah-observant and secular communities.

It was a mixed crowd: several Hollywood writers, a playwright and journalist, a Sephardic leader, an Internet entrepreneur, an Israel activist, an Orthodox outreach leader, a music producer, a philanthropist, etc. My co-hosts, Gary Wexler and Dan Adler, and I wanted the guest list to reflect some of the same cultural and ethnic differences Lau faces in his work.

Lau, who is the nephew of the former chief rabbi of Israel, was not there just to speak. He also came to listen. We talked about a lot of things, mainly around Jewish identity, but as the evening progressed an overall theme bubbled up: tolerance.

Some guests craved more tolerance — they seemed almost befuddled by the level of intolerance in Israel between the Orthodox and secular communities.

For others, there was more ambivalence: Is there a limit to tolerance when it comes to God-given truth? Should belief in one truth be something that should also be tolerated?

But it was a third perspective that, in my mind, really cut through — a view that says the Jewish nation must aim higher than just tolerance if it is to maintain its sense of common purpose and shared destiny.

It must aim for connection.

That was Lau's message, and also his life's purpose. As he sees it, being Jewish means being responsible for one another. It's not enough to tolerate each other, if that means turning our backs on the other. We have a timeless Torah, the rabbi said, that belongs to all of us and can help connect us. Lau's ongoing challenge is to make this Torah more welcoming and sensitive to the secular Israeli Jew.

The morning after our dinner, I was at a conference at UCLA Hillel titled "Building Jewish Los Angeles: A Leadership Conversation," where about 40 community leaders gathered to talk about how to strengthen the local Jewish community and help "chart its future."

Just like at the dinner, there was plenty of diversity among the attendees. Over the course of three hours, enough good ideas were expressed that even if we could do only 10 percent of them, our community would get an immediate boost.

But here's what got me about our talkfest: I can't recall anyone bringing up the word tolerance. I heard a lot of words like cooperation, connection, coordination, cohesion, innovation and education. But tolerance? Not so much.

It was as if we all realized that tolerance is only a beginning, not an end, and that settling for just tolerance means settling for a community of discrete and disconnected bubbles — hardly an ideal roadmap for building a thriving and engaged community.

Of course, once we got down to practical stuff — like what to do next and who should do what — things got more complicated. It's easy to agree in principle, but turning principles into action means compromise and sacrifice.

It means struggling to find common ground.

Later that Friday night, at a private home in Pico-Robertson, I met an epic struggler, Rabbi Seth Farber, from Jerusalem. He's an Orthodox talmudic scholar whose organization, Itim, helps disenfranchised Israelis navigate through the maze of the Rabbinate. If, for example, the Rabbinate rejects your marriage application because you can't prove you're a Jew, if it rejects your conversion, won't give you a get or simply makes your life miserable, you call Farber.

He's a halachic commando. He'll send a private eye to a remote village of Chechnya to find a copy of an old get. He'll videotape witnesses to prove a halachic point. He'll find obscure loopholes in the law. His consuming passion is to assist Israelis who identify as Jews and want to be Jews (like 300,000 Russian immigrants) but who have run up against the brick wall of the Rabbinate.

On Shabbat afternoon, during a panel discussion at Young Israel of Century City with four distinguished religious Zionist rabbis from Israel — Shlomo Riskin, Ari Berman, Farber and Lau — there was so much talk of bringing back compassion and inclusiveness to Jewish law, it was easy to forget that they were Orthodox rabbis. But theirs was a primal scream against the status quo — against a politicized and dogmatic Rabbinate that has refused to allow innovative and inclusive halachic solutions to Israel's most vexing civil problems.

Like Lau on Thursday night and our community leaders on Friday morning, Farber and his colleagues are engaged in a noble struggle: breaking down the walls that separate Jews and helping us connect with one another.

Going beyond tolerance is not easy, but in the great Jewish story, what is?

"Teaching our contributions to humanity would not only build Jewish pride, it would encourage Jewish kids to grab the baton and try to make their own contributions."

THE MISSING CLASS

April 23, 2009

I have an idea that I think could really improve Jewish education. It's so simple and obvious that I wasn't going to write about it, since I figure everyone's already thought of it. The idea came to me after a rabbi told me about his dream of broadcasting, on the Internet, a weekly class on Judaism designed for the huge number of Jewish kids who aren't getting a Jewish education.

This got me thinking: If I had only one hour a week to encourage Jewish students to connect with their Judaism, what would I teach them? What Jewish subject would have the greatest chance to instill Jewish pride and make a student say, "Yeah, that's something I want to be a part of?"

Would it be a class on the Torah portion of the week? The Talmud? History? The rituals of our faith? The meaning of Shabbat and the holidays? Israel? Tikkun olam? Jewish literature? Prayer?

In other words, would it be one of the many subjects already taught in Jewish schools, or would it be something different?

I found my answer when I took a group of kids to see the Lakers play at Staples Center. Have you ever seen the look on a kid's face when his team is winning? Have you seen the loyalty that these kids have for their home team? When my 10-year-old son and his buddies cheer for their beloved Lakers, they feel more than excitement — they feel like they're part of something.

I thought: Why can't we instill in all Jewish kids that same kind of pride and loyalty for their Jewish "home team"?

So here's my simple and obvious idea for a class that ought to be taught in every Jewish school in America:

Jewish Contributions to Humanity.

That's right, I think it's important that we teach Jewish kids how their religion and their "home team" have made the world a better place. How much better?

Here is prominent historian Paul Johnson from "A History of the Jews":

"All the great conceptual discoveries of the intellect seem obvious and inescapable once they have been revealed, but it requires a special genius to formulate them for the first time. The Jews had this gift.

"To them we owe the idea of equality before the law, both divine and human; of the sanctity of life and the dignity of the human person; of the individual conscience and so of personal redemption; of the collective conscience and so of personal responsibility; of peace as an abstract ideal and love as the foundation of justice, and many other items which constitute the basic moral furniture of the human mind. Without the Jews it might have been a much emptier place."

Or check out these words spoken in 1809 by our second president, John Adams:

"I will insist that the Hebrews have done more to civilize men than any other nation. If I were an atheist, and believed in blind eternal fate, I should still believe that fate had ordained the Jews to be the most essential instrument for civilizing the nations."

Here is what author and scholar Thomas Cahill, in his 1998 "The Gifts of the Jews," has to say about "this oddball tribe, this raggle-taggle band, this race of wanderers who are the progenitors of the Western world":

"There is simply no one else remotely like them; theirs is a unique vocation. Indeed, the very idea of vocation, of a personal destiny, is a Jewish idea.

"Without the Jews, we would see the world through different eyes, hear with different ears, even feel with different feelings. And not only would our sensorium, the screen through which we receive the world, be different: we would think with a different mind, interpret all our experience differently, draw different conclusions from the things that befall us. And we would set a different course for our lives.

"Without the Hebrew Bible, we would never have known the abolitionist movement, the prison-reform movement, the antiwar movement, the labor movement, the civil rights movement, the movements of indigenous and dispossessed peoples for their human rights, the antiapartheid movement in South Africa, the Solidarity movement in Poland, the free speech and pro-democracy movements in such Far Eastern countries as South Korea, the Philippines and even China.

"These movements of modern times have all employed the language of the Bible."

This is not about being or feeling superior, but about contributing to the world, and since biblical times, there's little doubt that Jews and Judaism have been fundamental to human progress. But how many Jewish schools in America are teaching this to their students — not as an afterthought to a history class, but as a bona fide curriculum that is taken as seriously as Chumash or Navi or how to build a sukkah?

My guess is, not many.

This is a missed opportunity. Teaching our contributions to humanity would not only build Jewish pride, it would encourage Jewish kids to grab the baton and try to make their own contributions.

It would also remind them that the Jewish story is more than one of persecution and suffering; that before and after the pogroms and the Holocaust, the Jewish way has always been to share our gifts with the rest of the world.

Of course, we need to feel comfortable speaking highly about ourselves. The Jewish tradition of self-criticism is wonderful, but we can overdo it. If you ask me, we're overdue for a pushback to the hypocritical and growing Jew bashing that has put so many Jews on the defensive.

This pushback can start in our schools, by teaching a new generation of Jews about their people's eternal value to the world, and instilling a Jewish pride based on knowledge and not just tribal emotion.

So here's hoping that Jewish educators across the country will develop this idea in time for the next school year. Worst that can happen, we'll make a few more fans — and God knows we can use them.

"It also dawned on me that of all the questions we can ask at Passover, of all the questions we can ask of our children, neighbors and those we have forgotten, perhaps the most powerful one is the simplest of all: What's your story?"

LEANING SIDEWAYS

April 16, 2009

I learned something new at our seder this year, and it had nothing to do with the story of the Exodus. I was ready for a seder full of questions. I had done my homework, gone to classes, read essays and books. I prepared questions that I would ask the kids, questions that would encourage them to ask their own questions. Like my friend Rabbi Chaim Seidler-Feller impressed on us at one of our Torah salons, a seder is like a mini-Beit Midrash, a table of learning, debating and understanding.

Armed with my questions and shivering in the cold of Montreal, I walked after synagogue services to my sister Judy's house for the first seder. The place was loud and festive. The kids were playing and reconnecting with their cousins. Grown-ups were catching up on the past year. And my mother was in my sister's kitchen acting as if it were her own. It was a scene right out of Woody Allen's "Radio Days" — everyone competing to see who could speak the fastest.

I looked at the joyful chaos around me and wondered if I'd be able to introduce some learning into the evening. How would I cut through the festive mood to kick off a discussion on the deeper meaning of slavery? How would I ask sober questions on whether there is holiness in the wicked son?

As our noisy group took their seats at the table, Rabbi Sherre Hirsch's recent book came to mind: "We Plan, God Laughs." It was clear that God was now laughing at my plan for a neat and orderly seder with lots of meaningful discussion. How could I compete with all this happiness?

We went through the haggadah, did all the dipping and the rituals and even threw in some explanations and discussions with the kids, but let's face it, the theme of our seder was family joy, not ancestral angst.

Little did I know, however, that once we had completed the rituals and begun the meal, an unexpected Passover lesson would await me.

It came not from Moses or Pharaoh, but from my 94-year-old uncle, Tonton Michel.

My uncle has been attached to our family since he was a kid in Morocco, though technically, we're not related. He's been married to the same woman, Annette, for 68 years. They've never had children. They have no relatives in Montreal. But they're so close to our family that we've always called them uncle and aunt.

They've been fixtures at our seder and holiday tables since the mid-1960s, when we all moved to Montreal. Although I have probably seen them hundreds of times, I don't recall ever having a real conversation with them. We never did anything more than small talk or exchange expressions of affection.

But this year was different, because my sister decided that Tonton Michel would sit next to me.

With the festive noise of our seder showing no signs of abating, I decided it was a good night to finally get to know my uncle.

So I leaned sideways to ask a few questions, and spent the next hour listening to his stories.

I learned that growing up in Morocco, one of his closest friends was a Muslim man who had a partly Jewish name, and who was probably a descendant of the Marranos several centuries earlier. I also learned that Jews in Morocco were clever businessmen.

Of the many stories that he shared, his favorite was that of an old Jewish merchant in Casablanca who made sandals using discarded tires.

When a customer complained that the same sandals sold for a lot less somewhere else, the Jewish merchant explained that his sandals were worth more because he used Michelins.

My uncle reminisced about seders 80 years ago in his Jewish neighborhood of Casablanca — what his mother cooked and who would come over, how he met his future wife, and how he loved the night of Mimouna (held the night after Passover ends) when Arab neighbors would help the Jews prepare the traditional sweet tables.

While he had fond memories of many of his Arab neighbors, he recalled how certain Arab expressions betrayed a demeaning view of Jews, and how things started becoming more hairy for Jews after the Six-Day War. Moving to Montreal made him feel safer, but you could tell he still misses the old country.

My uncle kept pouring out stories and I kept leaning over to ask him questions — none of them following any Passover script. Instead of the Pharaoh, we talked about the king of Morocco. There were no questions about the deeper meaning of slavery or the symbolism of matzah. Nothing about the personal significance of our people's master story.

The only story that held my attention was that of my 94-year-old uncle. The questions were not historical, but personal. It wasn't "tell me about our ancestors," but rather, "tell me about you."

After 40 years of spending time with Tonton Michel, I finally heard his story.

I broke the rules of the seder: I leaned sideways not to eat matzah but to listen to my uncle. But, as I reflected later, our collective master story is really an accumulation of millions of personal stories like the one I just heard.

It also dawned on me that of all the questions we can ask at Passover, of all the questions we can ask of our children, neighbors and those we have forgotten, perhaps the most powerful one is the simplest of all: What's your story?

It's a question we need to share especially with the old and vulnerable, those members of our community who can so easily become, in the words of Rabbi Ed Feinstein, "socially invisible."

When I saw the look on my uncle's face after he had told me his own story, it was like seeing a man come back to life.

I didn't just learn about personal liberation, I witnessed it.

"It follows that if any party should be selling, it is Israel. Yet, incredibly, it is always the reverse: The Palestinians are selling a peace they can't deliver, while the Israelis are buying a peace that doesn't exist."

MIND-STATE SOLUTION

March 25, 2009

I'm not sure, but I think I have a solution to the Israeli-Palestinian conflict, or at least another way of looking at it. It hit me the other day after I broke bread at Pat's Restaurant with some people connected to Americans for Peace Now, a leftist Jewish organization that actively promotes the two-state solution.

Now, you should know that whenever I hear the words "peace now," something inside of me cringes. I have never understood how Israel could make peace now with an enemy that hates her no matter what she does.

Over the years, I've asked this question of a number of people across the ideological spectrum: "If Israel dismantled all the settlements in the West Bank tomorrow, would it stop Palestinian hostility and violence toward Israel?"

I never once got a yes.

Why? I think it's because most people intuitively understand that dismantling settlements is not the same thing as dismantling hatred. The hatred that has been taught for years in Palestinian schools and summer camps, through television shows and billboards and in mosques is not just aimed at Jewish settlers but at all Jews and at all of Israel. This kind of hatred is too deep to be washed away by well-meaning gestures.

So I came to my Peace Now lunch with some apprehension — and a lot of prejudice.

I can't say I connected ideologically with my lunchmates, but I did end up connecting emotionally. The reason was that I trusted their deep commitment to Israel and their sincerity in their search for peace.

There was something very Jewish about their attitude toward the conflict. First, the idea of hope, of never giving up. Where would the Jews be today if we didn't have hope?

There was also the idea of taking responsibility for our situation — of not blaming others for our fate. Again, where would the Jewish nation be today without that character trait?

My peace-loving lunch companions are not naive. They know about the spread of Jewish hatred in Palestinian society, and they understand the fear many of us have that a Palestinian state could easily become a terrorist state. But they believe the ideals of peace and a two-state solution are so valuable to Jews and to Israel that it is worth pursuing relentlessly, even if it means paying a significant price.

It's this idea of paying a price for peace that made a lightbulb go off.

For nearly two decades, Israel has gone to one failed peace meeting after another with this question in mind: How much are we willing to pay for peace? In doing so, they have acted as if the Palestinians actually have something to sell.

Apparently, no one ever stood up during one of those meetings to say to the Israelis: "Wait a minute, you're not the buyers, you're the sellers!"

Why sellers? Because everyone knows that when Israel signs an agreement with an Arab country, it is capable of honoring it. On the other hand, it's no secret that the Palestinians, with or without Hamas, are in no position to deliver peace to Israel.

It follows that if any party should be selling, it is Israel. Yet, incredibly, it is always the reverse: The Palestinians are selling a peace they can't deliver, while the Israelis are buying a peace that doesn't exist.

Is it any wonder that all the peace plans keep failing? That groups like Peace Now keep banging their heads against the wall, hoping that more concessions from Israel will somehow bring us closer to that elusive solution?

The problem with pressuring Israel to buy peace through concessions is that it perpetuates the illusion that the Palestinians have something to sell.

What the peace process needs more than anything is for the Palestinians to be able to deliver their end of the bargain. Until that happens, any question of creating a Palestinian state is moot.

My solution? Have the sides switch roles or mind-states.

Israelis should act like "peace owners," and Palestinians should act like "peace buyers." With a buyer mentality, Palestinians will be more likely to make their own offers, rather than passively rejecting Israeli offers, which is what they often do.

As buyers, Palestinians would also learn that Israel needs a minimum security deposit: Stop teaching Jew-hatred to your children. Palestinians can't offer peace while they're teaching war. Tragically, the anti-incitement clause was the great ignored clause of Oslo — so for more than 15 years, Palestinian society fell back on its habit of demonizing Jews, which contributed to the growth of terrorism and rejectionist forces like Hamas.

Israel is hardly blameless in this picture, and it has made its share of mistakes. But settlements or no settlements, the fact remains that the great majority of Israeli Jews have been more than ready to pay a huge price for peace, including evacuating most of the West bank.

Had the Palestinians been smart, had they taken more responsibility for their situation and developed a culture of co-existence, they would have long ago made Israel an offer it couldn't refuse. They would have called Israel's bluff and made the process real.

Instead, we've all been treated to the continuing and sorry spectacle of global diplomats parachuting into Jerusalem to coax adversaries into yet another round of the "let's play peace process" game.

Leading the latest charge is our new can-do president, who believes that a solution is possible if only the U.S. becomes more "engaged." He will soon learn that no amount of American engagement or Israeli concessions can undo the reality that for the foreseeable future, the Palestinians are utterly incapable of delivering peace to Israel.

All this, of course, is very sobering for those of us who fear for the future of Israel as a Jewish democratic state. Going forward, the one thing we can be sure of is that groups like Peace Now will continue to pressure Israel to make concessions, and people like me will lament that the whole process is upside down.

"Is there any doubt that had the Palestinians chosen the 'Riviera' option, Israel would have welcomed it?"

THE GAZA RIVIERA

January 14, 2009

In the advertising business, clients pay us to dream. To dream means not to be too imbedded with reality, to be unshackled from any inconvenient fact that might interfere with the dreaming process, to be, like they say in self-help seminars, appropriately unreasonable.

The price you pay for dreaming is to expose yourself to abuse and ridicule. In a tough world, you never want to be accused of being naïve. The expression, "Are you dreaming?" didn't develop by accident.

What you can gain by dreaming, though, is significant. Dreaming is only limited by your imagination, so it can lead you to wild and break-through ideas. At the very least, it can give you a new way of looking at old problems.

Why am I telling you all this? Because the other day, as my mind was numb from yet another report from the Gaza war zone, I saw something that made me go off on a wild dream. It started with the sight of two Israeli soldiers as they drove into Gaza in an armored personnel carrier, and as I watched the soldiers, I recalled how much Israelis love to go to the beach.

As if I was hallucinating, I then imagined the same two soldiers in their beach clothes, in a convertible roadster, with a surf board sticking out and the music blasting, and instead of going to war, they were going to meet their buddies for a day of partying on the beach.

They were going to the jetsetters' newest fun spot: the Gaza Riviera.

By now, my mind was losing control. Images started flooding in. I saw this fabulous strip of hotels and casinos right by a sparkling ocean. I imagined thousands of proud Palestinians working with smiles on their faces to serve the thousands of tourists from around the world who were coming to their little strip of ocean paradise.

Behind this paradise, I saw a bustling economy, where the highest quality produce was grown and exported; where entrepreneurs built software companies, banks and advertising agencies; where a university attracted students from around the world; where local culture and the arts thrived; and where you could take the Orient Express train to Beirut, Cairo and, yes, even Tel Aviv.

And then I woke up.

But as I rubbed my eyes and crashed back to the reality of Grad missiles and bombing raids, I realized what the really crazy part of my dream was: It could easily have happened. That's right, the Palestinians could have built their own Riviera.

Think back to that infamous summer of 2005, the year of the Gaza disengagement, when Israel finally said: OK, you don't want us here, we're leaving — take it, it's all yours. Oh, and we'll even throw in our state-of-the-art farms and greenhouses, in case you want to continue growing some of the finest produce in the world.

Is there any doubt that had the Palestinians chosen the "Riviera" option, Israel would have welcomed it? That Israel would have responded to this show of good faith and optimism with corresponding gestures of cooperation and good will? That there would have been no need for "suffocating closures"? That, in fact, Israelis, known for their love of life and travel, would have been the first tourists to sample the delightful pleasures of this new Gaza?

Yet tragically, instead of choosing the Riviera option — the option of building for the future — the Palestinians chose the option of killing and dying for the past.

Instead of seizing the moment and showing Israel and the world what they could do with the land that they love, they showed the world that they still hate the Jews more than they love the land.

Instead of using the hundreds of millions the world showered on them to build housing, infrastructure and industry, they built bomb factories and hundreds of tunnels to smuggle rockets they could fire into Israeli towns.

Instead of making laws that would protect the freedoms and rights of their people and encourage investment and innovation, they imposed Sharia laws with such punishments as severing hands, crucifixion and hanging.

Instead of teaching love of life to their children, as Mark Steyn has written, they "marinated them in a sick death cult in which martyrdom in the course of Jew-killing is the greatest goal to which a citizen can aspire."

Finally, instead of using their Jewish neighbors as allies and trading partners, they provoked them into a destructive war in the hope that the world would renew its hostility for Jews and the Zionist state would be further undermined.

And to an extent, it worked. The world is once again blaming Israel for the Palestinians' suffering and condemning it for the deaths of civilians used cowardly as human shields.

And once again, Israel is losing the war of images.

But while the images of destruction coming out of Gaza are indeed tragic, there is one missing image that also merits our sorrow. This is the image of what could have been — what the Palestinians could have done with their precious land after Israel left Gaza three and a half years ago.

This is an image where the hero brands are Hilton and Sheraton, rather than Grads and Qassams; where captains of industry overshadow captains of terror gangs; where poets outshine bullies and guitars outshine guns; where the excitement of building for the future overcomes the aphrodisiac of permanent victimhood.

Yes, it's an image that requires one to dream in wild and unreasonable ways.

But an hour's drive up the coast from Gaza, you can see an image that was also once nothing but a dream, and that was built without any help from the United Nations or the international community.

It's an image of a thriving little Riviera called Tel Aviv, and for our Palestinian neighbors, it's a poignant and concrete reminder of what might have been.

"Israel, it seems to me, has decided that if it can't eliminate the terrorists' desire to murder Jews, the least it can do is significantly reduce their growing capacity to do so."

CAN WAR BRING PEACE?

January 7, 2009

I've always been annoyed by the term, "peace camp," the moniker commonly used by left-wing, peace-seeking organizations like Peace Now, the Israel Policy Forum and, more recently, J Street.

Because those organizations are very noisy about their desire for peace and their abhorrence for anything that smacks of a "military solution," they have crowned themselves with the glorious "peace camp" title.

The implication, of course, is that if you don't share their philosophy for attaining peace, you're in another camp – if not exactly the war camp, then maybe the stiff-necked, "force is necessary" camp.

In truth, however, I've never met a right-wing Jew who doesn't want peace. The divisive question is always: How do we get there? By being forceful and hard-nosed, or flexible and understanding?

One of the more powerful arguments advanced by the peace camp is that there is "no military solution" to the conflict. War is counterproductive and hardens the enemy. What we need are political solutions through smart and diplomatic engagement, like we achieved with Egypt and Jordan.

I have a lot of sympathy for the idea that wars can backfire and make things worse, as it did with the Second Lebanon War of 2006. That's why I agonized over whether Israel should escalate the war in Gaza and invade with ground troops. Like many others, I asked myself: Can we really win this kind of war? Will it really stop the rockets? What would come next?

Then, I came across something that hit me like a lightning bolt.

It was an item in Investor's Business Daily that reported that Hamas might already have rockets that can reach Israel's nuclear plant in Dimona.

Even if the claim was exaggerated, it made me wonder: If a terrorist entity like Hamas – one fanatically devoted to Israel's destruction – ever got hold of missiles that can take out Israel's nuclear installations, would they use them?

Is there any peace-loving leftist who can honestly answer, No, they wouldn't?

If Hamas bombs actually started falling on Dimona or Tel Aviv, would the "peace camp" still be harping against "military solutions" and calling for "immediate cease-fires"? Would J Street still find no moral distinction between the terrorist bombs of Hamas and Israel's long-delayed response to defend its citizens?

Israel, it seems to me, has decided that if it can't eliminate the terrorists' desire to murder Jews, the least it can do is significantly reduce their growing capacity to do so.

There are successful precedents for this approach. In a recent editorial, David Horovitz, editor of the Jerusalem Post, touched on one: "Operation Defensive Shield, carried out in the spring of 2002, was a carefully planned and effectively executed attack on the Palestinians' suicide-bomb infrastructure in the West Bank that remade the reality in the years ever since – precisely the kind of goal enunciated for Operation Cast Lead in Gaza."

The new reality that Horovitz refers to is that terror from the West Bank stopped because the enemy realized there was no way it could win a war against Israel. That realization was a prerequisite to restarting the peace process.

Robert J. Lieber, a professor of government and international affairs at Georgetown University, took it one step further in the Washington Post:

"Egypt and Jordan have made peace with Israel, not because they embraced the ideas of Theodor Herzl, the founder of modern Zionism, but because they concluded that the effort to destroy the Jewish state had failed and that refusing to come to terms with it was harmful to their national interests. Ultimately, peace will be possible only if most Palestinians and their leaders become convinced that terrorism and violence are a dead end and that they cannot under any circumstances prevail over Israel through the use of force. If today's conflict leaves a seriously weakened and politically damaged Hamas, that result is more likely to enhance the prospects for peace than to weaken them."

Of course, wars are tragic, messy and unpredictable – one errant bomb can derail the best plans. Lorelei Kelly, an expert in conflict resolution, wrote a powerful anti-war piece in The Huffington Post last week, where she explained that when fighting ideologies, "if you want ultimate victory, persuasion deserves as much firepower as coercion."

Kelly appealed to my intellect, but my viscera still couldn't shake the potential horror of Hamas rockets igniting a nuclear meltdown in the heart of Israel. I have this vision of Hamas terrorists gleefully cracking open a fresh crate of new missiles just arrived from Iran with the capacity to kill several thousand Jews at a time, and doing high-fives in anticipation of using them. Am I paranoid? Maybe. But this should give you an idea of the unlimited faith I have in Hamas' callous disregard for human life, whether Jewish or Palestinian.

From a PR standpoint, Israel is fortunate that the war in Gaza was started not by right-wing tough guys but by centrist leaders who have exerted enormous effort over the years to achieve peace. No one can ever accuse Ehud Barak, Ehud Olmert and Tzipi Livni of rushing to war, not when they tolerated thousands of bombs falling on their people before finally responding.

In the end, everybody has their breaking point – that moment when your survival instinct overcomes everything else. A lot of Jews, from the left to the right, seem to have reached that point.

But survival is one thing, and peace is another. It's far from certain that making war with Hamas will bring peace. The only thing that's certain is that as long as nextdoor neighbors like Hamas pose a terrorist threat to Israel, you can forget about peace – no matter what camp you're in.

"Clearly, this was not a life he was ready to simply clean out from his memory. His work has always been with real things that you can touch, and many of those things were still there in the upstairs room."

THE QUIET TAILOR

December 18, 2008

We all have times in our lives when it seems like nothing can go wrong. When one good move leads to another; when all the breaks go our way, and we simply can't wait to get up every morning. We feel invincible, on top of the world, hoping the feeling never goes away. These times can take on a mythical value within our larger life.

I was thinking about this the other day, when I went to pick up a suit at Paul's Tailoring on Pico Boulevard and stuck around to hear the story of the owner, Paul Drill.

Paul's shop has been a fixture in the neighborhood for 28 years. When you enter his shop, which sits adjacent to the Pico Glatt market a block east of Beverly Drive, you half expect to see trolley cars and '56 Chevys going by outside. His sewing machines are more than 50 years old. There are no computers, no cash registers, no ads on the walls, not even an employee to greet you.

There's just some old furniture and a sturdy, older man with a full head of white hair who hears the bell from the entrance door and soon appears to see what you need.

This is Paul the tailor, born 66 years ago in a little town outside of Kiev. Since the age of 18, he's made a living tailoring people's clothes. The world around him has changed, but his tools and materials haven't – it's still the same needles and threads and buttons and patterns and scissors and chalk markers and whatever else he needs to mold fabric to fit people's bodies.

His life in tailoring began when he was looking for work in his childhood neighborhood and saw through a window a tailor cutting a large swath of fabric. He loved how that looked: scissors swishing through soft material. That one moment would come to define the next 48 years of his life.

He started as a clerk and began taking sewing lessons, slowly moving up the ladder, before getting drafted by the Soviet army. After the war, he found a job in a "fashion factory" and went to a fashion college at night for four years, where he learned all the aspects of the trade.

When the Soviet Union began relaxing its immigration policy for Jews, he made plans to move to America with his wife and young boy. They landed in New York in 1976, and after working for a Manhattan tailor for a couple of years, he decided to take his family to Los Angeles, where most of his friends lived.

He carried a letter of recommendation in his pocket from his well-known former boss in New York, and that was enough to get him into the tailoring department at Saks Fifth Avenue.

Within a year, he was introduced to the woman who would transform his life.

Her name was Lina Lee, owner of an upscale fashion enclave in Beverly Hills. Impressed by Paul's many talents and old-world experience, she hired him to produce a high-end line of leather and suede designs under the Lina Lee label.

The line was so successful, that by 1980, he had to rent his own space to meet the growing demand. That's when he moved into his current location on Pico Boulevard.

When I was with him the other day, I asked him to give me a tour of the place. Paul is a shy, reticent man with poor English, but his face lit up when I asked for a tour. Before showing me the back room – where he does the alterations – he led me up some creaky steps to a large, dark, ghostlike room, where right in the middle was one of those huge work tables you'd expect to see in a shmatte factory.

This upstairs area is where for years Paul produced the hippest leather and suede fashions in town. Since 1993 – the year his specialty went out of style and the orders stopped coming in – the space has mostly been used for storage, but, amazingly, signs of his former, high-flying life are everywhere. He showed me stacks of leather and suede samples from Italy, Lina Lee labels and bags, delivery boxes still filled with merchandise, order forms – all untouched from his heyday more than 15 years ago.

It was as if he were ready to turn back time and start that exciting life again on a minute's notice.

As he walked me through the room, his words seemed to accelerate. Even his English got better. He explained in detail how the operation worked: the size of the staff, who did what, where they cut the patterns, the machines they used, where they stored the samples, how many pieces they would finish in an average week and, of course, how everything was always "rush, rush, rush."

Clearly, this was not a life he was ready to simply clean out from his memory. His work has always been with real things that you can touch, and many of those things were still there in the upstairs room.

He could still touch them. He could still touch his old life.

When we came back down, Paul seemed to slow down. His voice got a little lower, his English more choppy. A customer walked in with a baby in her arms to pick up a dress.

It's very likely that this customer, as well as the many regulars who walk in every day, have never seen the upstairs of Paul's Tailoring – the place where Paul used to run a fast-paced, high-end fashion factory.

The only Paul they see today is the quiet tailor, the one who'll occasionally reminisce about that time in his life when he would walk upstairs and feel on top of the world.

"As we freeze their assets, we should also freeze their egos."

STARVING THE MURDERERS

December 4, 2008

I was at a Thanksgiving dinner at my sister's house in Orange County, sitting next to a woman who couldn't take her eyes off her BlackBerry®. The woman wasn't being rude; she was texting back and forth with her friend Peggi Sturm, who was holed up in one of the hotels under siege in Mumbai.

The woman showed me one of Sturm's nervous texts – the word "scary" was in all caps (Sturm eventually made it out alive) – and she seemed dumbfounded. Here we were in the middle of a warm and joyous Thanksgiving celebration, even as she was in such close contact with the human carnage unfolding in Mumbai, and she simply couldn't fathom where all this evil was coming from, or what anyone could do about it.

The notion of this pleasant and polite Orange County mother confronted by the ugly face of cold-blooded jihadist terrorism halfway around the world left me speechless, too. What could I tell her? That I'm from Morocco, so I understand this kind of stuff? That I felt like strangling the murderers?

So I suggested she read a recent essay from the Shalem Center in Jerusalem written by its senior fellow, Martin Kramer, the world-renowned historian, author and biographer of Sir Winston Churchill. Although the essay isn't connected to the Mumbai massacre, it touches on the broader issue of dealing with Islamic fundamentalism.

Kramer's essay, titled, "What Do the Present Financial Crisis and U.S. Middle East Policy Have in Common?" draws an analogy between the headlong rush toward disaster in our financial markets and what he sees as a similar fate for our foreign policy. Behind both, he explains, is "a well-practiced mechanism for concealing risk."

"The risk was there," he writes of the financial crisis, "and it was constantly growing, but it could be disguised, repackaged and renamed, so that in the end it seemed to have disappeared. Much of the debate about foreign policy in the United States is conducted in the same manner: Policymakers and pundits, to get what they want, conceal the risks."

By far the biggest danger Kramer sees today lies in how we conceal the risks associated with Islamic fundamentalism (or radical Islam, or jihadism, or Islamism, take your pick), which the West does in two ways:

First, it ignores the "deep-down dimension of Islamism," which he describes as follows: "The enemies of Islam enjoy much more power than the believing Muslims do. But if we Muslims return to the faith, we can restore to ourselves the vast power we exercised in the past, when Islam dominated the world as the West dominates today."

The second concealment relates to concessions: "We are told that the demands of Hamas, Hezbollah or Iran are finite. If we give them a concession here, or a foothold there, we will have somehow diminished their demands for more concessions and footholds. But if their purpose is the reversal of history, then our gestures of accommodation, far from enticing them to give up their grand vision, only persuade them to press on."

He explains that no amount of "engagement" can change that dynamic. In the Middle East, Kramer says, "there is harm in talking, if your talking legitimates your enemies, and persuades them and those on the sidelines that you have done so from weakness."

He concludes that the least risky path for the United States is to "show the resolve and grit to wear and grind down adversaries, with soft power, hard power and will power."

What Kramer is saying, in essence, is that it's very risky to negotiate with evil forces that have a destructive and religious agenda, because they're not motivated by grievances that can be accommodated.

Just like the moderate David Horovitz, editor of the Jerusalem Post, wrote after the Mumbai attacks: "Much of the international community clings to the self-evidently risible notion that there are specific, legitimate grievances motivating the murders, and that these grievances can be sated and normal service resumed."

In discussing the premeditated nature of the attacks, Horovitz added: "This is only the latest bloody declaration of war by the death-cult Islamists, seeking now to destabilize India, but ultimately threatening all of our freedoms."

To our sophisticated Western minds, these are bitter and inconvenient truths that must be concealed. We much prefer making loud and grand gestures to create the illusion of forward movement. So we set up toothless U.N. commissions, or orchestrate fanciful peace-seeking spectacles like the one at Annapolis, and then we wonder why the only things that really move forward are violence and cynicism.

And when violence does strike, we get angry and bang on the table and make all this noise about our "Global War on Terror," which only feeds into the jihadists' pathology and apocalyptic visions – and helps them recruit even more jihadists.

Maybe it's time we take a deep breath.

As we mourn and pray silently for the victims of Mumbai, maybe we ought to consider a quieter, more lethal approach to fighting the multi-headed serpent of Islamic terrorism, one that doesn't play to the movement's craving for high drama and worldwide media exposure.

Our goal should be to starve the murderers – of money, attention and prestige. We should fight them with every tool and weapon at our disposal and with maximum worldwide collaboration – but do it without fanfare, without honoring them with a loud war. We should target their training camps and "take them out" with commando raids – but do it without telling

CNN. As we freeze their assets, we should also freeze their egos.

The only loud noise we should insist on is for moderate Muslims and their religious leaders to rise up in anger against their violent brethren who are desecrating the name of their God and their religion.

In short, we should treat Islamic terrorists like the losers and cowards that they are, and do everything we can to diminish their unearned status and prestige.

This is what I wanted to say to that mom from Orange County on Thanksgiving Day, but there were too many kids around.

"Organizations that thrive with little overhead are usually great at providing experiences – singing, learning, debating, poetry reading, Torah salons, meditating, community organizing, social activism, etc. – that really move people's hearts.

NO MONEY, NO CRY

November 26, 2008

I gained one of the deepest insights about money when I worked on a marketing project for a casino resort in Lake Tahoe. The client had asked our advertising agency to come up with a television campaign that would dramatize their resort and new summer program. They loved our idea for a commercial, until they saw what it would cost – about six times what they had in mind.

When I brought the news back to the troops at the agency, one of the junior copywriters, who had just joined us fresh out of college, asked a question: "If they can't afford $300,000, how much can they afford?" I told him the most they had budgeted was $48,000, which was a joke if you wanted to shoot a fancy commercial with lots of elaborate sets and many actors and even a few helicopter shots.

"Forty-eight thousand?" he said. "That's serious money. In college, we can make three movies for that."

The next day, the junior writer came into my office and showed me an idea for a commercial. It was radically simple – and hysterical.

The client approved it, and the commercial turned out to be not just very funny, but very successful. And it cost even less than $48,000 to produce.

That little episode came to mind recently as I've been hearing heads of

Jewish organizations complain about the current economic crisis. Fundraising seems to be down everywhere, pledges are not being met, building campaigns are being put on hold, and the conventional thinking is that things will only get worse.

So what's a nonprofit organization to do? If you depend on fundraising to fulfill your mission, how can you continue that mission if donations are drying up?

There's no easy answer, of course, but there is that insight I picked up from my Lake Tahoe experience: The hidden blessing of having less money is that it forces you to be more creative and resourceful.

In my Pico-Robertson neighborhood, a classic example of resourcefulness is the husband-and-wife team of Nouriel and Yaelle Cohen, the neighborhood angels who for years have been feeding and helping hundreds of needy families. They have no staff, no overhead, no marketing budgets, no committees and no consultants working on grant applications. They take things from people who want to donate them and give those things to people who really need them. It's mostly food (from restaurants, markets and simchas) but also furniture and household goods.

Their staff is their children and volunteers. Their warehouse is their living room and backyard. Their conference room is their kitchen table. Sure, they dream of one day having a real warehouse and doing a lot more, but, until then, their "mitzvah house" will have to do. As it happens, this mitzvah house is starting to fall apart, so a group of local volunteers is now trying to raise money on their behalf for repairs and renovations.

But regardless of how much they'll be able to raise, the key point is this: With very little money and plenty of moxie, the Cohens have managed for years to serve thousands of free meals and help hundreds of needy families.

Everyone's cause is different, but I think this kind of resourcefulness can come in handy for the Jewish community during these difficult times. Like the Stanford economist Paul Romer once said, "A crisis is a terrible thing to waste."

A good first step would be to learn from groups that do a lot with very little. One of the most lively and stimulating Jewish experiences in the city is located in a nondescript storefront on the Pico strip. It's called The Happy Minyan. They've been singing and dancing and inspiring hundreds of people for 15 years, and they've never had a building fund or a mortgage. Maybe that's why they're so happy.

Organizations that thrive with little overhead are usually great at providing experiences – singing, learning, debating, poetry reading, Torah salons, meditating, community organizing, social activism, etc. – that really move people's hearts.

If your organization is having trouble raising funds for a building or a major physical expansion, now might be a good time to consider more creative and less costly ways of fulfilling your mission.

Let's say, for example, that you need many millions to build a Holocaust memorial, but you're having trouble raising the money. You might want to scratch those building plans for now, and, with a fraction of that money, take the Holocaust message to every school in America – backed up with minifilms on YouTube and on social networks. Be nimble and think big: Play up not just the Holocaust itself but the Holocaust idea of survival against all odds, and recruit spokespeople from all walks of life who have overcome impossible challenges. Have people create their own films.

In other words, focus on the emotional software of your cause rather than the hardware, and you'll come up with more inspirational ideas – and save lots of money.

Here's what I would do if I were the head of a Jewish organization and my fundraising was hurting. I'd pick the five brightest people connected to my organization, and one very creative person not connected at all, and take them off campus for a four-hour brainstorming session.

During the session, I would have an easel with this simple question written on it: What meaningful things can we do to fulfill our mission with little or no money?

After four hours, at least five good ideas should emerge. Since they won't be money-driven, they're likely to be creative, soulful ideas that will potentially strengthen the organization (and, ironically, even your future fundraising).

And when you do this, try to include in your brainstorming group a hungry and eager college student who knows how to make killer commercials for very little money.

"In between PTA meetings and carpooling, she has continued her Batman-like escapades into the murky world of radical Islam and made a nuisance of herself any time she saw fit."

WARRIOR MOM

November 12, 2008

Like any parent, Esther Kandel is crazy about her kids. For years, she has led the typical Jewish parenting life: PTA meetings, carpooling, after-school activities, nightly homework and dinner with the kids, preparing for Shabbat and holidays, and so on.

But behind this normal life, she has led another, more mysterious life that few people know about – one that includes, among other things, going undercover as a spy to expose radical Islamic elements.

Back in 2002, when the Second Intifada was raging, she would regularly put on a hijab and attend Islamic conferences all over Southern California. She was there to document the hateful venom that often permeated these events, reporting her findings to private investigators of radical Islam in America.

Her obsession with fighting the evil of terrorism, she says, started on a Tuesday morning at the Cleveland airport. The date was Sept. 11, 2001. As she headed for her gate, she remembers seeing a security guard running at full speed toward her and screaming: "Everybody evacuate, the airplane's coming this way!"

It was a false alarm for Cleveland, of course, but not for New York or Washington, and the events of that day left a mark on Kandel that still fires her warrior instincts.

One of her first battles was in the winter of 2002, when she saw a report on honestreporting.com about a fake Palestinian funeral filmed by the IDF, which showed a "dead" Palestinian body that kept falling off the stretcher and getting back on – an obvious hoax.

Outraged, she got a copy of the videotape and spent hours on the phone with news producers trying to convince them to air it. Eventually, she got it on MSNBC, where Alan Keyes used the footage to illustrate, in his words, "the issue of Palestinian credibility in the wake of increasing indications that the claims of hundreds of dead and Nazi-style atrocities were greatly exaggerated, abused for propaganda purposes to achieve a political result."

Kandel was just getting warmed up.

Since then, in between PTA meetings and carpooling, she has continued her Batman-like escapades into the murky world of radical Islam and made a nuisance of herself any time she saw fit, even with members of her own tribe.

At a November 2007 conference in New York titled: "Hijacking Human Rights: The Demonization of Israel at the United Nations," sponsored by the Hudson Institute and two Jewish organizations, she stood up and publicly took to task Ambassador Daniel Carmon, Israel's deputy permanent envoy to the United Nations, who had lauded the work of UNRWA (the United Nations Relief and Works Agency) in sustaining Palestinian refugees.

Kandel, who had lobbied Capitol Hill to cut off U.S. funding for UNRWA, which she accused of massive corruption and publishing anti-Semitic textbooks, was subsequently quoted in the Jewish Week: "It doesn't help when we are trying to educate members of Congress about the fraud and evil-doing in UNRWA to have a representative of Israel say that UNRWA is a good thing. I feel undercut and undermined by the government of Israel on this issue."

No cause, however, has grabbed Kandel's passion like that of 55-year-old Mithal al Alusi, who has been called the "bravest man in Iraq."

Alusi is the secular and liberal Sunni politician who has incurred the wrath of Iraqi leaders for doing things like visiting Israel, protesting too loudly about human rights abuses and warning against the corrupting influence of Iran. After he first visited Israel in 2004 – and made a star turn at a counterterrorism conference – he was stripped of his bodyguards and his position in the transition government.

Kandel quickly heard about his situation and got in touch with Alusi, who sent her an e-mail saying he feared he would be thrown in jail or killed by terrorists. She tried to help, but all the doors were closed. Shortly thereafter, Alusi's two boys were brutally murdered. Undeterred, he told the Los Angeles Times: "They were stupid to think that by killing my sons they would make me soft."

Fired up by the boys' murders, Kandel spent several months flying back and forth to Israel and Washington, lobbying members of Congress to move Alusi to the safer Green Zone in Baghdad. She and Alusi, who flew to Washington, met with a motley crew of sympathizers – including people like David Frum, Christopher Hitchens, New York Sun journalist Eli Lake and Iraqi blogger Nibras Kazimi – and eventually hit pay dirt when the late Congressman Tom Lantos, himself a fervent Zionist and Holocaust survivor, took up the cause.

In May 2005, Alusi and his wife were moved into the safety of the Green Zone, along with his 70 bodyguards.

But now he is in danger again, because earlier this year he had the chutzpah to attend another conference in Israel. He was immediately stripped of his parliamentary immunity and, Kandel says, is at risk of being tried for treason.

When I spoke to Alusi a few weeks ago by phone from Baghdad, he seemed to feel he had more important things on his plate than his own survival. He desperately wants the world to know the extent to which Iran has infiltrated the Iraqi government.

"Almost everyone's corrupt," he told me. "Half of the Parliament is working for the Iranians or the terrorists, and the other half is distracted by money."

So while Alusi fights to get his important message out, Kandel and her allies are fighting to get him justice and protection so he can continue his fight.

It's not clear where this Pico-Robertson mother gets her unrelenting passion to defend a Mesopotamian man most of us have never heard of, or, for that matter, where she gets the energy to make 100 calls in one afternoon in support of one cause or another.

This, however, is clear: With two daughters in college and a son already in high school, this carpool mom will soon have a lot more time to play warrior mom – a pleasant thought for victims everywhere.

"I have a wish that our eloquent new president will have the audacity to tell the nation that, for most of us, 99 percent of our happiness is in our own hands."

YES, I CAN

November 6, 2008

Now that the election season is over, I want to share a personal revelation that I think can help bring Obama voters and McCain voters closer together. But first, a little background.

I've always loved a good conversation, especially with people whose views are different from mine. But this year, I have been vacillating between McCain and Obama, and without taking a clear stand, I found it hard to have any decent debates. I haven't met too many other vacillators.

I have, however, met plenty of hysterical partisans.

My McCain buddies have sent me countless e-mails warning me that an Obama victory might jeopardize the survival of Israel and endanger America, and my Obama buddies have been certain that the future of the Western world hangs on their man's victory.

If I tried to mention at a McCain table how an Obama victory would re-brand America globally, or how his ability to look at different sides of an issue might be a good thing for the country, or how there are advisers around him like Dennis Ross who could hardly be accused of being anti-Israel, I would invariably get an alarmed response demonizing the man. Conversation over.

If I expressed concern at an Obama table about his lack of experience, or his relationships with unsavory characters, or his politically convenient flip-flops on major issues, or if I brought up McCain's experience and independent nature, I would invariably get an indictment of McCain's warlike ways, or a demonizing of Sarah Palin. Conversation over.

People didn't just pick sides. They dug their heels into thick mud and barely moved. Unless you were surrounded by like-minded people where you could just pile on, you either had very short conversations or screaming matches.

So I came up with a secret plan. I shut my mouth. Instead of telling people how I felt about the candidates, I channeled the big "O."

Not the big O of Obama, but the big O of Observer. I became an observer and a listener. I soaked it up. I asked questions. I observed how people argued, what set them off and how people on both sides acted in similar ways. I learned that when emotions run so high and opinions are so intense, you learn a lot just by observing and studying the show.

And study I did. I read important writers on both sides. I read National Review and the Nation. I read the key blogs. I would go from the passion of Andrew Sullivan and Joan Walsh on the Obama side to the passion of Victor Davis Hanson and Mark Steyn on the McCain side. Somewhere in the middle, I would hear the moderating voice of David Brooks.

Because I have many friends whom I respect who are strongly anti-Obama, I tried to muster some animosity towards the man – but I couldn't. Maybe it was because I remember how my mother cried on a November day in 1963 when she heard on the radio that President John Kennedy had died. I was a little kid, having dinner with my family in Morocco, and all I remember thinking was: Why would my mother cry for someone who lives so far away?

No matter how many alarming blog posts I read against Obama, I simply couldn't ignore the few billion people around the world who might soon look up in admiration to our African American president in the White House – just like my mother looked up to Kennedy from her house in Morocco.

And no matter how many brilliant and valid critiques I would hear against Senator McCain, I couldn't stop thinking about the decent and heroic American that David Foster Wallace wrote about so lyrically when he covered McCain's "Straight Talk Express" for Rolling Stone magazine in the 2000 election.

Back and forth I went, seeing the power and weaknesses of both sides. Instead of engaging in exhausting debates, I channeled my passion away from ideology and toward understanding.

And by the time the winner was announced, I had received an unintended blessing from my dispassionate journey. A personal revelation, if you will.

It struck me that no matter who runs the White House – even after a historic victory that my grandchildren will talk about – they still won't be able to help me with the most important things in my life: How I raise and educate my kids, how I deal with my friends and community, how ethically I lead my life, how I give back to the world, how I grow spiritually, how I stand up for Israel and the Jewish people, how I live an eco-friendly life – in short, how I help my country by taking personal responsibility for my own little world.

Those things are not so much "Yes, We Can," but more "Yes, I Can."

In fact, I have a wish that our eloquent new president will have the audacity to tell the nation that, for most of us, 99 percent of our happiness is in our own hands. While we await universal health care, we should take better care of our bodies and our health and save the country billions. While we await a better education system, we should read to our kids every night and teach them the values that will make them productive citizens. While we await government action to fight global warming, we should go green in our own lives. While we await a fix to the economic meltdown, we should learn to budget and spend within our means, and, for those of us who can afford to help, have the kindness to help those who have fallen through the cracks of our debt-ridden safety net.

The truth is, despite the headiness of this historic moment, neither

President Obama nor President McCain could do for us what we need to do for ourselves and for our country. If our new president can inspire us to understand this truth, he will bring about the real change we need.

"If I forget to pray one day, I've hurt no one except maybe for God, and I know He'll forgive me. But if I offend, deceive, mock or dishonor another person, I've introduced real human pain into this world."

GOT FORGIVENESS?

September 25, 2008

Would you believe that most Jews, including Orthodox and ultra-Orthodox Jews, don't fully observe the High Holy Days? I don't mean the basic rituals, like going to synagogue, reciting the prayers, listening to the shofar and the rabbi's sermons, having the holiday meals and saying the blessings. Most Jews do all that.

And I also don't mean the spiritual element, like using this time of year to contemplate our mortality, reflect on the purpose of our lives, ask God for forgiveness and resolve to become better people and better Jews in the coming year.

No, what I mean is that most of us neglect what is arguably the most difficult and meaningful ritual at this time of year: Going to the people we've hurt, recognizing our hurtful actions and asking for their forgiveness.

This can be awkward and embarrassing, but our Jewish tradition has given us the perfect little window to help make this happen.

It's called the month of Elul, a time for self-examination and repentance that culminates during the High Holy Days. As the month of Elul comes to a close and we begin the daily selichot (prayers of forgiveness), the mood of repentance becomes more urgent.

This is the moment we are about to enter right now: The zero hour of repentance – the Days of Awe before the Day of Atonement when one of our key obligations is to muster our courage and humility, go to someone we have wronged and say "I'm sorry, I messed up, please forgive me."

The problem, of course, is that while we routinely do this with God, it's a lot less comfortable to do it with our fellow humans.

But the other, more acute, problem is that our Jewish faith has this little wrinkle: God cannot forgive us for the sins we've committed against another person until we have first obtained forgiveness from that person.

Ouch.

Theoretically, this means a rabbi can tell you that until you obtain the forgiveness of those you have wronged, it's useless to come to synagogue on Yom Kippur and ask God for His forgiveness – because He can't give it to you.

If a rabbi did that, who would show up to the big show?

Most rabbis challenge us at this time of year to engage in things like more mitzvahs, more tikkun olam, more tzedakah, more Jewish learning and more spiritual connection. But in truth, if they really wanted to challenge us and encourage personal transformation, they'd pick the one mitzvah that requires the biggest emotional sacrifice: Having to suck it up in front of someone you've hurt and ask for their forgiveness.

To his credit, the ultra-Orthodox writer Jonathan Rosenblum, in an article from a few years ago, took his own denomination to task on this subject:

"Too often we arrive at Rosh Hashanah feeling woefully unprepared and wondering what happened to Elul. As Kol Nidre approaches, we rush around to those nearest and dearest to us to seek their forgiveness. But our requests lack the specificity that would indicate that we have given any serious thought to how we have wronged the particular loved one whose forgiveness is sought. Nor are our ritual assurances that we forgive with a whole heart worth very much."

For too many of us, the modern-day excitement and pageantry of the High Holy Days – the marquee events, the glamorous sermons, the fancy clothes, the elaborate meals – have eclipsed the essential ritual, the one that deals with the pain we inflict on each other.

If I forget to pray one day, I've hurt no one except maybe for God, and I know He'll forgive me. But if I offend, deceive, mock or dishonor another person, I've introduced real human pain into this world. And by hurting one of His children, I've also hurt God— who must surely be spending the holidays waiting for us to forgive each other.

I count myself in the group that God has been waiting for. I've done the basic High Holy Day rituals and recited the prayers asking God for His forgiveness. But when it came time to recognize my mistakes and ask people for their forgiveness, I've chickened out and used the classic cop-out: "If I did anything to hurt you, please forgive me."

Like Rosenblum explains, "without a real chesbon hanefesh, some form of regular spiritual diary – of both the positive and negative – we are in no position to ask Hashem or our fellow man for forgiveness. Where there is no recognition of our failures, there can be no genuine regret, which is the starting point of teshuvah [repentance or return]."

On a more romantic level, Rabbi David Aaron of Jerusalem, in a recent article, reflected on the intimacy of forgiveness:

"The best time to remember your mistakes and wrongdoings and ask forgiveness of your beloved is in moments of love. The contrast between the bad times that were and the good time that is happening right now generates even greater feelings of love and appreciation."

Imagine, then, the love and appreciation that would filter through our community this year if the sound of the shofar at Rosh Hashanah became our clarion call to seek out those we have wronged – whether it be our spouse, sibling, mother, father, child, friend, neighbor, colleague, teacher, client, business partner, supplier or stranger – and, with love and courage, admit our mistakes and ask for their forgiveness.

By returning to each other and paying our spiritual dues, we would repair our souls, enter the Day of Atonement with cleaner hands, reduce the amount of pain in our little worlds and allow God the chance to forgive us.

Not a bad way to kick off a new year.

"He thinks Palin is the opposite of what they call in Israel a 'freyer' (a sucker or a fool), meaning that she'll see right through the deceptive tactics of sneaky lizards like Ahmadinejad of Iran or Assad of Syria, who he believes would outmatch a well-intentioned and articulate diplomat like Barack Obama."

SHOOTING SARAH PALIN

September 17, 2008

I was visiting with a friend and Israeli war hero the other day, a guy with great stories named Elan Frank, and all we could talk about was Sarah Palin.

Let me explain. Frank was awarded the Medal of Honor in 1982 after he rescued 25 Israeli soldiers caught in a nighttime terrorist ambush deep inside Lebanon. The conditions were so risky that Frank's co-pilot suggested they abort the mission. Frank ignored the advice, and under intense enemy fire, he made a daredevil 360 degree move to speed up the helicopter's landing and rescue the troops.

That was 26 years ago. Now Frank is a busy filmmaker.

Earlier this year, he called the office of the governor of Alaska to ask permission to shoot Sarah Palin for his new film, a documentary about powerful women of the world. Because he had spent a lot of time in Alaska, he'd heard about the feisty Palin and thought she'd be a natural.

Well, guess what? She said yes.

So there he was in Alaska a few weeks later, with his camera practically glued for several days to the eight-months-pregnant governor as she went about her daily business.

As fate would have it, soon thereafter Palin became the most talked-about woman on the planet, and Frank became the proprietor of film footage everyone wanted to see.

While I sat in his office last week, he took several calls from the press, including one from a producer at Fox television, who's flying him to New York this week to appear on Fox News' "On The Record With Greta Van Susteren."

Frank hasn't yet decided what to do with all the footage. Eventually, he hopes to make it part of his "Great Women" series and air it on a major television network.

I couldn't wait that long, so he gave me a sneak preview of several hours of raw footage, including lots of private, off-the-cuff moments.

Here's my conclusion after observing Palin in action: If you're rooting for Obama-Biden this November, there's reason to be nervous.

I don't say this because I discovered something new and extraordinary about Palin. Rather, it's that everything I saw reinforced the attributes that make her a winner.

For starters, she's a likeable adrenalin junkie who doesn't shy from public exposure. Palin gave Frank unusual access, so we got to see, on a typical day: Palin discussing legislative strategy with her chief of staff; reviewing the bidding process for the $40 billion Alaskan gas pipeline; making jokes about having to dust her office; schmoozing with lawmakers; asking pointed questions of her aides; inviting Oprah, on camera, to visit Alaska; speaking emotionally about fighting for oppressed women around the world; rushing under a snowfall to greet her 7-year-old daughter at a school bus stop; flirting with her husband and calling him "the boss"; playing the flute by a window; and, while talking to an aide on the phone in her kitchen and making dinner for her daughter, reminding the daughter not to stuff herself on potato chips.

Through it all, Palin was upbeat and cheerful – but you can sense an underlying edge. Frank's camera captured some of that edge by showing the forceful movement of her hands when she felt strongly about something, or the occasional subtle glare when something didn't please her.

There's little doubt about Palin's competitive streak; she couldn't have succeeded in the rough world of Alaskan politics without one. Yet, unlike other driven politicians like Hillary Clinton, whose steely demeanor and exaggerated enthusiasm can turn off or intimidate people, Palin uses her folksy charm to disarm people. It's the proverbial fist in the velvet glove.

Beyond that, there's one sobering thought for sophisticated liberals who are aghast at the possibility that this caribou-hunting evangelical supermom will snatch defeat from their jaws of victory.

She's a quick study.

Unlike a well-known current resident of the White House, she's not intellectually lazy or impatient with details. What I saw was a probing, engaged woman who's always on – and is anything but a naïve, small-town hick.

I wouldn't be surprised if she looks more and more savvy as the campaign heads to the finish line. Unlike her critics who see her as a shooting star who will flame out, I see an ambitious newcomer to the big time who's got enough street smarts to quickly improve herself. (The question, of course, will be how quickly she can catch up and make up for her lack of national experience.)

Frank saw all of those things and more when he hung out with Palin in Alaska. Frank himself is an independent who's staunchly pro-Israel, and whose primary concern as a voter is the global threat of nuclear-based terrorism.

He's not overly worried about Palin's lack of experience on the world stage. He's seen too many "experienced" and worldly politicians fall flat on their faces, and he sees in Palin a "natural-born leader" with good intuition who knows how to ask the right questions.

He thinks Palin is the opposite of what they call in Israel a "freyer" (a sucker or a fool), meaning that she'll see right through the deceptive tactics of sneaky lizards like Ahmadinejad of Iran or Assad of Syria, who he believes would outmatch a well-intentioned and articulate diplomat like Barack Obama.

So yes, Frank seems to have fallen under her spell. But Frank is no freyer himself. This is a war hero who spent seven years in the Israeli army fighting a wily foe. He knows all about deception. He doesn't trust easily. He can tell real from fake and tough from soft.

If Sarah Palin is anything, he says, she's real and tough.

And in a dangerous world, Frank sees the appeal of a lioness who's real and tough. Especially a lioness who learns quickly, loves her country and hates to lose.

"How could I have not known about such a seminal moment in Jewish American history – at an event that King himself called 'the greatest demonstration for freedom in the history of our nation'?"

BEFORE KING, IT WAS PRINZ

A few months before President John F. Kennedy was assassinated, a short Jewish man stood on the steps of the Lincoln Memorial and spoke to a large group of Americans:

"I speak to you as an American Jew. As Americans, we share the profound concern of millions of people about the shame and disgrace of inequality and injustice, which make a mockery of the great American idea.

"As Jews, we bring to this great demonstration, in which thousands of us proudly participate, a twofold experience – one of the spirit and one of our history.

"In the realm of the spirit, our fathers taught us thousands of years ago that when God created man, He created him as everybody's neighbor. Neighbor is not a geographic term. It is a moral concept. It means our collective responsibility for the preservation of man's dignity and integrity.

"From our Jewish historic experience of three and a half thousand years, we say:

"Our ancient history began with slavery and the yearning for freedom. During the Middle Ages my people lived for a thousand years in the ghettos of Europe. Our modern history begins with a proclamation of emancipation."

Thus began the least-remembered great speech in American civil rights history, one that had the dubious fortune of being immediately followed by another speech: Dr. Martin Luther King Jr.'s "I Have a Dream" speech, which America just celebrated on its 45th anniversary.

But before King's speech electrified the world and became an anthem for a generation, a German-born rabbi by the name of Joachim Prinz spoke on those famous steps. In front of 300,000 people at the Aug. 28, 1963, March on Washington, Prinz, the rabbi of a New Jersey synagogue and a community leader, offered a taste of tikkun olam to a human sea of freedom marchers.

"When I was the rabbi of the Jewish community in Berlin under the Hitler regime," Prinz continued, "I learned many things. The most important thing that I learned under those tragic circumstances was that bigotry and hatred are not the most urgent problem. The most urgent, the most disgraceful, the most shameful and the most tragic problem is silence.

"America must not become a nation of onlookers. America must not remain silent. Not merely black America, but all of America. It must speak up and act, from the president down to the humblest of us, and not for the sake of the Negro, not for the sake of the black community, but for the sake of the image, the idea and the aspiration of America itself...."

To be honest, my first reaction when I discovered Prinz's speech was embarrassment. How could I have not known about such a seminal moment in Jewish American history – at an event that King himself called "the greatest demonstration for freedom in the history of our nation"?

How did this little gem slip under the mainstream Jewish radar?

Of course, that can hardly be said for King and his speech. Go on jewishjournal.com, for example, and you'll see a nostalgic love letter to "I Have a Dream" from someone who saw it live, and in the Forward newspaper, a fawning essay on the moral and spiritual influence of King's speech on the Jewish community.

But search in the major Jewish papers for Rabbi Prinz's speech – the one that march organizer, Bayard Rustin, actually called the event's "greatest speech" – and what do you find?

Zilch.

For a noisy community like ours, that's puzzling. And a shame, too. Especially at a time when the already complicated relationship between Jews and blacks is being frayed by a virulent and viral anti-Obama campaign, it'd be nice to recall a time when the two groups fought so closely on the same side of history.

And there were few times when they were closer than on that hot August day of 1963, when King and Prinz, who were personal friends, made quite a one-two punch.

Prinz's speech complemented King's. Whereas King railed against the lingering effects of modern-day slavery, Prinz spoke as a descendant of biblical slaves who represented man's first struggle for freedom. While King brought the clear perspective of the victim, Prinz offered the more complex dual perspective of victim and observer.

It was as if Prinz, who died in 1988 at the age of 86, was saying to the black community: "Because we are white, we don't suffer from the same racism that you do. But as Jews, our experience as victims of prejudice goes back to our earliest days. That experience has helped us feel the pain of others. So we feel your pain, and you can be sure that we will not remain silent. Our tradition teaches us to fight not just for ourselves, but for all of our neighbors."

As things would have it, it was one of my neighbors here in Pico-Robertson, Daniel Fink, who awakened me to Prinz's speech. Fink, a long-time community activist and member of the local neighborhood council, came by recently for a late night tea. Our conversation meandered: two Jews talking. After a while, he began recalling his childhood on the East Coast. Fink got all misty-eyed when he recalled a man he had met almost 50 years ago whose influence he still feels.

The man was a local rabbi who would teach Fink and his teenage buddies Pirkei Avot (The Ethics of our Fathers) every Sunday morning. The rabbi's wish, Fink said, was that one day they would use these life lessons to help enrich their lives and the lives of others.

The name of the rabbi, it turns out, was Joachim Prinz.

And while a great many Jews may not presently know him, sometimes all it takes to change that is one neighbor.

"Yossi and Dror may not know each other, and they might live in two different worlds, but they share something in common – a character trait Jews of all stripes seem to have picked up from centuries of being Jewish."

YOSSI AND DROR

July 16, 2008

It took me a while to see the connection between Yossi Samuels and Dror Dagan. I met them a few days apart on my recent trip to Israel – Yossi in a poor, ultra- Orthodox neighborhood of Jerusalem, Dror in a wealthy suburb of Tel Aviv.

I met Yossi first. Immediately, he wanted to know what kind of car I drive. He knew all about Volvos, but I stumped him with the Acura NSX. Then he wanted to know who I was going to vote for. He likes McCain, and he warned me about Obama. He also loved talking about wines – he's a big Merlot fan.

We were sitting and schmoozing on a sunny patio deck in a residential center for kids with Down syndrome, a place I wrote about last week (Shalva). It turns out, though, that Yossi doesn't have Down syndrome.

He's deaf and blind.

It was one of those horrible accidents: At 11 months, a routine DPT vaccination from a "bad batch" rendered him blind, deaf and acutely hyperactive.

His parents, American ba'ali teshuvah who had made aliyah, decided to return to New York because the ultra-Orthodox community in Israel had no specialized care for kids like Yossi, and it was against their tradition to hand him over to the state.

In New York, he attended a special school during the day, but nothing helped. For years, while his mother had one baby after another, Yossi was the "wild animal" in the bunch. Nobody could figure out what to do with him. So his parents returned to Jerusalem. His mother made a plea to God: "If I see any sign of hope for Yossi," she said to the Almighty, "my husband and I will stay in Jerusalem the rest of our lives to help disadvantaged kids."

One day, Yossi met an expert who specializes in working with the deaf. After a few days of working with him, the expert told Yossi's parents that he had the ability to learn Hebrew words and letters through the feel of his hands and fingers. Within a few weeks, Yossi's five fingers were joyfully pressing against the hand of his teacher to spell words like "water," "glass," "bread" and even "wine."

Slowly, Yossi went from being a wild animal to a wild lover of life. He wanted to know everything. People who knew "finger Hebrew" took turns volunteering to read him the news, to teach him how to pray and put on tefillin, to tell him about the latest Corvette in a car magazine, and, more than occasionally, news of the latest vintage of Merlot.

That was 24 years ago, when Yossi was 8. A few years later, his parents opened the Shalva center.

When I met him, his left hand was virtually glued to the hand of a translator. Apparently, Yossi is so bright that over the years, by feeling the vibrations around people's mouths and throats (à la Helen Keller), he has figured out how to make certain sounds. One of those sounds is a loud, primitive grunt that lets you know he's happy. He was happy when he told me that he'd love one day to meet a pretty blonde – and, also, when he showed me how to finger-spell "I love you" (index and pinkie sticking out), which I did several times.

A few days later, I was standing in front of a mansion in a wealthy suburb of Tel Aviv, when a blue sedan pulled up. As the trunk opened automatically, an unmanned folded wheelchair, secured by a mechanical contraption, slowly came out and snaked its way to the driver's door, which was already open. The driver, Dror Dagan, opened the wheelchair with his left hand and, with a quick motion of his powerful arms and torso, pushed himself into the chair.

For the next few hours, at an afternoon party, I nudged him into telling me his story. He had been in an elite commando unit during the Second Intifada. On his last mission, he tried to help a terrorist's wife who was pregnant and had fainted, and got a bullet in his left eye and one in his chest. Bleeding profusely and semi-unconscious, he remembers hearing "Dror is dead." After several weeks in intensive care, he survived, but the doctors told him he would probably be paralyzed for life. He fought the prognosis and recovered some motion in his hands and upper body, but a year later his condition remained precarious.

He did tons of research and found the top surgery center in the world for his condition (in Denver), but he needed $300,000 for the operation. Because the operation was so rare, the army bureaucracy balked at paying for it, so Dror raised the money himself by going door to door in a wealthy neighborhood.

Eventually, with the help of a phone call to the chief of staff of the Israel Defense Forces, he got the army to pick up the tab. He tried returning the money he'd raised to the donors, but they wouldn't take it. He flew to Denver for the operation, which removed traces of the bullet from his spinal chord. The operation was successful, and he spent many months in rehabilitation.

Today, still in a wheelchair but vigorous and healthy, Dror has used the money that the donors refused to take back to launch the Dror Foundation, which helps injured war victims navigate through the complex bureaucracy to get the best possible care.

Dror Dagan's dream is to walk one day. When he's not working with the foundation, he spends hundreds of hours exercising his paralyzed legs in a pool.

Yossi Samuels' dream is to keep meeting people and talking about cars, wine, Israel and the American elections – and, maybe one day, to meet a pretty blonde.

Yossi and Dror may not know each other, and they might live in two different worlds, but they share something in common – a character trait Jews of all stripes seem to have picked up from centuries of simply being Jewish.

We don't like to give up.

"In the field of newborn genetic screening, Israel's contribution to the world has been Israeli impatience."

FROM PICO TO SHEBA

July 3, 2008

I'm dying to tell you about a fascinating afternoon I spent with an Israeli scientist at the Sheba Medical Center in Tel HaShomer, but first, I want to tell you how I ended up there.

It started on a recent Friday afternoon with a visit to Supercuts on Pico Boulevard, located between Young Israel of Century City and Nagila Pizza, right in the heart of the hood.

One of the pleasures of living in a neighborhood is that you're always bumping into people. Well, on the day I took my little boy for a haircut, there in the shop's corner, sitting and waiting patiently while perusing a car magazine, was my friend and neighbor Rabbi Joel Rembaum, the spiritual leader of Temple Beth Am.

When the rabbi heard that I was leaving soon for Israel, he put his magazine down and told me about "amazing new things happening in the field of genetics" at the Sheba Medical Center. I was scheduled to present an ad campaign to the Foreign Ministry on Israel's contributions to the world, so this struck a nerve.

After about my third "You're kidding!" the rabbi saw that I wasn't just being polite, so he put me on the phone with a local philanthropist and member of Beth Am, Marilyn Ziering, who has been very active in this field.

One e-mail led to another, and a few days later, I'm sitting with my Turkish coffee in a laboratory in Tel Aviv talking to Dr. Shlomo Almashanu about phenylalalines, spectrometers, metabolites and other things connected to the genetic screening of newborns – including the day Almashanu had to plead with an Arab father to rush his sick baby to a hospital.

Almashanu runs the Sigi and Marilyn Ziering National Center for Newborn Screening at the Sheba Medical Center, the largest medical center in the Middle East, which gets more than a million outpatient visits a year.

The key visits to the Newborn Screening Center come in the form of 600 to 800 medical envelopes, which arrive every day at 4 a.m., and contain the blood samples of every baby born in Israel – Jewish, Muslim, Christian, Buddhist or any of the 100 nationalities that people the Jewish state.

Over the next 16 hours, Almashanu's staff of 10 will care for these blood samples like little jewels and, using the very latest technology, test each sample for 10 treatable genetic disorders.

Because of everything I've heard about Israeli know-how, I assumed the technology had been developed by an Israeli company. It wasn't. It's American.

What Israel has brought to the party is something else: Speed. This is critical because at birth, every day is like a week.

Take, for example, the genetic disease called PKU (phenylketanuria), which can lead to severe mental retardation and neurological disorders. Babies with this condition are unable to metabolize an amino acid (phenylalanine) needed for normal growth development. In infants with PKU, the amino acid accumulates and can quickly wreak havoc on the baby's brain.

This can cause enormous damage in just a few days. But if you can catch the disease quickly, like, say, within five days of birth, the baby can be fed a special formula that contains only a very small amount of the amino acid, and brain damage can be prevented.

Unfortunately, in most hospitals around the world, genetic diagnosis takes about two weeks. Not in Israel.

Over the past year, Almashanu and his team have created a high-tech/low-tech system to get a genetic diagnosis in, yes, five days. I won't bore you with all the details, but the key features are an instant, simultaneous registration of the baby's basic data at the hospitals and the screening center; a customized bar code system based on a social security number given immediately at birth, which minimizes human error and enables instant, centralized tracking of all the steps in the screening process; and, for the low-tech pièce de résistance, a mini-army of private, caffeine-injected couriers who drive through the night to collect the samples and get them to Almashanu's lab by 4 a.m., seven days a week.

In the field of newborn genetic screening, Israel's contribution to the world has been Israeli impatience.

Almashanu himself is a calm man, but there was one day recently when he was not calm at all. His lab had diagnosed an infant with a genetic disorder that can lead to sudden infant death syndrome. The doctor called the father of the baby boy and instructed him to take the newborn to the hospital immediately. For 24 hours, Almashanu kept checking with the hospital, but the baby hadn't arrived. After several more urgent calls from the doctor and the hospital, the father finally brought the baby in. By now, he was barely awake. They saved the baby's life with a few minutes to spare.

Two years ago, before the new system was implemented, the baby probably would not have made it. In fact, the father, an Arab man from East Jerusalem, had lost other children at birth. He assumed he would also lose this one.

Almashanu is obsessed with solving problems. The afternoon I was with him, he talked to the head of a hospital in East Jerusalem about finding more Arab couriers, because many Jewish couriers are fearful of entering East Jerusalem.

It's funny how we can make so much progress with technology, create million-dollar machines that tell us the story of our genes and help save our lives, and still, so much of life comes down to little things like who's available to drive into a neighborhood, or who's willing to make a million phone calls to pester a father to take his baby to a hospital.

And, of course, who you happen to bump into when you take your kid to the local barbershop.

"Amid the chaos of living a life of never-ending conflict, Grinstein explained, Israel has developed the resourcefulness and unique skills one can only develop when living on the edge."

THRIVING ON THE EDGE

June 26, 2008

Is there any hope for peace in Israel? Are things getting better or worse? Does war and conflict dominate Israeli consciousness? After spending a week in the Holy Land with very little sleep and lots of Turkish coffee, talking to bright people from the left to the right, I can report with absolute certainty that I have no idea.

This is true conflict – not being able to reach clear and coherent conclusions.

It's what happens when you meet very smart people with very different worldviews.

Let's start with Rabbi Michael Melchior, head of the dovish Meimad Party. This is the original man from hope. Over several coffees late one night in the lounge of the David Citadel Hotel, Melchior riffed on the importance of introducing spiritual values and a common God when trying to find common ground with our enemies. He spoke of numerous encounters he's had over the years with religious and political Muslim leaders, and how the picture is not as dark, or black and white, as it often seems.

He senses a growing (if grudging) tolerance of the Jewish presence among some of Israel's bitterest enemies, including Hamas. He is by no means naïve or a pacifist; he repeated to me several times that "even one rocket on Sderot is unacceptable." But he asked a tough question on the day the controversial cease-fire with Hamas was announced: "Why is it so bad that there is now hope that bombs will stop falling? We could have gone in and lost a hundred soldiers and achieved the same armistice we are getting now."

The next morning, before my first coffee, I heard a withering rebuttal from Caroline Glick, the Jerusalem Post columnist with an intense following in right-wing circles who had just published a column, "Israel's Darkest Week."

Glick, who showed up for breakfast with a lingering cold, has a crystal-clear worldview. The enemy's primary and enduring interest is Israel's destruction; hence, it must be defeated. Israel is run by "corrupt and incompetent wimps" who prefer half-baked measures to decisive action, a weakness that has emboldened our enemies. She believes that real peace will only come after military victory.

She considers the Gaza cease-fire a disaster because it legitimizes and strengthens a terrorist entity, which in the end will result in a greater loss of Jewish lives.

Glick's real genius lies in her deep knowledge of geopolitics. In her new book, "Shackled Warrior: Israel and the Global Jihad" (Gefen) she argues that Israel is fighting an existential war with both hands tied behind its back, and she elucidates as well as any political analyst the rationale for her uncompromising views. If Glick were one of those right-wing crazies whose favorite punctuation mark is the exclamation point, she wouldn't be taken so seriously. But she's an articulate and hard-nosed analyst who has little patience for mushy optimism and who believes Israel is on the front line of a global war against radical Islam.

I got yet another worldview when I visited the Shalem Center in Jerusalem and sat down with historian and best-selling author Michael Oren.

Shalem is one of those powerhouses where you walk down the halls and bump into people like Nathan Sharansky (which I did), Yossi Klein Halevi or any number of deep Zionist thinkers. Michael fits right into this world. When I entered his office, he mentioned that he'd been up late the night before finishing an editorial for the Wall Street Journal titled "Israel's Truce With Hamas Is a Victory for Iran."

Oren's conclusion was similar to Glick's on the cease-fire, but the more I spoke with him, the more I noticed the nuance in his views. He recalled a meeting he had recently with American Army generals, who, at the end of the meeting, asked him: "So what's the solution?"

To which he answered: "Solution? Since when are there solutions in the Middle East?"

Oren doesn't believe the Palestinians are ready or able to sustain a sovereign state, and he harbors no illusions as to their acceptance of a Jewish state, but he's highly informed about the military and is anything but cavalier when talking about potential military solutions.

He melds the finesse of Melchior with the no-nonsense quality of Glick. He sees the Palestinian conflict as requiring careful managing, rather than a desperate search for a fix, and he'll take Israel's problems any day of the week over the Palestinians' privileged position as the world's most coddled victims.

Like I said, smart people, different worldviews. The funny thing is, while I personally lean to the Glick view, I found myself nodding enthusiastically to all the views I heard, even to the dovish and soulful optimism of Melchior. Maybe it was the caffeine overdose.

Whatever it was, it took a pre-wedding reception in Tel Aviv, of all places, for me to hear something that brought it all home.

My friend Gidi Grinstein of the Re'ut Institute was asked to say a few words in honor of the bride and groom: Israeli actress Noa Tishby, who was marrying an Australian television personality. In front of a crowd that included many first-time, non-Jewish Australian visitors to Israel, Grinstein spoke of the miracle of the little Jewish state; how Israel has managed to succeed beyond all expectations despite being surrounded by existential threats – and he concluded with a simple but powerful idea.

Israel thrives on the edge.

Amid the chaos of living a life of never-ending conflict, Grinstein explained, Israel has developed the resourcefulness and unique skills one can only develop when living on the edge. These skills have fueled Israel's ability to thrive under any circumstances.

He could have added that maybe another skill of thriving on the edge is having very smart people with very different worldviews.

"When she finally told Dr. Hamburg that even with painkillers her suffering was becoming unbearable, he didn't downplay it. To the contrary, he told her it was 'useful pain': It meant that the treatment was working."

EVA'S PRAYER

June 19, 2008

It's not often you see someone pray to God with all their might for something to happen, and then, when God doesn't make it happen, thank Him profusely and even celebrate.

My friend Eva Brown prayed to God with all her might.

She was praying the day she called me a few months ago and said, "Can you come over now? I need to see you." By a stroke of luck, I had just finished a meeting in her area, and I went right over.

It was one of those bright California afternoons that make you feel guilty if you're not in a sunny mood. And I was in a great mood, until I got to Eva's place, a little bungalow in West Hollywood where she has lived for over half a century. With the sun's rays piercing through the drapes of her immaculate living room, Eva sat on her sofa and gave me the news: She had stage IV leukemia.

Her spleen was so swollen by the tumor that fluid had entered her chest. At 81, she was too frail for surgery. Before doctors could start aggressive chemotherapy, Eva would need a bone marrow test. She was told the earliest it could happen would be two weeks. When she got to the doctor's office, he changed his mind and said it needed to be done in a hospital. That meant another two weeks. All along, the pain was getting worse.

That's when Eva started praying.

She saw all these obstacles as a sign that her time was up. Her daughter was not well. The thought of losing her had always haunted Eva. So she figured this was her chance to be the sacrificial lamb that might save her daughter.

"Don't take her, take me," she prayed to God day and night, while reading Tehilim (Psalms).

As she was telling me all this, my discomfort grew. This wasn't the Eva Brown I had come to know – the feisty Holocaust survivor who for years had talked to thousands of people about the preciousness of life. This Eva Brown was ready to throw in the towel.

But I just listened, awkwardly, not agreeing with her resignation, but also wanting to provide comfort and support. As she saw things, after years of teaching people how to live, maybe her new mission would be to teach people how to die: how to accept one's fate with grace and dignity – how to live while you're dying.

We agreed that we would film her last statement, which we did a few weeks later. It was not pleasant. The video is a soul-searching, painful summary of her life.

In the meantime, while Eva was anticipating the next world, her good friend Sara Aftergood introduced her to another doctor, Sara's husband, David, who after talking to Eva immediately put her in touch with a specialist, Dr. Solomon Hamburg. The new doctor and Eva hit it off. Hamburg, a child of Holocaust survivors, took her on as his personal mission. The bone marrow test was done in his office in a day. The chemo would start a few days later, every other Monday for eight weeks. Hamburg had no clue that Eva had been praying for God to "take her." All he wanted was for Eva to live.

During the chemo treatments, Eva would call and tell me about the incredible physical pain she was going through. It seemed that every part of her little body was aching. She was in such pain she no longer had the strength to pray. When she finally told Dr. Hamburg that even with painkillers her suffering was becoming unbearable, he didn't downplay it. To the contrary, he told her it was "useful pain": It meant that the treatment was working.

He pleaded with her to hold on and fight.

He wasn't the only one who helped Eva fight through the pain. For years, Eva has had an extended family down the street at Maimonides Academy. The head of the school, Rabbi Boruch Kupfer, often came to visit. One day, knowing what Eva was going through, he asked her what they could bring. Eva wasn't shy: Food, she said, and lots of soup. She had no strength to cook, and she loved soup.

Well, don't ask. Overnight, the leaders of the Maimonides PTA – Kathy Hiller and Susan Toczek – turned into managers of a catering operation. For several months, hot, homemade food cooked by Maimonides families was delivered to Eva's door, along with words of comfort from regular visitors like Marci Spitzer and Sabina Levine.

It was clear that everyone in Eva's life wanted her to fight and to hang in there, not least her ill daughter. But the pain was so deep she had trouble thinking straight. She started to see God everywhere. She saw God in her daughter's eyes. She saw God in all the people who wanted her to live. She even saw God in the fact that she was in too much pain to pray for Him to "take her."

Maybe, she realized, God was simply saying no, it's not your time to go.

This helped her regain the will to live. Armed with the food deliveries from Maimonides, the dedication of Dr. Hamburg and the love she got from all over, she made it a personal project to conquer the pain of chemotherapy. Like she says now, pain became her "full-time job." It's not like she had no experience: Surviving 10 concentration camps in one year at the age of 16 had given her plenty of experience in full-time suffering.

As the weeks went by and her battle continued, her condition slowly improved.

On the Friday before Shavuot, Eva called to give me the news: Her cancer was in remission. The tumor had shrunk and was dormant. She still had some life left in her, and was full of gratitude to everyone who had helped her get through the ordeal.

Having regained some of her strength, Eva is slowly returning to public speaking, and praying with all her might that her daughter will get better.

She's hoping that God, once again, will know how to answer her prayers.

"Imagine going to celebrate your parents' 60th wedding anniversary. What kind of gift would you bring? Would it be personal? Would it have special meaning?"

A BIRTHDAY GIFT

May 15 2008

Here we are, Jews in every corner of the world, awash in a frenzy of celebrations for Israel – all because of a birthday. And not just any birthday, mind you, but one that ends in a zero.

In a marketing-obsessed world, milestones give us an easy way to promote our brands. For lovers of Israel, promoting the brand of Israel is important business, especially since the country has taken a real beating over the years. So naturally, when a chance comes up to give that brand a little shine – like a 60th birthday – we run with it.

That's why this year, Israel@60 has become the hot Jewish brand.

Every Jewish newspaper in the world has devoted a special section. Every Jewish community is doing multiple celebrations. Israeli embassies and consul offices are busy squeezing every ounce of Israel@60 good will from their local communities. World leaders are sending messages of congratulations. Elites from everywhere are gathering in Jerusalem at the invitation of President Shimon Peres. And, of course, every Jewish writer of note is weighing in with their personal reflections on the state of the Zionist project. (My favorite is Yossi Klein Halevi's piece in this week's issue.)

There's something intoxicating about all this activity. I feel like I'm getting drunk on Israel. The Jewish world is rising up and giving my cherished Israel a celebration for the ages.

So why, then, do I also feel a certain emptiness?

Is it because I'm too aware of the growing dangers that Israel faces? Or that I know most of the world will go right back to hating us once the party's over, or that these kind of big-bang celebrations just leave us with one big hangover?

Maybe, but I think there's more. I see a missed opportunity. I love the sense of pride that the celebrations have fired up, but I wish someone had launched the Israel@60 campaign with this theme: "What will you give Israel for her birthday?"

That's right: What will you give Israel for her birthday? What I think is missing from all the hoopla is a birthday gift from each of us to the Israel we love.

And I don't mean money. Money is the gift for normal times. A 60th anniversary is not a normal time. It's a time to celebrate, yes, but also to reflect, take stock, look deep inside of ourselves – and offer a special gift.

Imagine going to celebrate your parents' 60th wedding anniversary. What kind of gift would you bring? Would it be personal? Would it have special meaning?

Now imagine going to celebrate Israel's 60th anniversary. What's the most personal and meaningful gift you can make? What is your unique passion or talent? What can you bring to the party to show your love for the honoree?

Whatever your thing is, it's worth bringing. If you're a musician, organizer, writer, artist, environmentalist, cook, teacher, activist, comedian, doctor, architect, rabbi, Web designer, business tycoon or filmmaker, whatever your passion, it can become your personal gift to Israel.

Make a film. Write a poem. Start a Web site. Help at a soup kitchen. Organize a trip to Israel. Find a cause dear to your heart. In short, look at what Israel needs, and see how your talents match up.

So, what about me, what's my "thing" for Israel?

These days, the advertising guy in me would love to promote a side of Israel the world rarely sees – the good side. God knows the anti-Israel propaganda machine has done a remarkable job of turning Israel into a globally reviled country. And God knows Israel has more than enough critics who expose her many mistakes and weaknesses. But who is balancing the picture? Who is showing the other side? Who is spreading the word on Israel's many contributions to the world?

Of the $1 billion a year in Jewish philanthropy, how much do you think goes to advertise in the mainstream media the numerous contributions Israel makes to humanity? Virtually zero.

So this is my birthday gift to Israel: Ads4Israel.com.

It's a new organization whose mission will be to create and run ads worldwide that show Israel's incredible gifts to the world, in such areas as combating disease, developing alternative fuels, fighting world hunger, creating life-changing technologies, revolutionizing agriculture and much more. There are literally hundreds of areas where Israel has helped make the world a better place, and Ads4Israel will do its share to let the world know. The Web site will offer a variety of ads that donors will be able to support and help run.

Why ads? They're dramatic, quick and efficient. You can reach 100 million people with a powerful message in a few seconds. Grass-roots efforts, conferences, articles, books, Web sites, etc., are all valuable, but when 99 percent of the planet has been poisoned by three-second visual soundbites about Israel, the best way to fight back is with equally powerful soundbites.

Will this solve Israel's image problem overnight? Nothing can. But we can at least raise immediate awareness of Israel's value to the world, and that's a gift.

We each have a gift. What will be your birthday gift?

"As Sylvain Abitbol explains it, the expulsion and exodus of more than 850,000 Jews from Arab countries is among the most significant yet little-known injustices against humanity of the past century."

THE OTHER REFUGEES

April 24, 2008

Is there a more loaded word in the Arab-Israeli conflict than "refugee"? Is there anything more visceral or emotional than the sight of millions of Palestinians living in miserable refugee camps for three generations?

If any one thing has symbolized the Palestinian cause and put Israel on the defensive, it is this image – this powerful and constant reminder to the world that Israel's creation 60 years ago came with an "original sin," and that Palestinians deserve the "right of return."

You can debate the fairness of this claim, but in our world of easy sound bites, the image of Palestinian suffering has become an albatross around Israel's neck. The fact that few Jews would ever agree to this right of return – which would erode Israel's Jewish character – has made this an enormous obstacle to any reconciliation between the two people.

But here's the question: Will Israel ever be able to claim the high ground when it comes to justice for refugees?

This week in Montreal, where I am spending Passover with my family, I met a man who thinks the answer is yes. He is one of the leaders of the Jewish community here, and he is actively fighting for justice for Middle Eastern refugees.

Jewish refugees, that is.

As Sylvain Abitbol explains it, the expulsion and exodus of more than 850,000 Jews from Arab countries is among the most significant yet little-known injustices against humanity of the past century. For hundreds of years, and in many cases for millennia, Jews lived in countries such as Algeria, Egypt, Lebanon, Lybia, Morocco, Syria, Tunisia, Iran, Iraq and Yemen. In several of these countries, the Jewish population was established more than 1,000 years before the advent of Islam. From the seventh century on, special laws of the Dhimmi ("the protected") subjected the Jews of the Middle East and North Africa to prohibitions, restrictions and discrimination – not to mention harsh conditions of inferiority. Still, many Jews managed to prosper despite these circumstances.

Things took a turn for the worse after the birth of Israel in 1948. Between the 1940s and 1980s, the Jews of Arab countries endured humiliation, human rights abuses, organized persecution and expulsion by the local governments; Jewish property was seized without compensation; Jewish quarters were sacked and looted and cemeteries desecrated; synagogues, Jewish shops, schools and houses were ransacked, burned and destroyed; and hundreds of Jews were murdered in anti-Semitic riots and pogroms.

To this day, Arab countries and the world community have refused to acknowledge these human rights violations or provide compensation to the hundreds of thousands of Jews forced to abandon their homes, businesses and possessions as they fled those countries.

But activists like Abitbol are fighting back, all the way to the White House and the U.S. Congress. Abitbol, the first Sephardic Jew to lead the local Jewish Federation in Montreal and now co-president of the Canadian Jewish Congress, connected with this movement a year ago when he joined the board of Justice for Jews from Arab Countries (JJAC). Together with other organizations like the American Sephardi Federation (ASF) and the World Organization of Jews from Arab Countries (WOJAC), the movement, which is officially called the International Rights and Redress Campaign, toiled for years in obscurity.

A few weeks ago, they hit the jackpot.

That's when the U.S. Congress overwhelmingly passed the first-ever resolution to grant recognition as refugees to Jews from Arab and Muslim countries. House Resolution 185 affirms that all victims of the Arab-Israeli conflict must be treated equally, which means it will now be official U.S. policy to mention "Jewish refugees" whenever there is mention of Palestinian refugees in any official document.

It's a huge victory, but only a beginning. The United Nations and the world media are the next fronts in this battle for Jewish justice. Abitbol, a sophisticated man in his mid-50s who's fluent in French, English, Arabic, Hebrew and Spanish, has no illusions about Israel's precarious image in the world. But he's far from being a cynic. He's passionate about fighting for the rights of Jewish victims, and he is also a Jewish refugee (from Morocco). Yet he hardly acts like either a refugee or a victim.

Over tea at my mother's house, he reflected on the major influences of his life. One of the things that stuck with me was something Abitbol said he learned early in his career, when he was in sales. Abitbol, who has two engineering degrees and is chairman of an innovative software company called uMind, calls the technique "listen and adapt:" You adapt your strategy and your communication to the values of your audience.

He gave me a fascinating example. While in Dubai recently on business, an Arab businessman confronted him on the situation in Israel. Abitbol, seeing that the man was a devout Muslim who believed that everything comes from God, gently explained – in Arabic – that if Israel has survived so many wars over 60 years, maybe it's because it is "Inshallah" (God's will). Abitbol got the other man's attention.

Same thing when he spoke recently at a United Nations conference in Geneva on the subject of Jewish refugees. Directly facing representatives of Arab countries, he used the language of indignation and human rights that Arabs have used so successfully against Israel for so many decades, only this time it was on behalf of Jews.

Of course, he added that there is one major difference: Jews didn't put their 850,000 refugees in squalid camps so they could have a power-ful image on the evening news. They helped them resettle, so that one day, one of them would learn five languages and fly to Geneva to speak up on their behalf.

"The story goes on, and it's an epic one, full of high drama and human conflict. Unfortunately, most of it is not in your haggadah."

WHERE'S THE PASSOVER STORY?

April 17, 2008

I t's one of the great mysteries of the Jewish tradition. Every year, Jews around the world gather around a seder table to retell the story of our people's liberation from slavery. You can read a thousand articles, talk to a thousand rabbis, and they'll all say the same thing: At the Passover seder, we retell the story of the Exodus.

There's only one problem with this statement: It's not really true.

At least not if you go by the traditional definition of story.

Pay attention to every word when you go through the haggadah this year, and ask yourself: Where exactly is the story? Especially all you folks in Hollywood – agents, screenwriters, producers, actors – who live and breathe stories every day. Is this an actual story you are reading? Where's the buildup? The character development? The narrative flow? The climax?

The haggadah, as handed down by our rabbinic sages, breaks all the rules of good storytelling.

Sure, there are snippets of story here and there: "We were slaves to Pharaoh in Egypt, but Hashem our God took us out from there with a mighty hand and an outstretched arm"; "The Egyptians did evil to us and afflicted us and imposed hard labors upon us," and so on.

But the bulk of the haggadah is a mercurial mash-up of commentaries and biblical exhortations. A minute into the "story," for example, we are mired in a Talmudic discussion between Rabbi Elazar ben Azaryah and four other rabbis in Bnei Brak on the subtleties of a particular phrase in Deuteronomy – as they debate not the Exodus itself, but simply when and how often they should study it.

What comes next? Well, had the writers concerned themselves with the basics of storytelling, they might have continued like this:

"The year was 1445 B.C.E. The Israelites are now captives in Egypt, and the time of Joseph, the Jew who became prime minister in Egypt, is long forgotten. The ruling Pharaoh fears their numbers. The Israelites are an estimated 2 million in number. Moses, who had been raised in Pharaoh's court, is now living as a shepherd in the desert.

"As he is tending to his flock, Moses sees a burning bush that is not consumed by the flames. He goes to the bush, and, to his astonishment, God speaks to him from it: 'Come now, and I will send thee unto Pharaoh, so that you may bring forth my people, the children of Israel, out of Egypt.'

"It took some convincing to get Moses to agree to the task. Moses was not a good speaker and he feared that he would fail. But still, he listened to God and set out with his family on the long trek to Egypt."

The story goes on, and it's an epic one, full of high drama and human conflict. Unfortunately, most of it is not in your haggadah.

Instead, after the Talmudic debate in Bnei Brak, the haggadah continues with one of the great non sequiturs of Jewish liturgy: The Four Sons. Think about it. What do these four characters have to do with the story of the Exodus? In Hollywood parlance, they don't even establish a subtext, or plant the seeds for a future plot twist. They just show up.

So what gives here? Why is our annual night of storytelling so devoid of actual storytelling? How can we ask Jews to relive the story of their people if we don't explain it to them – and make it part of the official liturgy? How can we expect them to embrace and discuss a story that looks so disjointed and full of holes?

Sometimes I think we should contact the Creative Artists Agency and ask them to produce the world's most compelling retelling of the Passover story. Can you imagine the haggadah that an elite team of Jewish screenwriters and producers could create? Families and seder participants would be riveted to the page. The tension would build as each person would take turns reading from this extraordinary story – and no one would think of asking, "When do we eat?"

This all sounds so logical and wonderful that I feel like calling CAA right away. But before we rush off and rewrite our 2,000-year-old liturgy, it's worth asking one key question: Why would our brilliant sages tell the story of the liberation of the Jewish people in such a mercurial and fragmented way?

The usual answer is that we are encouraged to fill in the holes with our own questions and discussion. This response has never satisfied me. I don't know about you, but I'm more likely to discuss a story and ask questions if the story is told clearly and completely.

No, I think it's possible that our sages had something deeper and more subtle in mind. Maybe, just maybe, our sages were elusive in their writing because they didn't want us to get overly attached – to our own story.

This thought occurred to me during a recent Friday night meal at my place with two great thinkers from Israel (Avraham Infeld and Gidi Grinstein). We were talking about the need for Zionism to renew itself, and in doing so, to make sure it doesn't stay too stuck to its old narratives. Yes, it is critical to remember the stories and lessons of our past, but not in a way that deadens our thinking in the present or stops us from considering new ideas for the future.

In that spirit, it could be that our sages gave us a more grainy and less explicit version of the Passover story so that we could review it from a healthy distance – and not get so enmeshed in the drama that we fall prey to triumphalism or victimhood. In other words, they wanted us to own the story, rather than have the story own us.

Maybe that's the great hidden lesson of Passover: We can become slaves to anything, even to our own amazing story.

"There must be millions of stories throughout the ages of how little Jewish communities came to be, many of which we never hear about because they don't have any particular drama or relevance beyond their immediate surrounding."

PURIM ON THE PRAIRIE

April 3, 2008

What blew me away about the synagogue wasn't the painting on the wall of the old Moroccan rebbe Meier Baal Ness, which I had never seen anywhere else -- not even in Sephardic synagogues -- and which brought back memories of going on pilgrimages with my family as a child in Morocco.

Nor was it the charity baskets -- one at the entrance of the shul that contained food for a homeless shelter, the other in the back of the shul that was part of a bat mitzvah charity project.

Nor was it the megillah reading by a Portuguese Jew with a melodic style and Ladino enunciation I had not heard before.

No, those things were interesting and aroused my curiosity, but what really blew me away were the cows.

Hundreds of cows.

Cows that I saw as I drove for miles through the rugged farmlands of Central Oregon before reaching a dirt road that took me to a little synagogue planted right in the middle of five acres of prairie desert.

It was a shul called Shalom Bayit, the pride and joy of the Jewish Community of Central Oregon.

The first person who greeted my daughter and me was a man in his mid-50s dressed in drag, with a bright green wig, lots of jewelry and a pretty red dress with an open back. His name was Rabbi Jay Shupack, and he reminded me that everyone must get dressed up on Purim and be really silly. He wasn't too impressed with the clown bowtie I was wearing on my all-white outfit, so he quickly rummaged through a basket of costume hats and offered me a few.

This was my introduction to the little Jewish community of Bend, Ore., where my daughter Shanni goes to school and where I found myself last week searching for a Purim party and a megillah reading -- 700 miles and a few worlds away from Pico Boulevard.

As the rabbi was reading the megillah, engaging the congregants with questions and drawing parallels between Haman and Ahmadinejad, one thought preoccupied me: Who are all these Jews in weird costumes, and how did they get here?

There must be millions of stories throughout the ages of how little Jewish communities came to be, many of which we never hear about because they don't have any particular drama or relevance beyond their immediate surrounding -- quiet stories that stay forever lodged in the memory of the locals.

The story of the Jewish community of Bend is one of them. It's about a group of Jews from places as far away as South Africa, Denmark and Israel, and from areas all across America, who found themselves and each other on a wide-open land and became Jewish settlers.

It's about Jews like Izzie Oren, an Israeli rancher who fought in the Yom Kippur War and who decided one day to open a dude ranch in Oregon, who became a founding member of Shalom Bayit.

It's also about Alice Shapiro, who was living in Ohio 15 years ago when she decided to look for another place to live. She remembered that on a cross-country tour she took with her family years earlier, she had fallen in love with "the special air of Bend," a fragrant mountain and desert air she yearned to rediscover.

In the midst of the Purim partying, Shapiro recalled that when she first came to Bend, there were only a few Jewish families who would arrange occasional prayer services in church basements and private living rooms.

Eventually, they all decided to get serious and hire a rabbi, and out of the five rabbis they interviewed, guess which one they picked? The one who did a puppet show with his wife to tell the story of Chanukah -- during his interview.

Rabbi Jay Shupack, a yeshiva boy from Philadelphia who was part of the Jewish Renewal movement and who was once a cantor for a Chabad in San Diego, is one of those Renaissance Jews who's hard to figure out, because you get a sense he'd be comfortable with any Jew, from the most ultra-Orthodox to the most liberal.

He's also very comfortable with nature, which might explain why the Shalom Bayit synagogue is powered by 36 solar panels that produce one-third of the electricity they need, and that he dreams of building a wind-mill one day that will power the whole shul.

While Rabbi Shupack was going on about the great leaders of the shul -- people like Steve Leventhal, who was there at the very beginning -- he also mentioned the shul's resident "bubbe," Marion Tannen, who's almost 90, and its resident "zayde," Monroe Weinberg, who's in his 80s and who still writes songs that he plays on his ukulele to entertain the kids.

Today, the community has reached a milestone: With about 100 families and a budding Sunday school program, it has outgrown its space. So they've set up a committee that is helping plan their future and answer questions like: Should they do a major expansion? Should they invest in more educators? Should they start a new building fund?

You hear all these familiar issues, and it's tempting to think that Shalom Bayit is just like any other shul you might find here in Pico-Robertson.

But it's hard to forget the cows.

I took a walk outside during the Purim festivities, and as twilight fell on a land that looked like it reached all the way to the sun, I couldn't help asking myself: Which neighborhood is more Jewish, the one with a hundred shuls and kosher markets and storefronts that bathe your eye in Jewishness, or the neighborhood with one tribe of Jews surrounded by miles of endless land?

I thought I knew the answer a week ago, but after my Purim in Bend, I'm not so sure.

"When the shock wore off, part of me felt like an idiot for having been so 'realistic,' and for not taking more seriously the optimism of these courageous munchkins."

RAYS OF LIGHT

March 20, 2008

A couple of events over the past week have given me a nice dose of optimism for the Jewish people. The first event was a Little League baseball game in a Jewish league called Blue Star, where my son Noah's team, the Rays, were playing a very talented team called the Jays.

For a while, I thought I was in one of those "Bad News Bears" movies, where one team fumbles everything while the other team is smooth and confident. And just like in the movies, near the end of the game, the Jays scored five runs to go up 6 to 1 (they have a "mercy" rule in this league where they stop an inning if you've scored five runs).

Now it was the Rays' last chance. These cute little kids came into the dugout and, instead of being demoralized by the five runs they had just given up, decided they were going to rally. No kidding. In their first two games, they had barely managed to get one or two hits, and only walks and an error gave them their only run. It'd be a miracle just to get someone on base -- let alone score five runs!

You could just imagine the thought bubbles over the parents' heads: "These kids are in for some hard lessons, like you better learn to lose and it takes more than enthusiasm to make it in life."

But these little guys didn't know from grown-up realism. It's as if they completely forgot their past failures at scoring runs, and this was simply a brand new inning where anything could happen. While I was bravely trying to match their enthusiasm, all I was thinking was: There will be peace in the Middle East before the Rays score five runs against the Jays.

Well, 30 minutes later, I was feeling a lot better about peace in the Middle East. Don't ask me how, but the Rays scored those five runs. Grounders, errors, fly balls, a few walks, gutsy running, an amazing double and lots of wild cheering from the dugout -- including an improvised backward twist of their cap that they called the "rally caps" -- gave the Rays a miracle comeback that they'll probably still remember when they're grandfathers.

When the shock wore off, part of me felt like an idiot for having been so "realistic," and for not taking more seriously the optimism of these courageous munchkins. For the first time in years, I started thinking without cynicism about the incorrigible optimism that some of my friends on the political left have always had for peace in the Middle East -- an optimism I have rarely taken seriously.

It took a little miracle at my son's baseball game to make me consider the possibility of other miracles. When I shared this story with a friend who is to my political left, he took over my role as the cynic and joked that when it came to peace with our enemies, Israel might as well be "miracle proof." Of course I knew where he was coming from, but on that cool and windy Sunday in the San Fernando Valley, the miracle of Noah's Rays was so mind-blowing that I was in a mood to think only of miracles -- even unimaginable ones.

The second event that has fueled my optimism happened at my friend Rabbi David Wolpe's Sinai Temple. For those of you who were around about seven years ago, you might remember that a good chunk of the Orthodox community wanted to run the Conservative Rabbi Wolpe out of town for suggesting at a Passover sermon that the Exodus might not have happened exactly how it is explained in the Bible. Although Rabbi Wolpe's ultimate message was to promote faith and mitzvahs despite any doubts one might have about the literal veracity of Bible stories, this idea got lost in the front-page coverage of the Los Angeles Times, and the controversy sparked a firestorm that simmers to this day.

You can imagine, then, my shock and awe when I saw Orthodox rabbis and all these Orthodox Jews gathered at Sinai Temple on a Monday night to help launch an organization called Standing in Unity. About 200 Jews of all denominations were there to listen to Rabbi David Baron of the Reform Temple of the Arts, Rabbi Yitz Jacobs of the Orthodox Aish HaTorah, Rabbi Wolpe and the Israeli Consul General Jacob Dayan speak passionately about Jewish unity in honor of the eight fallen yeshiva students of Jerusalem.

What was remarkable was that the Orthodox were not simply participants, but were instrumental in putting the whole event together. Rabbi Jacobs talked about transcending our differences by focusing on the things that bind us, like preserving Jewish lives and Jewish peoplehood. Rabbi Wolpe connected Mordechai's message to Queen Esther in the story of Purim -- that she was given the unique power of a queen precisely to help save the Jewish people -- with the idea that our generation has been given unique powers and resources precisely to help our brothers and sisters in Israel.

Everyone -- Reform, Conservative and Orthodox -- spoke about Jewish unity.

Of course, it was easy to be a cynic and remind yourself that only tragedies seem to bring Jews together; or that Jewish unity is a tribal idea that undermines the importance of healthy self-criticism; or even that a night of unity hardly makes for a movement.

But cynicism and even realism don't allow for miracles. Jews coming together despite their sharp differences is a little miracle, even if it took a crisis to make it happen. It's like the story Rabbi Jacobs told of the British soldier during the Falklands War who pointed his gun at a lone Argentine soldier left in a foxhole. The Argentine covered his eyes and started saying the "Shema," at which point the British soldier, who was also Jewish, dropped his gun, hugged his "enemy" and said the "Shema" with him.

It was a week to be reminded that miracles do happen, in foxholes, baseball dugouts and even synagogues.

"After many years of being immersed in the Israeli PR battle, I've concluded that we're not likely ever to win it, and no, it's not because of anti-Semitism. It's because of something in our genes."

WHY ISRAEL MUST KVETCH

March 13, 2008

I f there's one question I've heard a thousand times from Jews all over, it is this: Why is Israel so bad at PR? I know that when Jews ask me that question, they're also saying, "Suissa, you're in the business, can't you do something?"

Jewish emotion never ceases to move me. I look at the pain in people's eyes when they see how the world hates us even after thousands of bombs land on our cities; I see our collective grief when Jews are murdered; I read the passionate e-mails exhorting us to stand up to our enemies, or those encouraging us to make peace with our enemies, and it's clear that Jews are anything but indifferent.

One thing Jews are always peeved about is Israeli PR. We want to know why the world continues to hate us, why we can't seem to get any credit for the good that we do, and why our image seems to get worse every year.

Well, if you're expecting some good news, stop reading now.

After many years of being immersed in the Israeli PR battle, I've concluded that we're not likely ever to win it, and no, it's not because of anti-Semitism.

It's because of something in our genes.

This was brought home to me during Condoleezza Rice's recent trip to the Middle East. Here's a quote from a New York Times' editorial on the result of her visit: "Her only accomplishment was persuading Mr. Abbas to resume peace talks with the Israeli prime minister, Ehud Olmert."

Think about that. Israel suffers through thousands of bombs launched indiscriminately on its sovereign land from a territory it relinquished to its enemy, then finally decides it has had enough and enters that territory to try to stop the bombing, and while the bombs keep falling on Israel, who decides to throw a hissy fit and stop the "peace process"? It's our "peace partner," Mahmoud Abbas, who calls our efforts at self-defense "worse than a Holocaust" and compels Rice to visit him with hat in hand and plead with him to return to the peace table.

That, my friends, is brilliant PR.

It's also the kind of PR we never do. Why? Because the Jewish way is not to throw hissy fits but to look responsible. It's in our genes; the gene of the stoic Israeli who can get things done without complaining.

Don't get me wrong. Taking responsibility is a great thing. It helps you build countries. It's just that in the snake pit of Middle East PR, it's the kiss of death.

Arabs understand this, Jews don't. Jews are task-oriented, not PR oriented.

It might be insane for any nation to tolerate thousands of bombs raining on its civilians, but to get so upset as to walk away from a peace table? That's too irresponsible.

The Arabs have always known that the way to get the world's sympathy is to studiously avoid responsibility – and constantly kvetch. How often have we seen Arab negotiators come out of peace meetings with a glum and pessimistic look on their faces, while our Israeli negotiators, with their steely resolve, report that they are committed and determined to keep pushing for peace?

Listen to Prime Minister Ehud Olmert after his country suffered through months of bombings, including the recent brutal murder of Jewish students in Jerusalem: "Despite terrorism and despite the pain, we are not relinquishing the monumental task of making another dramatic step that can bring us closer to building the foundations for true peace between Israel and the Palestinians."

Those are the words of a taskmaster, not a PR meister.

What creates good PR is pessimism, not optimism; being offended, not accommodating. Smart PR is geared to the people who spend nanoseconds thinking about your cause, which is about 99 percent of the planet. Those people don't look at your body of facts; they look at your body language.

When your body language shows no emotion, when you don't even react to being stabbed in the back, you look guilty. In the Middle East, the way to fight the PR battle is not to stay calm, but to show more outrage than your enemy.

If defending Israel's image was a priority for Olmert, he would regularly criticize the behavior of his "peace partner" Abbas, who continues to preside over the indoctrination of hate in Palestinian society, and who, while pretending to be a peacemaker, praises terrorists and reiterates his refusal to recognize Israel when speaking to the Arab press.

But unlike Abbas, Olmert doesn't kvetch about his adversaries. In fact, our formidable Mount Rushmore of stone-faced leaders – Olmert, Peres, Barak and Livni will kvetch a lot less about the murder of Jews than the Palestinians will wail about Israeli housing permits in Gush Etzion. That's why they cream us in PR. They're always wailing.

Sometimes I fantasize about being Israeli prime minister for a day, just so I could hold a press conference and say stuff like this to the world: "How would your country feel if two of your cities had been terrorized by 7,000 bombs since September 2001? Would you preach restraint? As the leader of a sovereign country, my first responsibility is to protect the safety of my people. I report to them. Until our peace partner Mr. Abbas starts to teach the language of peace to his people and shows that he's dead serious about fighting terrorism, we are very pessimistic about any peace process."

Irresponsible? Maybe, but don't be so sure.

Let's face it: No matter how responsibly Israel acts, Palestinians are always kvetching. And the more they kvetch, the less they feel like doing or building anything. Maybe Israel should give the Palestinians a taste of their own medicine and force them to grow up. And if they choose to remain history's biggest crybabies, at least they'll have a harder time blaming us for their misery.

If you ask me, it's the responsible thing to do.

"We will never be a Buddhist-like nation that wallows in peace and serenity in a quiet mountain enclave. That's not our calling."

AT PEACE WITH CONFLICT

February 28, 2008

O ne of the bonuses of living in exile is that you can see Israeli society more clearly, one lunch, party, speech or cappuccino at a time. When I'm in the Holy Land, I lose myself in a noisy, beautiful, hectic, joyful and soulful blur.

It's as if I'm inside a boat in a stormy sea. Here in the Diaspora, Israel comes at you in neat little waves. Over the past month, I've had encounters with four passionate Israelis, and each, in their own way, has helped me make sense of the craziness of what it is to live the Zionist dream.

My first encounter was at Beth Jacob Congregation, where on a recent Shabbat morning I went to hear right-wing Jerusalem Post columnist Caroline Glick, who has developed a cult-like following among fellow right-wingers.

Here is this petite, gentle-looking brunette who doesn't look a day older than 30, but listen to her speak and you'll see they don't come any tougher. During three long sessions that continued through late Saturday night, Glick showed a mastery of the geopolitical dynamics that challenge Israel on a daily basis.

Glick doesn't apologize for her contention that military victory against an uncompromising enemy is the smartest policy. Because she brings so much knowledge to the table, she comes across not as an extremist, but as a reasonable and logical thinker.

Of the many words she spoke, one phrase stood out: "It's not about us." Israel can dismantle settlements and make concessions and have peace meetings until hell freezes over, but that won't change a thing, not least the nature of our enemy. This is an inconvenient truth, but as Glick passionately expressed it, it is a truth we must deal with if we are to survive.

My second encounter was with two wounded heroes of the Lebanon war, whose first names were Haran and Idan, and who were in town to help an organization called Friends of Israel Disabled Veterans.

Over egg rolls and sushi at Shanghai Gardens on Pico Boulevard, they bantered, laughed and playfully needled each other, before Idan began telling me his story. He was at the head of a platoon that had just finished an eight-hour operation to take over an enemy hill. At around 4 a.m., he noticed that two Israeli tanks were stuck in the valley below – what they call in military lingo the "dead zone," because you're a sitting duck to enemy fire – and he immediately commandeered towing and armored vehicles to rescue his comrades.

They got hit with a "bad-ass missile," as he called it, and a firefight ensued. Israeli tanks came to rescue the rescuers, and in the chaotic seven kilometer trek back to the safety of the Israeli border, Idan, who was nearly unconscious from the barrage of shrapnel that had pierced his body, could only remember hearing these words: "Yaffe, stay with us!"

Yaffe was his nickname, and his comrades were pleading with him to stay alive.

I asked Idan what went through his mind as he was fighting for his life, and he recalled the promise he had made to his girlfriend, Yael, that he would never leave her. When he saw that I was a little shaken by his story, he lightened things up a bit by telling me that Yael had recently broken up with him, and that he was now dating someone else.

I had no luck getting Idan to say anything negative about the Israeli army, or even all those corrupt Israeli politicians we so often complain about here. He and Haran looked like party animals who would rather spend their nights in a Tel Aviv disco than in a combat zone, but as they both said to me: "When our country calls, we go."

My third encounter was with a talent agent who represents two of the lead actors in the Israeli movie "Beaufort," which was nominated for an Academy Award. At a raucous reception in a private home in Beverly Hills, with Israeli television cameras and reporters covering the scene, the agent talked to me at length about how Israeli artists struggle to get their work produced, distributed and recognized internationally. Before we parted, she said in a wistful tone: "If Israel put the same amount of money into the arts that they put into weapons, we would be the most creative country in the world."

Finally, I met with political analyst and author Yossi Klein Halevi. In a little French cafe nestled in Topanga Canyon, my friend Halevi said that most Israelis were willing to pay a heavy price for real peace, but that there was a general consensus among the people today that since a real peace is not in the cards, they should "tough it out" until the circumstances become more favorable.

Halevi held the same passion to defend his country as Glick; the same love of life as the wounded warriors; and the same love of art and culture as the actors' agent. He seemed to carry within him the views and struggles of all Israelis.

Maybe that is to be expected from a spiritual seeker who struggles to make sense of the bigger picture. As we entered my car to drive through the canyon, he couldn't wait to play me this new CD of beautiful Yom Kippur melodies, as if to say: "This kind of beauty helps us all see the bigger picture."

As I reflected on my four encounters, it struck me that maybe the Jewish destiny is not to obsess over peace and to end conflict, but instead, to be at peace with conflict. We will never be a Buddhist-like nation that wallows in peace and serenity in a quiet mountain enclave. That's not our calling.

Our calling is the struggle. Whether we are struggling with war, peace, art, ideas or God, living with conflict is our story, our collective journey.

The Israelis who met me here in exile seemed to be at peace with that.

> "What I gathered, after listening to Rabbi Abady, was that in the Torah-observant world, having a world-class kollel is like a city having a world-class symphony orchestra."

REBBE ROAD

January 31, 2008

I f the great Maimonides ever came back to life and found himself in Los Angeles, chances are he'd look for a house on a small street called Detroit, between Oakwood Avenue and Beverly Boulevard, one block west of La Brea Avenue. There are no holier streets in Los Angeles.

This little discovery happened thanks to my 10-year-old daughter, Mia, who informed me recently that she had volunteered me to be a driver for her upcoming class outing. Little did I know what kind of class outing it would be: a minitour of a very Jewish neighborhood – not my neighborhood of Pico-Robertson, but the neighborhood of Hancock Park.

Our tour guide was Mia's fifth-grade Chumash teacher at Maimonides Academy, Rabbi Moshe Abady. The tour is actually called a "Kollel Tour," because the feature attraction is a visit to the two kollels, or Talmudic study halls, of the neighborhood.

You will never understand the Orthodox world until you understand the idea of the kollel, which originated in Eastern Europe in the 19th century as a way to keep yeshiva students in a Torah-learning environment after they get married, and also nurture Torah scholars, teachers ("rebbes") and experts in halacha, or Jewish law, who would make rulings for their communities.

In America, the kollel movement was started after World War II by

Rabbi Aharon Kotler, the founder of Beth Medrash Gohova, a large yeshiva in Lakewood, N. J. Since then, kollels have opened across the country in all major cities, becoming a key catalyst for the growth of the Orthodox and ultra-Orthodox movements in America.

On the West Coast, the oldest and best-known kollel is called the Kollel Los Angeles, started by Rabbi Chaim Fasman 30 years ago and located on Beverly Boulevard, across from the Coffee Bean & Tea Leaf, the only cafe where I've seen Cholov Yisroel milk, which is imported from Israel and is favored by many ultra-Orthodox.

The first kollel we visited with Rabbi Abady was a smaller Chasidic kollel on La Brea Avenue called Yechiel Yehuda, where we met with full-time student Chaim Unger, who gave the schoolchildren a minioverview and answered their questions. I don't remember his exact words, but I have a clear memory of his message and body language: There is no better way to be a Jew and to serve God than to study His Torah.

How do you make money, one child wanted to know. Unger said that the kollel helps a little, his wife works a little and they basically just get by. I couldn't resist asking how he could physically sit down and learn all day and most nights. Didn't he ever feel like moving or running or swimming, just to get the blood pumping? He gave me this strange look, mumbled something about his wife having a Stairmaster and then explained how the study of Jewish law can be so draining that it is like a workout.

Rabbi Abady then walked us over to the Kollel Los Angeles, where the kids had lunch and heard from two more full-time kollel members. The message was the same: Learning Torah is heaven. I've rarely met such happy people. There is nothing they'd rather do than spend all day analyzing the intricacies of a talmudic tractate.

When I met up with Rabbi Abady a couple of weeks after the tour on a rainy Sunday night at the Coffee Bean across from the kollel, he acknowledged that one of the criticisms of kollels in general is that it doesn't seem fair that married men with children should study full time and not work. But, he says, students are screened carefully; the money they get from the kollel is too little to attract slackers; women consider it an honor to be married to a Torah scholar and, most importantly for the community, kollels can transform the Jewish life of cities and neighborhoods.

Here in Los Angeles, the kollels of Hancock Park have been feeding the community for years with leaders and Torah scholars – such as Rabbi Gershon Bess, who is part of the leadership of the Rabbinical Council of California, heads the highly successful Kehilas Yaacov synagogue and is a world-renowned halachic expert, and Rabbi Yaacov Krause, who runs the prominent ultra-Orthodox Toras Emes day school and is the head rabbi at Young Israel of Hancock Park.

What I gathered, after listening to Rabbi Abady, was that in the Torah-observant world, having a world-class kollel is like a city having a world-class symphony orchestra. The orchestra attracts the best musicians; the kollel attracts the best students. Even if you are not a classical music aficionado, there's a civic pride in knowing that your city has something majestic and superior.

For the Jews of Hancock Park and for many others, a world-class kollel is something majestic and superior.

And that includes the Jews on that little block of Detroit Street, where Rabbi Abady started his class outing as if he was a tour guide with a "Map to the Stars." With a look of reverence on his face, he walked us down the block and showed us how virtually every house belonged to a Torah scholar and prominent member of the Orthodox and ultra-Orthodox communities.

Over coffee Sunday night, he jokingly called that block the "holiest street west of the Mississippi," while reminding me that many of these scholars have been involved with the local kollels, primarily the Kollel Los Angeles. Hancock Park would never be what it is today without the kollels, he said.

In that case, my friends of Pico-Robertson, fasten your seatbelts. The rabbi confirmed that a world-class kollel is quietly starting in our neighborhood, under the tutelage of two Torah giants of Hancock Park:

Rabbi Baruch Gradon and Rabbi Daniel Danishefsky. It is currently being housed in Beth Jacob Congregation, and from what I hear, it's already attracting major talent from Lakewood.

The great Maimonides, if he returns, will now have another neighborhood to look at.

> "Karsenty, a Sephardic Jew and Internet entrepreneur, thinks he lost the first trial because the president of France at the time, Jacques Chirac, sent a personal letter in support of his opponent."

J'ACCUSE

December 13, 2007

P
hilippe Karsenty is not sure exactly when he snapped. He does re-call a certain morning in Paris when one of the employees in his software firm walked into his office, and, instead of talking busi-ness, brought up something rather unexpected: "What did you do yes-terday in Gaza? When will you Jews stop murdering Arab children?" the employee asked.

It was the day after the shot heard around the world – one of the many shots that rang on Sept. 30, 2000, at the beginning of the second intifada, the day those "brutal Israeli occupiers" allegedly killed a young Palestinian boy named Mohammad al Dura as he crouched for cover near his panicked father.

Within hours, virtually every television station in the world had played and replayed the now-famous tape of that tragic scene. I remem-ber being confronted myself by one of my closest friends, an assimilated Jew who knew I was a supporter of Israel, and who was quite shaken by what he had just seen on the evening news. There wasn't much I could say, because I, too, was pretty shaken after watching the same images.

It was a low point for Israel, and for her supporters.

For the next few months and years, the picture of the crouching, dy-ing boy unleashed a global wave of resentment against Israel and became the icon par excellence to incite further terrorist violence against Jews and the Jewish state. To this day, the Al Dura image continues to proliferate throughout the Muslim world, in everything from postage stamps, billboards and T-shirts to memorials, films and television shows.

For the Palestinians, it has been a PR bonanza – the money shot that says it all in one second: helpless victim of violent oppressor.

The only problem is, there's compelling evidence that it's all a hoax.

Beyond the stuff I've read over the years (most notably, an exposé by James Fallows in the Atlantic Monthly), I've recently seen evidence with my own eyes. I saw, for example, footage that was kept out of the original news clip, which shows the "dead" boy lifting his hand from his face, almost as if to say: "Can I get up now, or are you still filming?"

I also saw footage, taken during those infamous 45 minutes when Israeli soldiers were said to be shooting, that shows the impossibility of the angle between where the Israelis were stationed and the boy and his father. At the same time, I saw a Palestinian "director" staging two scenes of "wounded" Palestinians being carried off to ambulances, with one of the participants applauding after a scene was completed.

I saw close-ups that showed there were no gunshot wounds to the father or the kid – during the time they both appeared dead and immobile – with the only "red stuff" being on a rag that appeared to be a prop. I saw a camera tripod conveniently placed a few feet from the crouching boy. In short, I saw overwhelming evidence that the whole thing was staged; but perhaps the most chilling thing was the edited French newscast that cobbled together all these staged scenes, creating the impression that the Israelis killed a helpless child.

All this was shown to me by a French gentleman named Philippe Karsenty.

More than 100 years after another Frenchman named Emile Zola wrote the famous "J'Accuse!" (I Accuse!) declaration of anti-Semitism by French officials in the Dreyfus Affair, Karsenty has been fighting an uphill battle for the last five years to expose what he calls a "slander against the

Jewish nation."

As he was enjoying some Parisian-style French fries the other day at Shilo's while on a short visit to America, Karsenty's passion on this subject could not be contained. He didn't wait to finish his fries before he pulled out his laptop to show me the evidence. This is the same evidence that is now being shown in his ongoing trial in France against the French television station that sued him for libel a couple of years ago – and won.

But after they turned the tables on him, he is turning the tables on them.

Through his appeal, which began last month, the evidence of a hoax has been gushing out, and the number of his supporters, even among the anti-Israel intelligentsia in Europe, is growing. It helps that his accusers in court have been anything but forthcoming, producing, for example, 18 minutes of original footage instead of the 27 the cameraman swore he shot.

Karsenty, a Sephardic Jew and Internet entrepreneur, thinks he lost the first trial because the president of France at the time, Jacques Chirac, sent a personal letter in support of his opponent. But now, with the next hearing coming up in Paris on Feb. 27 and more evidence coming out, the momentum is shifting to Karsenty's side. (One sure sign of momentum is that he's already stimulating interest from Hollywood to turn his crusade into an "Erin Brockovich"-type movie.)

Karsenty is clearly an ambitious man, and his ambition is fueled by outrage.

Outrage at the anti-Israel and anti-Jewish bias in Europe and in his home country of France, where he says he was maligned as a "conspiracy nut," and where Israel is usually "guilty until proven innocent." Outrage at the anti-Semitism that was awakened by the Al Dura global "PR campaign." Outrage at the general incompetence and timidity of the Israeli diplomatic corps, who rarely publicly confront the lies against their country.

And, finally, outrage at the Jewish groups who jump to scrutinize and criticize Israel over every roadblock and outpost, but who have remained remarkably quiet over this Palestinian deception that has contributed to so much violence against Jews.

Ironically, he's not especially outraged at the Palestinian deceivers. As he says, calmly: "They lie. That's what they're taught to do. That's how they fight."

Karsenty would rather fight with the truth.

"For every million we raise for children in Africa, certainly a worthy cause, how many hungry Jewish kids will we not feed or help send to a Jewish school?"

TIKKUN FOR WHICH OLAM?

November 1, 2007

I f you want to be popular in the Jewish world today, just say tikkun olam. Everywhere you go it seems that Jews of all stripes are jumping on this universal bandwagon.

It's not just the Reform, Conservative, Reconstructionist, secular, progressive and humanistic groups. Many Orthodox are also getting involved.

What's going on? What is it about this notion of "repairing the world" that makes Jews go gaga? And who decided that we the Jews – with less than half of 1 percent of the world's population – should become the Great Fixers of Humanity?

Recently, in one day, I got to experience three different views of tikkun olam. The last view was so politically incorrect, it was almost embarrassing.

Let's start with the first one. It's lunchtime at the Magic Carpet on Pico Boulevard, and I'm enjoying myself with two prominent progressive Jews of the community. It's the kind of lunch where you get a big "l'chaim" just by blurting out words like social justice and universal health care. If you want a really big hug, just say "Palestinian rights."

This is classic tikkun olam: There are problems and injustices in the world, and it is our duty to try to fix them. Economic injustice; reforming the criminal justice system; promoting interfaith dialogue; fighting hunger and homelessness; fighting global warming; helping the dying children of Darfur; and so on.

This approach has talmudic roots in the mishnaic term "mipnei tik-kun ha-olam," which can be translated as "in the interest of public policy." As you can read on the Web site MyJewishLearning.com, the term refers to "social policy legislation providing extra protection to those potentially at a disadvantage – governing, for example, just conditions for the writing of divorce decrees and for the freeing of slaves."

In modern-day America, classic tikkun olam has evolved into full-blown social activism that for many Jews is the primary expression of their Judaism.

I got my second view of tikkun olam several hours later when I attended "An Encounter With Jewish Spirituality" at the home of Rabbi Abner Weiss in Westwood. Rabbi Weiss is one of those renaissance Jews: an Orthodox scholar, author, trained psychologist, expert in kabbalah and leader of a congregation (Westwood Village Synagogue). He has just launched this new "Encounter" program to provide a "kosher" Jewish yoga and meditation experience for those who haven't found spirituality in traditional Judaism.

In his introduction, the rabbi went back to the time of Abraham to talk about a world "not lit, but in flames" and how we partner with God to put out the flames. Abraham was the first hero of tikkun olam, not as a holy priest, but as an everyman who "chose God," "loved without reason" and performed simple acts of loving kindness.

But in kabbalah, the rabbi went on, "Tikkun olam is a lot more than social activism."

In this "spiritual" view, all mitzvot have the power to change the world. Because the mitzvah has a Divine origin, it also has a Divine effect. Thus, lighting the Shabbat candles, making a blessing before you eat or honoring your parents has the same cosmic power to "repair the world" as any demonstration in front of the federal building to raise the minimum wage.

While lauding the work of social activism, the rabbi impressed on us that in the mystical tradition, tikkun olam starts from the "inside out" – we repair ourselves through deep contemplation and by clinging to God and His commandments, like Abraham did, which, in turn, gives us the strength, humility and wisdom to make our world holy.

That same night, on an Internet reader forum, I stumbled on yet a third view of tikkun olam, one I can charitably describe as "tribal."

It was a rambling, passionate rant that boiled down to this: "The Jews should take care of Jews, and let others worry about their own." In other words: Tikkun, yes, but for our own olam.

This wasn't just politically incorrect; it was downright offensive. How dare we focus on ourselves and forget the rest of the world?

But that response seemed too predictable, so I gave it some serious thought. That's when it got embarrassing. You see, I confess that the tribal rant struck a deep tribal chord in me, and brought out stuff that had been brewing inside for a while.

I wondered: Have we gone a little too far with our passion for tikkun olam? Can this grand love affair with "repairing humanity" become a run-away train that will take Jews further and further away from the binding glue of Jewish peoplehood?

For every million we raise for children in Africa, certainly a worthy cause, how many hungry Jewish kids will we not feed or help send to a Jewish school?

I know the classic response: "It's not either/or, we must do both." Well, that may be ideal, but in the real world, where 90 percent of Jewish tzedakah goes to non-Jewish causes, too many Jews are not doing both.

Let's face it: there's something quite intoxicating about tikkun olam – this notion of a little tribe looking out for the whole planet. After you've tasted that global Kool-Aid, who feels like schlepping to La Brea Boulevard to pack food boxes for needy Jews?

Don't get me wrong. It's not that I don't care about Muslim children dying in Darfur. But why can't we hold accountable the billion Muslims around the world who haven't lifted a finger to help their own brothers and sisters? If we encourage other groups and nations to take better care of their own, does that count as tikkun olam?

For Jews, what is the appropriate balance between "repair of the whole world" and "repair of the Jewish world"? Is it in balance now? Has our glorifying of tikkun olam contributed to the modest percentage of Jewish money that goes to Jewish causes – and the declining interest in Zionism among young American Jews?

If, for many Jews, social activism has become "the new Judaism," will this overshadow foundational Jewish practices like Shabbat and Torah learning that may not seem as "sexy" and "relevant"?

And should we pay more attention to the spiritual approach to tikkun olam that teaches us that all of God's mitzvot can help repair the world?

If you ask me, we're due for an honest debate on the untouchable – and touchy – subject of tikkun olam.

"For the rest of her life, she would grieve the 59 other hugs that would never happen – the hugs for her mother, four siblings and the 54 other relatives who never made it back."

"THEY KILLED US LIKE TERMITES"

October 18, 2007

W hen the girl was two years old, she became so sick with pneumonia that the doctors told her mother there was nothing more they could do, to just take her home.

Her father, a rabbi, arranged a minyan of 10 men to say special blessings. She lived.

At one point in her young life, she had received so many blessings for so many illnesses that her parents gave her a second name: Bracha.

At 16, she was sent to 10 different concentration camps. Near the end, she was forced to march for two weeks through the rain, without water or food. She survived on insects and wild mushrooms. By then, she weighed less than 65 pounds, and with typhus ravaging her body, she was barely clinging to life. When she was rescued by a Yiddish-speaking American soldier at 4 a.m. one morning, in an open, muddy field in western Germany, she could hardly move or say a word.

To reunite with her father in a Hungarian town called Miskolc, she had to tie herself to the roof of a train for three days, all the while breathing the fumes of the locomotive.

When she finally tracked down her father, she gave him "the hug that would never end." For the rest of her life, she would grieve the 59 other hugs that would never happen – the hugs for her mother, four siblings and the 54 other relatives who never made it back.

More than six decades after that bittersweet reunion, Eva Brown, a tiny 80-year-old walking testament to the ideal of survival, is sitting at my Shabbat table, doing what she does best: telling stories and smiling.

She's one of the happiest people I know.

Eva was my neighbor for many years before I moved to the Pico-Robertson neighborhood, and I would often see her walking to Cedars-Sinai to do her charity work. She would come over for holiday meals and play with the children. In her little bungalow, she told me how much she missed her husband of 50 years, Ernie, who passed away 10 years ago. We also had fun: She was my "date" once to the Maimonides' trustees dinner – a fancy affair for which she insisted that we take the Acura NSX sports car, not the minivan.

No matter where we were or what we talked about, her smile never went away.

At our Shabbat table, on the day after Simchat Torah, she was telling stories to my mother, my three sisters and some of my kids, tales of her dark days in those 10 concentration camps. The hint of a smile never faded from her face.

For a woman who's seen so much darkness and lost so much, and who often feels very alone, how do you explain this ability to keep smiling?

Is it the cliché that when you go through hell, you appreciate all the little blessings of life? No doubt, but I think there's more.

As I've gotten to know her better, I've seen that a key part of Eva's joy comes from her ability to remember not just darkness, but love. She's more than a survivor, she's a lover.

She remembers the love of her father, who told her to look in the mirror every morning and ask: "What can I do today to help someone else?"

She remembers the love of her younger brother Heschel, who was 10 years her junior and whom she raised like her own son.

She remembers the love of her soul mate and husband, Ernie, who for years would cuddle with Eva on his lap, rather than have her sit on a chair.

Her memories of love overflow into the present. Like the well in the backyard of her childhood home that provided water to sustain life, the deep love she feels for her family, including her two beautiful daughters and one granddaughter, is a well of joy that sustains her today. The more she feels love, the more she loves life.

For years, she has been expressing that love by sharing her story in schools, community centers and at the Museum of Tolerance. Now, her very own book, "If You Save One Life," which she wrote with Thomas Fields-Meyer, is out. She hopes that her story of conquering darkness will inspire others to do the same.

Occasionally, though, she is reminded that the darkness can win out.

She confided to me that a recent event had shaken her up. She had to fumigate her house. Her husband used to take care of these things, now she has to. As she was making the final preparations, something in her snapped. She was told to carefully wrap all the little items in the house that might be damaged by the fumigation – things like toothpaste and bars of soap.

As she was wrapping the toothpaste, she couldn't resist pouring out her soul to Jose, the fumigator from El Salvador. How could I be so protective of a stupid toothpaste, she asked him, while no one cared enough to protect the millions who died in that other fumigation 65 years ago? Jose saw the sadness on her face and wanted to hear more, so she told him her story. Finally, she yelled out: "They killed us like termites!"

This was not the cheerful Eva I knew, the one that is moved by love. This was the Eva that had earned the right to hate and get angry. The image of living termites being killed by gas was simply too graphic – it brought back memories that were too dark. She cried every night for two weeks, she told me, until she "ran out of tears."

She sounded a lot better, though, when she told me that Jose the fumigator wanted to bring his children over to hear her story.

Maybe that's the secret to Eva Brown's smile – knowing there are people out there who will always want to hear her story.

> "You can be wildly imaginative and successful in marketing and 'presenting' your cause, yet still continue to develop the Talmudic-like substance to back it up."

DAZE OF AWE

October 4, 2007

After two days of talking marketing with Jewish organizations, I've come to appreciate that marketing is not a very Jewish idea. Think about it. Marketing is all spin and presentation. What did we, the Jews, do at our first great marketing opportunity?

The year was 70 C.E. The center of our existence – the Holy Temple – had just been destroyed. Did we reach out to the world and strengthen our standing by launching an "image campaign" to attract more adherents to our faith?

Or did we go off and spend 1,900 years trying to improve our product?

Indeed, for centuries, our Jewish sages worked to interpret, refine and better understand our Holy Book. And, in the process, they taught us that the Jewish way has little to do with the flash and seduction of marketing, and a lot to do with the substance of introspection and refinement.

Having said that, most Jewish organizations today will tell you they "need marketing."

Maybe that's why fellow marketer Gary Wexler and I got an enthusiastic response to our Days of Awe offer of free marketing advice to the Los Angeles Jewish community.

A total of 26 Jewish nonprofit organizations registered for individual sessions on Sept. 18 and 19 at the Crowne Plaza Hotel on Beverly Boulevard at the corner of Pico.

It was an intense and dizzying experience. For two days, while Rabbi Shlomo Schwartz was giving out New Year blessings in an adjacent area, Gary and I huddled in a bunker-like conference room where we engaged in "speed meetings" with a wide cross-section of the Jewish world – and had to come up with marketing ideas on the spot.

We could probably write a book about our two-day whirlwind, and maybe one day we will. But for now, here's a taste of some of the groups who came and what we said to them.

We met a hospice group that deals with one of life's more sensitive areas: helping people who are at the end of their days. They wanted their specialty to become more recognized. Our suggestion: Create a new mitzvah for the Jewish world. Just like you have bar mitzvahs and shivas, this mitzvah would be called "The Last Cycle." It would have its own rituals and receive the same reverence and attention to detail given to other life cycles.

We also met a leader of an old, run-down shul in the Pico-Robertson neighborhood that had lost its rabbi and many members and was desperate for any idea. We suggested banners on their storefront to promote the shul as the "real shtibl in the hood" with "nothing hip," just "davening and a little herring."

A JCC in the San Fernando Valley, which had lost use of its key asset – the swimming pool – was also eager for a big idea. We suggested having kids build the world's biggest Chanukah menorah in the empty pool using recycled soda cans, inviting the mayor and the city's press , and creating a rebirth of excitement based on unique community-wide events.

A small Holocaust museum had a problem: What do you do when the city already has one of the world's best, the Wiesenthal Center's Museum of Tolerance? Our suggestion: Instead of playing up the notion of a "martyr's memorial," play up the more dynamic idea of "survival" – and make it a more hopeful, universal and future-oriented experience.

The Jewish Federation of the Greater San Gabriel and Pomona Valleys wanted to continue to pull the two communities together. Our idea: Do an event – like a community Passover seder – right at the border of the two areas, and continue the "Events at the Border" theme throughout the year.

The Israel Institute Green Technology Fund came in with a Power-Point presentation outlining how they can harness the skill of Israeli scientists to contribute green technology to the world. We gave them a new name for their pitch – "A Convenient Truth" – and helped them with strategies for high-powered fund-raising.

For a group that wanted to keep the Yiddish language alive, we suggested having "Yiddish Cooking Nights," in homes throughout the community, that would combine the Yiddish language with the all-time No. 1 Jewish marketing hook: food.

On and on it went like this, with one group after another sharing their stories and challenges, and each hoping for a little marketing injection – in thirty minutes.

We saw all kinds of groups: a new community mikveh; a Reform temple; an Orthodox high school; college and high school outreach groups; two Jewish universities; a Chasidic Jew's Kung Fu program for disabled kids; the Board of Jewish Education; Jewish World Watch; Koreh LA and even venerable institutions like Hadassah.

Each cause had its own drama.

Some touched us especially deeply, like the Jewish group that travels to tiny villages in Ethiopia to care for fellow Jews. We suggested they create Ethiopian events and Shabbatons throughout the Los Angeles Jewish community to build awareness for this unique culture, and start a campaign asking for Jews to help out another "old Jewish neighborhood."

In truth, Gary and I were touched by all the groups, and the gratitude they showed us. At the end of two days, although we were in a bit of a daze, we felt exhilarated – and hopeful God would go easier on us on Judgment Day.

Looking back, we were also struck by the candor of the people we met. Many of them admitted that marketing was out of their comfort zone. They felt it was too intangible – they were more comfortable just servicing their cause.

Of course, they also realized that if not enough people knew or cared about their cause, there would be no cause.

We wanted them to see that it's not either/or. You can be wildly imaginative and successful in marketing and "presenting" your cause, yet still continue to develop the Talmudic-like substance to back it up.

Jews, of all people, should feel no guilt about marketing. Seriously: We spent 1,900 years refining and improving our product. It's not like we haven't earned the right to show it off – even if that's not exactly, you know, the Jewish way.

"Your followers are Jewish first and Conservative second. So are you. Focus less on the subtleties of your denomination and more on the richness of Judaism. Celebrate great answers, not just great questions."

CONSERVATIVES' NEW DISH

September 20, 2007

I read a remarkable quote a few days ago from a prominent member of the Conservative movement: "We've been searching for an identity for a hundred years now."

A hundred years?

In the business world, products can fail in a year or two if they don't have an identity. But in religion, maybe God gives you a pass from the realities of the marketplace.

Or maybe not.

Over the past couple of decades, the Conservative movement has been in a steady decline. A couple of years ago, one of the leaders, in his outgoing speech, described the movement as suffering from "malaise" and a "grievous failure of nerve."

Everyone has a theory for why this has happened.

Mine is that they do have an identity, but it's the wrong one: A great debating society.

When you think of the Conservative movement, you think of fascinating, complicated debates that aim to reconcile traditional halacha (Jewish law) with modern sensibilities. The leadership always seems to be going through some noble struggle to craft rulings that will delineate the permissible boundaries of their movement.

Now, the new powers have spoken, and after a 17-month "listening tour" and strategic review, they have decided to recommend ... more debate.

From what I gather, they've had enough with "top-down" leadership, and now it's time to let the "people" in on the process. They're calling it the "mitzvah project," whereby people will be encouraged to debate within their communities their personal views and feelings on mitzvahs, including, presumably, which ones of the 613 they feel like doing.

If you ask me, it sounds like they've thrown in the towel.

They haven't figured out how to revitalize their movement, so they're handing off the problem to the masses and calling it a grand community experiment to help define the movement.

That sounds noble, but there's a problem: when you're schlepping from carpool lanes to soccer practices with screaming kids in the minivan, you're not in the mood to define religious movements. Professors, rabbis and scholars might live for the grand debate, but normal people don't. They're consumed with their own problems, like family, money, relationship and health. When they finally squeeze in time for religion, they want more than fascinating debates.

They want real nourishment.

For years, noisy, public debates – including some important ones on gender and gay issues – have had an enormous relevance to the process of Conservatives' self-definition, but significantly less relevance to the nourishing of their flock.

As a result, the burden has fallen on individual communities, where local success stories are often due to charismatic and enterprising rabbis. It's a shame the national leadership hasn't led the way. But they can. They just need to expand their horizons. I would offer these suggestions:

First, de-emphasize the word Conservative and focus on Judaism.

Your followers are Jewish first and Conservative second. So are you. Focus less on the subtleties of your denomination and more on the richness of Judaism. Celebrate great answers, not just great questions.

Second, nourish your people with Judaism that connects to their lives. Unlike their rabbis, people don't get paid to go to synagogues or conferences. They want to know: How will Judaism help me navigate through life? How will it enrich it? They don't care whether their religion is organized or disorganized, as long as it's relevant.

Launch a series – in video, Web, print and live classes – that would be called: "What Does Judaism Say About...?" Each section would deal with an issue people care about: money, marriage, social justice, raising kids, ecology, art, business ethics, health, intimacy, tikkun olam (healing the world), pleasure, charity, community, relationships, etc.

Have your experts craft this "nourishment" from the Torah literature they already teach, but would now tailor to the everyday interests and concerns of your people.

You can call it the Jewish Nourishment Project.

The more people feel that Judaism nourishes them, the more they'll want to do mitzvahs, rather than just debate them. And when they do engage in debate, it will be from a point of knowledge – not only feelings and opinions.

The third suggestion is to nourish your people's hearts and souls with spiritual experiences. The Conservative movement has some of the best and most spiritual "nourishers" in the Jewish world. Rabbi Ron Wolfson, for example, and many others have developed innovative ways of making the synagogue experience more welcoming and inspiring. Borrow from your local achievements to create national programs. Give spirituality a bigger priority in your seminaries. Create an annual spiritual convention. Help Jews elevate, not just debate.

Finally, think portable. Take your movement on the road and to college campuses. Reconnect with the thousands of Jews who have been nourished by one of your biggest success stories – Camp Ramah. Become known as a movement that provides Jewish knowledge and spiritual joy for all generations, even when they're not in synagogue.

Make the head offices of the movement a Web-driven resource

center to help disseminate your Jewish nourishment. Create your own global Webcasting network.

In short, re-brand yourselves as great Jewish nourishers – of the mind, body and soul.

Your efforts will always include fascinating debates and sensitive rulings. But these aren't enough. If you want to thrive in the next century, you'll need to start nourishing the Jewish world with what it is hungry for.

And that is good old Judaism, served up smart, deep and delicious.

"Memories of seders, Shabbat meals, hot soups on winter nights, summer picnics, afternoon snacks – big meals, small meals or spectacular meals, always coming out of tiny kitchens."

MEME'S IN THE KITCHEN, MAKING MEMORIES

September 8, 2007

I remember the moment well. I had just picked up my 74-year-old mother at LAX, and as we entered my new house in the Pico-Robertson neighborhood, I proudly showed her the new kitchen.

Compared to her kitchen in Montreal, this one was the size of the Roman Coliseum. It took her about an hour to fully inspect it. I think she opened every drawer and cabinet. She was so impressed, she muttered a few words in Arabic I had never heard before. She got a kick out of those little transparent decal stickers on the cabinets – which I got at Shmulie's Books & Gifts on Pico Boulevard – that delineate milk and meat dishes.

But what I think really moved her – what got those 20/20 eyes of hers to open just a little wider – was the potential. The potential for some very serious cooking.

I've never seen Bob Dylan in a recording studio. But I can just imagine. He probably knows just what he wants. He can speak the engineer's language, tell the bass player how to improve a rhythm, make changes on the fly, fix a lyric, add some harmonica when he feels like it. He's in creative heaven. Within a few hours, a "Blowin' in the Wind" or "Dirt Road Blues" is born.

That's sort of my mother in the kitchen. The difference is she weighs more, she doesn't sing, she doesn't wear sunglasses, she has no angst, she doesn't smoke or drink, she has no help and, once she's done creating her art, it immediately gets consumed.

What remains from her creations is not a lifetime of playing and listening, but a lifetime of memories.

But oh, what memories.

It didn't take long for my mother (her grandchildren call her by the French "Meme," which sounds like "meh meh") to create memories on her first trip to the hood.

Within a week, her anisette-flavored galettes – flat, crunchy cakes, which she served my father every morning for 49 years along with his Turkish coffee – were politely interfering with Rabbi Abner Weiss's Torah salon. I distinctly recall Rabbi Weiss taking a break from his class as he saw a tray of Meme's galettes approaching – the man wanted one. No one seemed to mind.

She used a special pastry roller for those galettes. I'm sure you could find one like it at Pottery Barn. Hers came from her grandmother, who used it to make the same galettes in a Jewish neighborhood of Casablanca. The roller has that worn-out look, but you can see the kind of sturdy construction that suggests it could probably crank out galettes for two more generations.

As the weeks of her visit here went by, and her rule over my kitchen became complete, the household began to revolve not just around her food, but around her.

Grouchy kids getting ready for school in the morning? Nothing like the aroma of a few hot moufletas (Moroccan crepes), with Meme in her bathrobe spreading some melted butter and honey, to lighten the stress of an upcoming algebra test.

Playdates coming over after school? How about an elaborate fruit platter and marzipan cookies to tide you over until Meme's juicy Keftas (spiced up burgers) for dinner?

For several months, in addition to the weekday surprises she would prepare every night for the kids, a parade of Shabbat guests feasted on

Meme's delights like spicy Moroccan fish, truffle and meatball tagine, an array of delicate Mediterranean salads and, for Shabbat lunch, her signature, unmistakable Dafina, the Moroccan cholent.

Put it this way: By her second month here, she was on a first name basis with at least one meat-cutter at Pico Glatt, and she was beginning to pick up Spanish.

All this, however, seemed to be a build-up to the meal that will go down in family lore. If you should ever come across any of the 20 or so guests who came to Meme's second Passover seder – created during an intense 10-hour burst of activity in her new kitchen – ask them about that meal.

For about four hours, a group of sophisticated and happy grown-ups were engaged in lively conversation – and kept getting interrupted. As soon as Bob Ore, a French playwright, would go off on one of his wild, comedic riffs, something would come to interrupt. When the editor of Moment magazine tried to explain a new piece she was planning on Norman Mailer to a movie producer sitting next to her, something would interrupt. When the creator of Harissa.com tried to tell us about the different kinds of Sephardics around the world who had taken to his site, or when Louie Kemp tried to enlighten us with a story on the Lubavitcher rebbe, something again would interrupt.

All night long, something would come to interrupt.

These glorious interruptions were Meme's creations, one sensuous platter at a time. If a Hollywood cinematographer could have filmed the evening, it would have rivaled the food scenes in "Like Water for Chocolate." To this day, when I meet someone who was there, the conversation invariably comes back to that night of a thousand delights. By the time the meal was over, we had all surrendered. The conversation had clearly shifted to the food. Meme had won, hands down.

After four months creating this culinary heaven, Meme had to return home. The relatives there were clearly getting impatient with our monopolizing of the family treasure. We had no choice. We gave Meme back her passport. But not before she made moufletas, with a big smile on her face, for about 200 guests at the traditional mimouna party celebrating the end of Passover.

Which brings me to a few weeks ago, when I got an e-mail from The Jewish Journal, asking me if I would write about my mother's cooking for the Rosh Hashanah food issue, accompanied by color photos, recipes, the works. Now I'm thinking: the editors there probably don't know that Meme's been back in Montreal for awhile. That big kitchen she took over during those memorable months, well, it hasn't been the same without her. How can I do a Meme food story without Meme?

As luck would have it, my kids and I were about to go to Montreal for a big family wedding. Would Meme be up to preparing a full Rosh Hashanah feast in the middle of all the festivities, in her tiny kitchen? And where would I find a professional photographer on such short notice?

It's great when God smiles on your projects. My sister, Sandra, ran around town getting the special ingredients – including pomegranates and dates on leaves – for the traditional blessings Sephardim do at the Rosh Hashanah table (see side bar). My other sister, Kathy, got the rest: meat, fish, couscous, vegetables, etc. And my third sister, Judy, did the real heavy lifting: she took a group of hyperactive kids on an outing – any outing, we told her – very far away from Meme's tiny kitchen.

This was serious business. The photographer was coming over in a few hours, and a complete Rosh Hashanah table had to be laid out, in all its glory.

That same morning, the photographer called to cancel – she said her flash blew out. But get this: Our original No. 1 choice, a star photographer who is a friend of the family, Raphael Ohayon, had just become available because the wedding he was supposed to shoot that night ... got cancelled! I can't tell you how guilty I felt that I was grateful for the cancellation.

I was also grateful for my brother-in-law, Paul Starr, who has this talent for fixing broken circuits on kitchen stoves very early on Sunday mornings.

So now we had all the ingredients, and in the middle of the tiny kitchen was Meme, with Kathy assisting, doing her usual dance frying bastillas, caramelizing onions, roasting lamb, steaming couscous, chopping up vegetables and mixing them with dried fruit and nuts, simmering pumpkin soup – and all this while taking mazal tov calls from overseas.

As I absorbed the scene from a distance, my own childhood memories returned. It must have been the tiny kitchen, which is all I saw growing up.

When Meme cooked in the big kitchen back in Los Angeles, she created a whole new set of childhood memories – for my kids. But here in her tiny kitchen in Montreal, these were my childhood memories. Memories of a small apartment kitchen where Meme cooked for 100 people who came for my brother Samy's bar mitzvah, in 1967. Memories of seders, Shabbat meals, hot soups on winter nights, summer picnics, afternoon snacks – big meals, small meals or spectacular meals, always coming out of tiny kitchens.

I wondered: Can our children's memories have the same meaning today, when so many of them see only spaciousness, abundance and luxury? Can you feel love as deeply when it emanates from a large modern kitchen, as when it comes from a tiny kitchen?

If I asked my mother those questions, I'm sure she'd tell me to stop getting so schmaltzy and to send her a plane ticket pronto, so she can get back to that big, spacious, luxurious, sun-drenched kitchen right here in the hood – where more than a few people with sharp memories are awaiting her return engagement.

"How's that for a disconnect? The language of Osama bin Laden and Hamas can teach the Jews some important subtleties about their own faith."

SHMUEL OF ARABIA

August 23, 2007

I t must have been quite a scene in that little courthouse in Jerusalem. Rav Qapah, a Yemenite Jew who sat on the Jerusalem Beit Din (court of law), was hearing a case involving a commercial dispute between a Jew and an Arab.

At one point, the beit din heard testimony from an Arab judge who was serving as a witness. Rav Qapah asked his first question in Arabic. The Arab judge did not answer. Rav Qapah asked again. The Arab judge just sat there, speechless.

Rav Qapah wondered if the Arab judge could not understand his Arabic. After a long pause, the Arab judge said no, that was not the problem. He was speechless because, as the story goes, Rav Qapah's Arabic was so pure, so perfect, so luminous, the stunned Arab judge thought he was hearing the voice of the prophet Muhammad himself – from a Jew, no less.

That was many years ago. Today, here in the Pico-Robertson neighborhood, Rav Shmuel Miller cracks up when he tells that story. He's got a whole bunch of them, stories that speak to the ancient connection between Jews and the Arab language.

In fact, Rav Miller has more than stories. He's an expert in Arabic.

He can learn Torah in Arabic, and often does. In the pristine shul that he built in his backyard, he teaches his sons and others how to study Jewish texts in Arabic. If it were up to him, there'd be many more Jews learning Arabic.

It's not obvious why this Jewish man would have a passion for a language that today is too often associated with suicide bombers and radical Islamists. Here is a French Orthodox rabbi who has studied at the top yeshivas in Europe; an expert in Talmud, philosophy and mysticism; a lover of Jews, Torah and the Hebrew language; a sofer who writes mezuzahs and Torah scrolls in perfect Hebrew calligraphy; and yet, when the subject of Arabic comes up, his eyes light up like he's one of the kids at the Munchies candy store on Saturday night.

I know the emotional arguments. I've been hearing them for years from my parents, aunts, uncles and their friends who grew up in Morocco. They have nostalgia for the past. They love Arabic music, and they're crazy about the language. It's a little like my Ashkenazic friends who wax about the joys of Yiddish. There are words in the Judeo-Arab dialect spoken by my parents that light up the heart like no word in French or English can.

I remember this one word I was particularly fond of: "Shlemto." If one of her kids would do something wrong, my mother would use that word to convey that "I really love this kid, but I really wish he wouldn't do that, but at the same time, I want everyone to know how much I still love him even when he does something that really annoys me."

That's with one word. There are many others.

In the Morocco that I remember, Arabic was the daily language of emotion.

But what about for Rav Miller, a rabbi who was born and raised in France? His first language is French, then Hebrew. Where does his mad love for Arabic come from?

If you see him, you get some clues. There's a regal, Lawrence of Arabia quality to him. Short beard. Piercing eyes. Always upright. He looks like he'd fit right in with the romantic mystics of the Middle Ages.

But beyond that, after hanging out with him for the better part of a year since I moved to the hood, and seeing him give classes at my place on everything from the patriarchs to Spinoza, I have a simpler explanation for his Arabian passions.

He loves Arabic because he loves Judaism.

Take his love affair with Maimonides. He wanted to read "The Guide to the Perplexed" in the language in which it was written, so he studied it in Arabic. He says this gave him a deeper, "more palpable" understanding of Jewish ideas. For example, the word in Arabic that Maimonides uses for the Hebrew daat (knowledge) is eidrak, which refers to a knowledge that you "apprehend" or "take in." It is a union between the modrak, the one who understands, and the modrik, the one who is understood. Whereas the Hebrew daat denotes something external and impersonal, the Arab eidrak defines a knowledge that is more personal and contemplative, one that ultimately becomes part of you.

Similarly, by studying Rabbi Yehuda Halevi's Kuzari in the original Arabic, Rav Miller got a more subtle take on the problematic notion that Jews are the "chosen people." Looked at superficially, the idea of being "chosen" can easily offend other groups by suggesting racial superiority. In Arabic, however, the notion of the Hebrew segula (chosen) is more layered. The Arab term khassuss speaks to a one-to-one intimacy with God. In the original Arabic text of Rabbi Halevi, Jews are more likely to be the "particular, singular, private" people, rather than the more blunt "chosen" people. It's about intimacy, not superiority.

How's that for a disconnect? The language of Osama bin Laden and Hamas can teach the Jews some important subtleties about their own faith.

That does take a little getting used to.

Maybe that's why Rav Miller has no illusions about Arabic classes ever catching on in the Jewish world. Of course, that won't stop him from continuing to give his own classes to his inner circle, and from spending long nights poring through ancient Arab texts written by Jewish sages.

One thing he won't do is talk about politics. That's not his trip. He did make a slip the other day, however, when he made an offhand remark wondering what it would be like if Jewish leaders started talking to Arab leaders in Arabic.

I have no idea if that would help the peace process, but I am sure of one thing: More than a few Arabs would be left speechless.

"We are nurturing a generation of Jewish noshers who only want to lick the icing off the Jewish cake."

DUMBING DOWN JUDAISM

July 26, 2007

You can't talk about Jewish philanthropy without talking about Jewish priorities. For many years now, a huge priority for the American Jewish community has been to fight assimilation – what is elegantly called "Jewish continuity." It's a priority that is rarely challenged. How do you argue against Jewish continuity?

Well, the other day, I had lunch at Shilo's with a Talmud professor who's not overly worked up about Jewish continuity. In fact, my lunch guest, Rabbi Aryeh Cohen of the Shtibl Minyan, wouldn't mind if the Jewish world lost its obsession with Jewish continuity and started worrying about something he considers more important.

What kind of Judaism the Jewish world wishes to "continue."

In this view, Judaism itself has been diminished by our obsession with "survival" and "continuity." By coddling and pandering to keep Jews from leaving the faith, we have trivialized our faith and turned it into fluff. Look around and you'll see how Judaism has slowly evolved into a consumer brand of sweetness and convenience – into Judaism lite.

Not crazy about doing Shabbat? Come Friday night for a fabulous musical and social experience. No tickets for High Holy Day services? Just show up at any Chabad and they'll treat you like royalty. Never been to the Holy Land? If you're young, no problem – it's your birthright and you can go for free.

If you find synagogue services too boring or complicated, we have an array of "spiritual" services where all you have to do is read English and hold hands and chant in unison. If you're single and you want to meet someone but your time is precious and limited, come have a latte and "speed" through a string of possible Jewish mates.

You know nothing about your Judaism? Don't feel bad, you're not alone. There are hundreds of introductory classes for you to choose from. There's Judaism for the "Clueless but Curious," "Kabbalah for Dummies," even a user-friendly "High Holiday Survival Guide."

If you're more into culture and attitude, there are magazines and Web sites that will show you how to be Jewish and cool. You don't believe in God? Don't worry, there's a whole movement for you with the word "human" in it. Just remember: our No. 1 concern is that you stay Jewish, even if you know nothing about your Judaism.

It's almost as if American Judaism, in its desperate struggle to keep Jews from vanishing into the gentile mainstream, has become a marketing carnival. And Jewish philanthropy – driven by a Holocaust-level fear of losing Jews – has helped fund this carnival.

At our lunch, Rabbi Cohen lamented the price we have paid to reach this point: the dumbing down of Judaism. In twisting ourselves into pretzels to reach out to vanishing Jews, we're marketing Judaism as a faith that can comfort, entertain and even elevate you – but will rarely challenge you or make too many demands, intellectual or otherwise.

We are nurturing a generation of Jewish noshers who only want to lick the icing off the Jewish cake. Even the budding spiritual revival we hear so much about is based more on the need for personal empowerment and self-fulfillment than it is on deep knowledge of the Jewish tradition.

Our marketing of Judaism has created consumers, not thinkers.

My neighbors and friends who live a few doors from me, Rabbi Joel Rembaum and his wife, Fredi, told me on a recent Shabbat afternoon that the Jewish world needs to do more inreach, and less outreach. What they

DON'T GET ME STARTED

and Rabbi Cohen were saying is that we need to create a new generation of educated Jews from kindergarten up, rather than expend so much of our resources on throwing lifeboats to unaffiliated and disconnected grown-ups.

For me, that's probably going too far, because I've seen how outreach has brought so many young adults to reconnect with their Judaism. As I see it, any connection is better than no connection. Still, there is one mantra that I hear everywhere I go – whether we're talking about outreach or inreach.

This is the mantra: Thousands of Jewish families cannot afford to send their children to Jewish day schools, and it is outrageous that the Jewish community cannot raise the money to subsidize these children.

It's so obvious that it's almost embarrassing: Is there a better anti-dote to the dumbing down of Judaism, and the eventual assimilation of Jews, than having Jewish kids get a Jewish education? Maybe the reason Jewish continuity efforts have been so unsuccessful (half of our adults still marry outside the faith) is that it's hard to stay connected to something you don't know much about.

For the large number of Jews who stay committed to their Juda-ism after getting a Jewish education, you can bet that when they grow up they'll demand more from their spiritual leaders than "Judaism for Dummies." If they have studied Talmud and other texts, they will be more likely to introduce knowledgeable debates into their congregations and communities, and, generally, add more depth and vibrancy to the Jewish conversation.

When we lament the lack of great Jewish thinkers in our generation – who are the Heschels, Soloveichiks and Bubers of our day? – we are also lamenting what Judaism has lost through their absence. I don't know about you, but I'd pay anything to hear what someone like Heschel would have to say about the great Jewish issues of our day. The knowledge that one can only get from a Jewish education is the first step to creating great Jewish thinkers, rather than simply clever ones.

But as we know, "Jewish education" is not as sexy a fundraising hook as "we're losing Jews!" "the world hates us!" and "we can never forget!" Never mind that Jewish education holds the secret to a stronger Jewish continuity: It strengthens Jews by strengthening Judaism, and it strengthens Judaism by strengthening Jews.

The real dumbing down of Judaism today is that the Jewish philanthropic world hasn't figured that out yet.

"It was visceral, it was sincere and it didn't come from talking points. It came from his heart, and I guarantee you it played well in Wisconsin."

HAVE JEWS LOST THEIR MOJO?

June 7, 2007

I took a break from the hood the other night to speak to a large Conservative synagogue in Palos Verdes called Congregation Ner Tamid – and I used a word that got me in trouble. The occasion was a showing of "Obsession" – a documentary on the rise of radical Islam and the worldwide terror that has accompanied it – and it was sponsored by CAMERA, an organization that counteracts anti-Israel bias in the mainstream media.

"Obsession" assaults you with the hatred that fuels the fire of radical Islam.

The film points out that the majority of Muslims are not radical Islamists, but when it homes in on the radicals, the words and images make your skin crawl.

You see an old sheik, speaking to what looks like 100,000 people, pulling out a sword and exhorting his screaming flock to kill every Jew they can find. One radical Muslim after another is shown giving motivational speeches on the fine art of Jew-hatred. And Jew-killing. Lots and lots of Jew-killing.

But here's the crazy part: There's not a word from the Jew-haters about the dreaded Occupation. Not a peep about roadblocks or fences or the oppressive policies of the Zionist occupier, which, as we are so often reminded, lie "at the heart" of our enemies' discontent. The Jew-haters are honest: they want Jews dead. All Jews. Roadblocks or no roadblocks. West Bank or no West Bank.

Talk about an inconvenient truth.

When you see all this Jew-hatred, it's tempting to be dismissive and say "These are only the radicals; there are many more moderates." Or to get all cynical because "The radicals will always want to kill us. So what's new?" These are great coping mechanisms that help us maintain our composure. But here's what's new: The radicals aren't just getting bigger and bolder on the battlefield, they're also, amazingly, winning the PR war.

Who would have figured that two years after our heart-wrenching evacuation of Gaza – two years of continued relentless attacks from an enemy that brazenly calls for our destruction – we'd be the target of a boycott from British professors? Again, it's tempting to get all blasé and say "Been there, done that."

But this blasé attitude is a reason why we are losing the PR battle: We assume that getting all worked up about stuff doesn't really make a difference, or that it's not very becoming of Jews. The practical thing to do is to stay composed and look for solutions.

Well, here's a practical idea: Let's all take a time-out from "solutions" and get a little worked up. Let's stop being so composed and start being outraged. Because if we continue like this, the whole world, except for America and Micronesia, will be boycotting Israel.

Israel needs the Diaspora to get more emotional right now – because emotional outrage wins PR battles. Our enemy understands that a lot better than we do. The most effective TV interview I ever saw happened about five years ago on a major network, while Israel was in the midst of numerous suicide bombings. The anchorman asked Knesset Speaker Avraham Burg, a very composed and sophisticated man, why Israel could not arrest these suicide bombers. Well, you should have seen the outrage on Mr. Burg's face.

With clenched fists and an almost growling voice, he said something like: "But how do you expect us to do that when they can blow up in one second?"

It was visceral, it was sincere and it didn't come from talking points. It came from his heart, and I guarantee you it played well in Wisconsin.

After seeing the Jew-hatred in "Obsession," it was hard not to get worked up when I spoke at the Palos Verdes synagogue. I wanted the Jew-haters of the world to know that we have as much passion to defend Jewish lives as they have passion to destroy us.

But I got a little carried away. I said that we need to have our own Jihad – a Jihad for life – and to show the enemy that we believe in it as much as they believe in their "Jihad for death."

A fellow Jew rose up in indignation. My clever twist did not amuse him. No matter how much I tried to explain the subtleties of turning our enemy's word on its head to convey our own "noble struggle," the word went too far for him.

I understood his discomfort, but maybe that's precisely why we need to go there.

Our PR timidity has backfired on us. I'm not saying we should emulate "Wrestlemania" announcers (how sincere do they look?), but I am saying that we need to get bolder and more emotional. It makes us more human.

For example, when the bombs fall on Sderot, instead of empty clichés like "no terrorist is immune" and "this is unacceptable" and so forth, we should have the guts to run ads all over the world and get on CNN and the BBC and say things like: "We gave them land, and they gave us war." "This proves that the occupation was never the key problem," and "How would England respond if the same amount of bombs fell on Manchester?"

These are not think-tank words, they're real words. If we can deliver them with the same intensity Mr. Burg used five years ago, the world will better understand the justness of our cause.

The amazing thing about the PR battle is that it's probably the only area right now where we can win. The political, military and diplomatic landscapes are a mess, but the PR landscape is wide open. Especially post-disengagement, there are numerous PR victories that are ours for the taking.

In a brilliant article in Haaretz, Moshe Arens explains why you can't deter terrorists, you can only fight them. It's time for Jews of all stripes to get their mojo back, and join the PR fight.

Even if your only weapon is your PC, and your mouth.

"The night of Mimouna was all about bringing good fortune into your life. After eight days of prohibitions, Mimouna was the night you broke free, the night anything was possible."

THE MAGIC OF MIMOUNA

April 5, 2007

G o back a few centuries and picture yourself on a small street in a Jewish neighborhood in Casablanca, Morocco, as the sun is starting to set.

You've just finished the late afternoon prayers on the last day of Passover, and as you head home, you see Arab grocers setting up shop and laying out butter, milk, honey and, most importantly, flour and yeast. They are doing what their ancestors did for generations: helping the Jews of Morocco prepare for the ancient tradition of Mimouna, a night when the Jews celebrated the end of Passover by opening the doors of their homes to their neighborhood.

After sundown, Jewish men would rush to gather all the supplies – either by purchasing them or receiving them as gestures of good will from local Arabs – and bring them home, where the women would prepare elaborate sweet tables.

These tables were laden with delicacies, but the star of the show was a thin, mouth-watering Moroccan crepe called the moufleta, which you would roll up with soft butter and honey. Please trust me when I tell you that to this day, few things in life are as perfect as a couple of hot, sweet, tender moufletas – right after you've come off a strict eight-day diet of dry matzahs.

Moufletas were not the only sweet things floating in the Arabian moonlight on the night of Mimouna. According to folklore, Mimouna was known as the ideal night to meet your sweetheart. It was a night when doors and hearts were open, and young men and women, dressed in their finest, would move and mingle like butterflies from one party and sweet table to another. (I know, it sounds a lot more romantic than speed dating.)

The free-flowing and joyful atmosphere that made you feel the promise of finding love was not a coincidence. The night of Mimouna was all about bringing good fortune into your life. After eight days of prohibitions, Mimouna was the night you broke free, the night anything was possible.

For the Jews of Morocco, Mimouna was the Jewish holiday that celebrated optimism.

All night long, people would give the same greeting over and over again: "Terbach," an Arab word that roughly means, "May you win and be fortunate."

The word "mimouna" itself combines the Hebrew/Aramaic root "mammon," which means riches, with the Hebrew word "emunah," which means faith. Have faith in your good fortune: If Mimouna ever becomes a big deal in California, I bet the California Lottery would salivate to sponsor Mimouna parties.

As many of you know, the mainstreaming of Mimouna has already happened in Israel. The tradition has morphed from magical nights among neighbors to loud daytime barbecues in public parks, where politicians of all stripes come to sell their wares. I'm guessing the politicians want in on the good Mimouna vibes, which might explain why they've made it a national holiday.

From what I hear, the rabbis in Israel also got involved. They were afraid that people would rush out to buy their moufleta ingredients before the holiday was officially over, so they nudged Mimouna into the bright sun of the next day.

These rabbis obviously have no feel for romance – Mimouna is for the moon, not the sun. My memories of Mimouna nights in Casablanca can never mesh with the notion of an afternoon barbecue in a public park. Even though I was only a child, I recall feeling this mysterious, nighttime magic in the air. Even the nervous rush after sundown to gather the goods and prepare the sweet tables were part of the excitement.

But the magic of Mimouna was not just the sweet tables and the Arabian nights. There was something else.

When I talk to Sephardic Jews today who spent a big part of their lives in Morocco, they go on and on about Mimouna. It's like they're talking about an ex-girlfriend they were madly in love with and wish they had married. There's a sense of nostalgia, yes, but also of loss – a loss of what that one night represented.

It's true that they have tried to take Mimouna with them. In Montreal, where I grew up and where there is a large Moroccan Jewish community, people drive to fancy Mimouna parties all over town until the early morning hours. Even here in Los Angeles, there are Mimouna parties sprinkled all over the area, especially in Moroccan Jewish homes.

But everyone knows there's something missing. You could serve the world's greatest moufletas (my mother's), wear a gold-laced caftan and have a live Middle Eastern band, and there would still be something missing.

It's the neighborhood.

Mimouna represented the love and intimacy of a neighborhood. There's nothing like popping in to see 10, 20, 30 different neighbors on the same night, most of whom you see all the time – especially when you know your great-great-great-grandparents probably did the same thing in the same place.

According to tradition, Mimouna itself came out of a neighborhood need. Because many Jewish families in Morocco each had their own Passover customs, Passover week was the one time of the year when families would usually not eat in each other's homes.

Mimouna was a way for the neighborhood to dramatically make up for this week of limited hospitality – a night when things got back to normal, and everyone invited everyone.

If Passover was the holiday that drew you in – toward yourself, your home, your family – Mimouna was the holiday that blew you away, back to the neighbors, your friends, your freedom, your dreams, maybe even your future love.

Many years later, I find myself living again in a Jewish neighborhood, and I can't help wondering if my moving here had something to do with my memories of another neighborhood.

Especially on that one magical night of the year, when the moufletas were hot, the doors were open and everything was possible.

"Rabbi Friedman explained that the biggest obstacle in romantic relationships is what he calls the 'third thing.' This third thing is the all-consuming question one asks of potential soulmates: Are they fulfilling our needs?"

A NIGHT FOR THE SOUL

March 15, 2007

Have you ever heard words of Torah that made you really uncomfortable? Where you almost started to squirm, not because you were bored, but because you were rattled?

This happened recently when I had a "Torah in the Hood" salon at my place for about 20 Jewish singles.

The class was connected to Purim, and it was billed as "A mystical journey into a mysterious holiday." The speaker was the Chasidic mystic and philosopher Rabbi Manis Friedman, author of "Doesn't Anyone Blush Anymore?" which on its back cover has a raving blurb from a fellow mystic named Bob Dylan.

Little did we know during the polite chatting over Moroccan tea that we were about to be ambushed by the rabbi's provocative riffs on the human soul.

With the glow of candles reflecting softly on his long white beard, Rabbi Friedman didn't waste any time. He started by telling us that the struggle in Judaism is not to find the truth – because we already know it. The struggle is to realize we know it, and then make it compatible with our reality.

Argument is part of the noise that makes us forget we already know the truth. When we get drunk on Purim so that we can't tell the difference between "Blessed is Mordechai and cursed is Haman," it is to show us that beyond the state of knowing and reason – when our minds are plastered – our souls are intact and sober, and they know the truth.

The body might be drunk, but the soul is our designated thinker – it never stops knowing the difference between Mordechai and Haman, between right and wrong, between holy and unholy.

Rabbi Friedman was talking about the human soul as if it had a mind of its own, a very confident mind.

The soul doesn't need argument or reason to make its point. It knows that this is wrong because it is wrong, and this is right because it is right. The soul doesn't need to explain why you should go to the gym or visit the sick or control your anger or resist gossip or be Jewish. It is our Godly instinct. It just knows. It just is.

It was a little disconcerting to hear something as nebulous and intangible as a soul being talked about like a human asset at our disposal. But the notion that we could mine – even emulate – this asset was exciting.

According to the rabbi, we suffer from inner conflict, in part, because we don't allow ourselves to enter the state of "soulful knowing." Our rational minds are taught to process everything – to challenge, to argue, to debate, to struggle, as if those acts themselves had some overarching truth. In the process of all this processing, our egos become the heroes. We become self-conscious instead of soul-conscious.

When we're not in touch with our souls, we're also confused about our roles. Our egos make us worship uniqueness. But the Torah values roles above uniqueness. When we praise the Woman of Valor on Friday night, we don't praise her for being unique; we praise her for being trustworthy, respectful, resourceful and compassionate. We praise her knowing soul.

In this mode of living, there is little room for tortured debate, agonizing dilemmas or self-absorbed obsessions. The struggle becomes to lower the noise level in our minds, nourish our souls with Godliness and then allow our soulfulness to permeate our reality.

In short, the rabbi was telling 20 well-educated Jews to put their minds in the service of their souls. But wait, the real discomfort in our Torah salon was still to come, and it started when someone brought up a perennial hot topic in the singles world: Looking for a soulmate.

Rabbi Friedman explained that the biggest obstacle in romantic relationships is what he calls the "third thing." This third thing is the all-consuming question one asks of potential soulmates: Are they fulfilling our needs?

We are in love with our needs and, because love is blind, we are blinded by them. We're in love with love, status, security, sex, laughter, companionship, intellectual stimulation, spiritual inspiration or whatever else we might need at any point in time. When we meet someone, we don't see a real person; we see a potential need-filler.

But need-filling is not the same thing as soul-filling. Needs are noisy and shifty, while souls are quiet and eternal. When we care about each other's needs at the expense of each other's souls, we become needmates, not soulmates.

As the rabbi reminded us, our needs can play tricks on us. They can come and go and change without notice, and then what? Who is left facing us? Who is that person we are having dinner with?

In his soft, almost whispering voice, Rabbi Friedman suggested another way. Perhaps the path to true love is to lower the noise level in our minds and bring only one thing to the table: the desire to learn who the other person is, so we can touch their souls.

Romantic unions that are born in this fashion are not flashy, but they create real soulmates.

By now, after 90 minutes of this spiritual jazz session, Rabbi Friedman had challenged us to look at our minds and souls in a different way, and he turned our views on love and soulmates upside down. Not bad for a night's work.

What's more, he didn't let us off the hook by using obscure language that no one understands. As far as esoteric messages go, his words were remarkably clear. Maybe that's why they shook us up – and also drained us.

The reaction was not polite enthusiasm. It was more like, "What was that?" People left slowly and silently, as if something deep and quiet inside of them had been touched.

Their souls, perhaps?

"You see, Jacob has a unique style and a unique voice. He has Down syndrome, so you have to listen carefully to get everything he says. In fact, to understand Jacob really well, you have to listen as well as he does."

JACOB'S LADDERS

March 8, 2007

Every neighborhood has its gathering places. In my neighborhood, you'll find one if you head west on Pico Boulevard from Robertson Boulevard, past the ethnic aromas of the "center" hood and into the kosher Ice Blended Mochas of the "west" hood, where, right next to an Office Depot, The Coffee Bean and Tea Leaf rules.

That's where you're likely to meet a young man named Jacob Katz. Jacob is a happy-go-lucky, kippah-wearing, 23-year-old Jew who mixes ice-blended coffee drinks and takes care of customers at the Coffee Bean. Talk about a neighborhood hangout. When Hillary Clinton wrote the book "It Takes a Village," she could have started here.

Pop in to the sunny patio on any afternoon and you're likely to see Rabbi Yosef Kanefsky at a corner table giving a private Torah class; a Conservadox aspiring pop star who used to study in a Jerusalem seminary promoting her upcoming live show; a few perfectly coiffed frum supermoms taking a break from the carpooling; a couple of born-again Chasids from the Happy Minyan talking about a Jethro Tull concert; and a retired couple from Palm Springs making their weekly visit to their old neighborhood ("We bought a house on that street for $37,000. You know what it's worth now? I don't know why we got rid of it. Is that your daughter? How old is she? Hey, we have a granddaughter the same age.").

Late afternoon, the patio gets invaded by YULA high-school students coming to unwind after a long day of Talmud, algebra and Shakespeare. The more eager students lay out their homework next to their lattes. The funny thing is, everyone seems to know Jacob.

You see, Jacob has a unique style and a unique voice. He has Down syndrome, so you have to listen carefully to get everything he says. In fact, to understand Jacob really well, you have to listen as well as he does.

Because Jacob Katz is a human sponge.

Ever since he was a child, he's had a talent for listening, and for absorbing everything around him. But as he got older, this talent morphed into something more universal: "I want this" and "I want that." As his mother Frieda recalls, Jacob developed this unlimited capacity to want things.

It didn't matter what, Jacob wanted it: I want a computer, I want to learn how to drive, I want to listen to the Beatles, I want to go to college, I want to go to the movies. You name it – if it was cool, Jacob wanted it.

So one day, he looks up at one of the coolest places in Los Angeles, just a few blocks from his house, and he says, "I want to work at Coffee Bean." And guess what? He gets the job.

Don't think it was a cake walk. He had to fill out a lengthy application, and after meeting with the store manager, he impressed him enough to get an interview with the district manager, a religious Christian woman named Jan. Obviously something clicked. She hired Jacob, and he started training that same week.

That was six months ago. Today, Jacob laughs all the way to the bank every two weeks to deposit his paycheck.

He laughs in other places, too. He laughs when he takes the bus twice a week to Santa Monica College, where he's learning all kinds of things, including how to type 30 words a minute without looking. From what I hear, Jacob's pretty well known around campus.

This week, Jacob is doing research on the Internet for a little dvar

Torah he'll be giving at the Etta Israel Shabbaton at Beth Jacob Congregation. Etta Israel is the popular local organization that caters to kids with Down syndrome and other special needs, and it's where Jacob studied Judaism every Sunday for seven years.

Many years ago, Jacob's mother stood up at an Etta Israel dinner and said something that people still talk about. What she said was remarkably simple.

She said that all the things that Jacob did over the years – special classes, speech therapies, life skills training, etc. – were really important, but that one thing in his life was even more important: friendships.

Since he was very young, Jacob has been blessed with friends. Friends of his sister and three brothers are his friends, too. He has friends at Etta Israel, friends where he prays every morning (Young Israel of Century City), friends at the gym where he works out, friends all over the hood.

One reason he has so many friends is that he keeps in touch, and he doesn't ask for much. I love getting his calls: "Heyyy David, it's Jacob" is how he always starts, in his deep baritone voice. A little schmoozing, a few laughs, a few "I love yous," and we're done. I think he gets a kick that the person at the other end of the line knows who he is.

At the neighborhood Coffee Bean, where he works four hours a day, four days a week, they definitely know who he is. Yet despite being so loved and having so many friends, guess what? Jacob wants more.

The other day, while sipping a pomegranate ice tea, and after singing his favorite Beatles tune ("Ticket to Ride"), he confided that there is one friend he still doesn't have – his lifetime soulmate. Like millions of single Jews, Jacob wants a great Jewish shidduch.

When you look at his track record with the things that he wants, and how single women in this town go crazy for Ice Blended Mochas, I wouldn't count him out.

"If we keep 'confessing' to an already hostile world, for example, that we are too harsh in defending ourselves, should we be surprised if that same world concludes that we deserve to be punished – that we had all this terrorism coming?"

THE FREEDOM TO SHUT UP

March 1, 2007

D id you hear about the local court in Israel that sentenced a newspaper editor and a reporter to a year in jail for criticizing the prime minister? Or how about the 100 men who were arrested at a private party in Tel Aviv because they were "dancing and behaving like women"? Or the Israeli court in Haifa that ruled that the testimony of a man is worth twice that of a woman?

You probably haven't heard, because these abuses didn't happen in Israel. They happened in Israel's neighborhood, in countries like Egypt, Jordan and Saudi Arabia, and as you might imagine, there are plenty more where those came from.

What does any of this have to do with a column about the Pico-Robertson neighborhood? This week I feel like going a little broader.

There's a controversy that has bubbled up in the Jewish world today around this question: Is it good for Israel when Jews go public with harsh criticism of Israel?

One recent example is a Jewish group that has been presenting on college campuses a stinging, single-minded and, in the eyes of many, exaggerated critique of the Israeli army. Presumably, this type of collective soul-searching demonstrates the Jewish values of fairness and good faith and ought to generate some goodwill in return.

Of course, Jewish criticism against Israel or its policies is nothing new – but not all criticism is created equal. Criticism that rails against the corruption in Israel's government, for instance, is an example of a political system trying to clean up its act to better serve its people.

But Jewish criticism that publicly undermines Israel's morality and ability to defend itself is another matter, and it can backfire.

If we keep "confessing" to an already hostile world, for example, that we are too harsh in defending ourselves, should we be surprised if that same world concludes that we deserve to be punished – that we had all this terrorism coming?

And if this public self-criticism happens only on our side – because the other side doesn't allow it – aren't we creating a false reality that puts inordinate responsibility on Israel for whatever goes wrong? When we complain that Israel's global brand image is worse than that of murderous regimes, isn't our public self-flagellation at least partly to blame?

In short, shouldn't supporters of Israel be more careful with what it allows its enemies to hear?

As I write these words, I feel like an 80-year-old World War II veteran who spends his days looking at his medals. Nothing, absolutely nothing, can make you more exhaustingly boring and unsophisticated today than suggesting for one second that a Jew should watch his mouth.

For the Jews who don't think twice before criticizing Israel in public, there's no such thing as a bad debate. Go ahead and trash the Israeli army over civilian casualties, watch the enemy exploit this weakness to create even more civilian casualties and then let's all celebrate the beginning of a "terribly important" debate.

Jews who are careful about not helping the enemy don't have this fetish for debate. They see their home being broken into by people about to hurt their kids. Then, as they look at the faces of their frightened children, they have a choice to make: Do they argue with their spouse – in front of the burglars – about who was supposed to call that security company to install the new alarm, or do they figure out a way to protect their children and leave the debate on the alarm for later, in private?

These Jews' mouths might be shut, but their eyes are wide open. They see that when Israel tried to give its enemy what it said it wanted (example: Gaza), things got even worse. They believe in peace, but not suicide, and they believe that in times of danger, knowing when to be discreet can be just as courageous as knowing when to speak out.

This is their guiding question: Does an enemy who wants to kill my family deserve to see all my insecurities?

So clearly, despite the ingrained Jewish habit of self-criticism, there are millions of Jews today who don't think it's a great idea to villify the Israeli army in front of American and pro-Palestinian college students.

Instead of buying you good will, it's more likely to buy you bad PR.

Having said all that, in our collective obsession with Israel, Jews of all political stripes have missed a major opportunity: shining a light on the rest of Israel's neighborhood.

While the world's press records every Israeli mistake, millions of Arabs are being silently persecuted across the Middle East – gays who are arrested for being gay, women who are humiliated for being women, reporters who are attacked for reporting, Christians who are persecuted for being religious, poets who are jailed for writing the wrong poems.

Where is the outrage? Where are the "Breaking the Silence" campus road shows? Where is the liberal support for these Arab victims of human rights abuse who don't have a fraction of the freedoms that Arabs in Israel enjoy?

The notion of shutting Jewish mouths is a moot point – nobody can shut a Jew up. If a Jew exercises the freedom to shut up, it's a personal choice, and it's usually for good reason.

But for all you progressive Jews out there who believe it's in the grand Jewish tradition to always speak out, there are 300 million Arabs who don't live in the vicinity of Israel, and who could surely use a road show.

"What is it about the pull of neighborhoods? Can't I just drive those extra five or ten minutes to get to my old coffee joint?"

WELCOME TO THE HOOD

September 7, 2006

I've been living in the Pico-Robertson area for a month now, and I must say I'm a little dizzy. I put my new Volvo SUV on "drive" and it goes straight to Nagila Pizza.

I'm on a first-name basis with a Hispanic-looking guy called Freddie, who I think works there because he's always offering to clean my table, while I am trying to teach my kids to do the same. I assume that within a month, several of my kids' teeth will be cracked from the 25-cent cement balls they sell at Nagila, which I hear turn into bubblegum if you have a jackhammer handy. Anyhow, there's this great children's dentist who lives in the neighborhood and whose name is – I'm not making this up – Dr. Hirt.

I hear he's a member of Young Israel of Century City, which had a blockbuster summer because it's known to have the best air conditioning system among all the shuls of the Pico strip. I was there on my first Shabbat for mincha, and yes, you could definitely hang meat in that sanctuary; the temperature was somewhere between crisp and icy cold – the perfect counterpoint to Rabbi Elazar Muskin's sizzling sermon on the importance of not wasting precious time in our very short lives.

Besides the powerful air conditioning, I've been enjoying those little Shabbos bulletins that often lay like fallen leaves on empty chairs. On a recent Friday night at Aish (two blocks from my new house), one little item – inserted between Shalom Bayis Roundtable for Women and Sefarim Dedication Opportunity – caught my eye: "MISTAKEN HAT-ENTITY: There are many black hats hanging on the hat rack on Shabbos that look very similar to each other. Please make sure that the one you are taking is your own."

This is Talmudic-quality housekeeping.

One thing I've noticed in the Hood is an unusual interest in dry cleaners. I've counted about six that are within a few blocks of my house. At night, one of them reminds me of the Flamingo Hotel and Casino in Las Vegas; it's really well lit. I hear that the owner is Persian, and that the cleaner store opposite his is owned by his brother. I got this juicy tidbit at my new neighbors', the Castiels (where I was invited for Shabbat dinner), and I can't wait to check it out. Let's face it, two Persian brothers duking it out over Martinizing and fluff and fold? If it's true, that's a whole column right there. I wonder whom the mother roots for?

Speaking of mothers, this is the neighborhood that invented the Perfectly Coiffed Frum Supermom. They're easy to spot. They have good posture, they're quite perky and they have complete control over their kids. If one of their kids crosses the line, they will use words like "unacceptable" and "not OK." On their coffee tables, you will find books like "The Organized Student" or "Creating the Perfect Kosher Kitchen." Incidentally, they were quite ecstatic that a Jew moved to the neighborhood (as opposed to a non-Jew). I think that's why they keep bringing challah to my door.

Of all the stores I've visited so far, there's a special place in my heart for Needles 'n' Tees (personalized gifts & clothing for men, women & children). This, my friends, is a hole in the wall. My initial encounter with the owner (who has been there 35 years) did not go well, as I used his store to carry on a cellphone conversation in French with my mother. Since he had no idea at the time that I would, within the half hour, empty most of his shelves of these really cool Jewish educational games that would help me impress the Perfectly Coiffed Supermoms and get super play dates for my kids, he asked me to leave his premises. We're now on very good terms.

As I write this at 7 a.m. over an Americano at the local Starbucks, I realize how much I miss my old Urth Caffé on Melrose Avenue. What is it about the pull of neighborhoods? Can't I just drive those extra five or ten minutes to get to my old coffee joint? I suppose I could, but then again I wouldn't be loyal to my new hood.

Special thanks to
my rabbi Manis Friedman
the staff at the Jewish Journal
Kathy Shapiro
Yossi Klein Halevi
Arianna Huffington
Selwyn Gerber
Jonathan Fong
and, of course, all my friends in Pico-Robertson.

CPSIA information can be obtained at www.ICGtesting.com
Printed in the USA
LVOW041014191012

303583LV00001B/1/P